FROM LANDSMAN

TO

LANCASTERS

AND BEYOND

Ron Davies Ldh.
101 Sqdn.
Ludford Magna 1944

Ron Davies

Chevalier de la Legion d'honneur

To the memories of my first wife, Pat (died 1976)
And my daughter, Sue (died May 16th 2015)

RON   1940

RON 2017

From Landsman To Lancasters & Beyond

Published by Green Man Books 2018

15 Poulton Green Close, Spital, Wirral, CH63 9FS

(davidgregg @talktalk.net)

Copyright © Peter Davies 2018

Edited by Peter Davies

ISBN 978 – 1721247530

Printed By Create Space
Available from Amazon, Green Man Books
and other retail outlets

FROM LANDSMAN TO LANCASTERS & BEYOND

Editor's Note

This is the true story of the life and experiences of Ron Davies and his family. Towards the end of the 1990s, Ron started to pen a series of memoirs initially describing his father and mother's life in rural Wirral, from about 1910 onwards. As he reached his late teens, he became eager to escape the fate of a tenant farmer's middle son of that time - that of being strapped behind a ploughshare. Ron volunteered for the RAF as soon as war on Germany was declared, despite being in a reserved occupation. He went on to write about his wartime flying training in the USA, Canada and the UK. This includes an all too vivid description of a fraught, stormy, crossing of the North Atlantic, during which German U-boats ran amok and sunk a third of the convoy.

Ron has written in graphic detail, of his operational experiences as an aircrew member, during a 'tour' of operations in one of Bomber Command's (special duties) Lancaster squadrons. There will be times during this section, when the reader will try to 'make themselves small' as canon fire from Luftwaffe fighters, or ack-ack from ground defences, rip through the Lancaster's thin fuselage. Latterly, now in his nineties, Ron has also described his secondment to advanced 'bombsight' research and development units in the UK - and to South East Asia Command, in Singapore - around the time of VJ Day; a riveting story! Ron then vividly relives the social hardships armed forces personnel faced, when they attempted to settle down to a normal life in Post War Britain.

In a final series of memoirs Ron reveals what happened when, after a gap of fifty two years, he managed to contact his former aircrew colleagues, and his wartime bomber Squadron. Subsequently he made many visits to his old stamping grounds in Lincolnshire's 'Bomber Country' - which have provided additional and often tantalising material for his books. In these recent years other things have changed. The RAF has reached its centenary as has Ron's 101 Squadron. Finally, after decades of neglect, the great contribution of Bomber Command to the defeat of Nazi Germany has been openly acknowledged and celebrated. Ron was able to attend the touching dedication of the fine 101 Squadron memorial at the National Arboretum and meet old friends there. This year (2018) the International Bomber Command Centre and memorial was opened at Lincoln and Ron was able visit the carved steel panels recording the names of over twenty of his fallen comrades and mark them with poppies.

Through publishing the first book of his adventures and actively promoting their sales for local and national charities Ron has made new contacts and friends in the Military History community, given talks and attended meetings and exhibitions. Every trip and visit has been designed around a good pub lunch…an essential start for every grand adventure.

All of these, previously unpublished, memoirs have been integrated and edited to produce this book. The overriding priority has been to retain the 'voice' of a member of a heroic generation of whom, sadly, all too few are left. Expect also some 'interesting' socio/economic comment and a book that resonates throughout with many human interest stories, told with a wry humour. Despite the carnage of the War in Europe, I can assure you that you won't easily forget the tales of 'Lucky Johnnie Webb', or indeed, 'One of our airmen is missing', (chapter 12).

This is real history which is still unfolding. In 2016 Ron became a Chevalier de la Legion d'honneur along with, the now few, other living survivors of the Allied Liberation of France. So the farm boy and horse lover: the landsman, completes his long journey as a knight: a warrior on horseback. A flying Knight of the Lancasters.

Peter Davies

CONTENTS

Page

Preface 9
Introduction 10

PART ONE – Life In Rural Britain

Chapter 1 – Early Years. 13
Chapter 2 – Lancelyn Farm 20
Chapter 3 -- Darkening Clouds over Europe. 29
Chapter 4 – War Looms Closer – I Become a Full Time Farmer. 38
Chapter 5 – Called Up for the RAF – My First Home Leave. 48
Chapter 6 – Epilogue to Part One. 57

PART TWO – Taking to the Air

Chapter 7 – Farmer's Fields and classrooms. 60
Chapter 8 – RAF Ansty – Flying at Last. 66

PART THREE – Bound for the US of A

Chapter 9 – Crossing the North Atlantic – Encounters with the U-boats. 70
Chapter 10 – We step on US Soil - Jackson Field Academy. 73
Chapter 11 – Transferred to Canada. 80

PART FOUR – Home Once More – and Advanced Flying Training

Chapter 12 – Slow Progress to an Operational Training Unit. 86
Chapter 13 – Heavy Conversion Unit and Lancaster Finishing School. 95

PART FIVE – Operational at Last!

Chapter 14 – The First Three Weeks of the Invasion. 99
Chapter 15 – July 1944. 114
Chapter 16 – August 1944. 133
Chapter 17 – September 1944. 141

Chapter 18 – October 1944. 146
Chapter 19 – November 1944. 152

PART SIX – Vital Research and Development Flying – South Wales and Hampshire

Chapter 20 – CCDU Angle – South Wales. 156
Chapter 21 – The Unit Relocates to ASWDU – Hampshire. 162
Chapter 22 – The James' Crew Return To Ludford Magna. 165

PART SEVEN – South East Asia Command

Chapter 23 – The Far East Beckons. 166
Chapter 24 – Life in Kallang – Winning the Peace in Asia. 171

PART EIGHT – Post War Britian – The Discovery of The 101 Squadron Association

Chapter 25 – Post War Britain. 180
Chapter 26 – Fast Forward Fifty Two Years. 182
Chapter 27 – Into the New Millenium – 101 Sqn Reunions and Lincolnshire Lancaster Association Open Days. 185
Chapter 28 More Adventures Beckon. 201

Appendix I – Uncle Ned and the Ice Cream Factory. 224

Appendix II – The Short Life of Keith Gosling. 231

Appendix III – Wirral Grammar School for Boys. 243

Appendix IV – Lambs to the Slaughter & a Victoria Cross. 247

Acknowledgements 251

FROM LANDSMAN TO LANCASTERS

AND BEYOND

By RON DAVIES

PREFACE

It was Monday 4 September 1944. The airman was resting in a field some eight miles from his base at Ludford Magna (Lincolnshire). It had been necessary to put a good few miles under his pedals before he could even attempt to unravel the circumstances he now found himself immersed in. He was halfway through his tour of operations with Bomber Command, most of which, since D-Day had been in support of the Allied invasion force. In fact just that morning the news came through that the British 11th Armoured Division had liberated Antwerp.

The airman had latterly suffered severe ear problems exacerbated by a grim determination to continue flying. He was only now receiving appropriate medication and had been ordered to take a couple of day's leave. Slowly the warm sun and the distant whirr of a binder in the next field soothed his troubled mind. Even so the thoughts kept coming: how did he, a Cheshire farmer's middle son arrive 'here' and furthermore, could he survive the odds against completing his Tour of Operations?

Here is his story.

INTRODUCTION

The question I am asked by some people is, 'Why write a book at ninety-three years of age?' The answer is quite simple. Some two decades ago my second wife Dorothy was forced to stop playing golf due to her failing health. I then spent considerable time helping to keep her both active and occupied during the daytime. After she retired in the evening I spent hours jotting down notes and memories of yesteryear. Following her death in 2007, I began (as a therapy) to construct these words into some dozen or so individual stories. I had thought that on my own demise these tales would be passed on to posterity.

Recent global events have convinced me that the world is becoming an ever more dangerous place. Now would be an appropriate time for people (and their countries) to be reminded of the terrible consequences of a world war. I have made an effort to describe the effects of two world wars through both the lives of my own family and also of others I have met on my passage through life.

Another disturbing feature is contained within the remit of – Part One – Life in Rural Britain. Once again mega companies use their might to control the agricultural industry especially in the field of dairy produce. Over the past two years the 'big four' supermarkets have used their 'cut price' milk, to attract customers to their respective stores. For example, 'four pints for a pound'. On average now, farmers receive currently about twenty-three pence for a litre of milk which costs between twenty six and thirty pence merely to produce!

The German company Muller are reducing the price they pay for milk to produce their yoghurt products. Dairy farmers, as in the 1930s, are already rapidly going out of business. What next? No one will listen to this short sighted policy until it's too late. At least I have put pen to paper to register my protest. And, Oh yes, I still remember the workhouse brigade of the 1920s and shudder at the thought.

Dresden – February 1945.

It was entirely predictable that on 13 February 2015, exactly seventy years after the first raid on Dresden, there would be further one-sided media interviews. The BBC showed the Archbishop of Canterbury the Most Rev. Justin Welby explaining to the German people that he stood before them '…with a profound feeling of regret and deep sorrow', for the bombing of their homeland.

Many interpreted these comments as constituting an apology. These words came from a man who was not even born until some eleven years after the Dresden raid and who, as head of the Anglican section of the Christian Church almost certainly does not represent even fifty per cent of the UK population. The Channel Four news at seven pm followed this up when Jackie Long, one of the presenters, interviewed an ex RAF gunner who had taken part in the raid. He was asked whether he believed that he had participated in a war crime. The interviewer suggested that the raid could be compared with the atrocities being committed in Syria by Assad.

Not one person explained that the intensity of the fires was mainly due to the extensive wooden buildings erected by Germany to house the many thousands of forced labour workers most of whom bore the brunt of the casualties. Nor did anyone mention that the raid was carried out at the request of 'Kindly' Uncle Joe Stalin, who was yet again pleading for extra assistance. This was mainly to enable his own troops to arrive in Berlin before the American and British troops!

Perhaps I could direct the reader to chapter five and November 1940 where the Nazis report with obvious glee the 'Mile high fires' over Liverpool and had used land mines for the first time as 'Terror' (blast) weapons. In reality the US Air Force was supposed to have carried out the first (daylight) raid on Dresden but this was altered the following day due to adverse weather conditions and so the US was the perpetrator of the second raid twelve hours later. The media are quick to point out what is thought to be the more efficient way of bombing sensitive targets but other post war evidence indicates little difference to the results for area bombing.

Operation 'Meetinghouse' – Tokyo March 1945.

Approximately three weeks after the controversial raids on Dresden, the most destructive, none nuclear air raid in the whole of WW II, was carried out on Tokyo by the USAAF. In excess of 300 B29s carried out an incendiary raid which set a pattern for what were essentially firebombing raids which were to be carried out for several months more. In common with the British Air Ministry, the Americans had arrived at the conclusion that precision bombing was just not successful enough. Operation Meetinghouse destroyed circa sixteen square miles of Tokyo and killed approximately 100,000 people (Dresden, max. 25,000 killed).

Major General Curtis LeMay was in charge of the raids and afterwards continued to have a distinguished career. He was honoured by several countries for his wartime achievements. He became Chief of Staff of The US Air Force from 1961 until his retirement in 1965.

Contrast this with the fate of 'Bomber' Harris whose Bomber Command struggled for almost seventy years to obtain recognition in the form of the Bomber Command Memorial. Harris himself 'spoke of having abandoned hope of any worthwhile official appointment...' and '... decided... to take up a good business appointment in South Africa...'

[Bomber Harris by Henry Probert – p 360, 361].

We didn't just bomb Germany.

It is my intention that section five of this book should highlight the intense and comprehensive support given by Bomber Command to the Allied invasion forces, both in preparation for the June 6th D-Day landings and indeed for many months after. When many in the West were predicting that the war would be over before the end of 1944, Hitler invested a huge amount of money and scientific resources into producing the VI s and V2 s - weapons specifically designed for the 'Terror Bombing' of London. Bomber Command played their part by bombing underground storage facilities, launching sites and the Peenemunde Army Research Centre, the 'home' of the V2.

The price was high –101 squadron alone lost over thirty two aircraft and well over 200 aircrew, during my time on the squadron, from the last week in May to November 6th 1944. Even these figures do not include the Lancaster ditched in the English Channel on D-Day, when the crew were fortunate to survive. Neither do they include six aircraft which crashed away from base at Ludford and were completely wrecked – Nor do they include some two or three Lancasters which crash landed at Ludford with dead aircrew aboard – nor the Lancaster on a training flight on 15 September 1944 which crashed into Loch Lomond...

I think that says it all.

R.S. Davies – Wirral, Spring 2015

PART ONE

LIFE IN RURAL BRITAIN c 1910 – 1940

CHAPTER 1   The Early Years

I have tried to piece together the early days of my parents' lives, from the end of the nineteenth century to about 1925. After this time many of the events are an assortment of my memories and facts contained in documents kept at our home at Lancelyn Farm until the death of my mother in August 1976.

My father's birth certificate indicates that he was born on 6 January 1890 at Raby Village ASD, on The Wirral. He was born the second of nine children and would probably have left school before his teens. It was the custom of the times to attempt to obtain employment on a farm with living-in accommodation. My father must have done this because during the next decade he became a 'teamsman', a driver of a team of horses. By the time he was twenty-three he had a post and a tied cottage with Pimbleys of Clatterbridge, Wirral. The cottage was named Claremont Cottage and was situated on the periphery of the farm. It has long since been demolished. This stability enabled him to marry my mother, Lily Evans (a 'townie' from Rock Ferry). My mother was twenty-one years old, lived in Bedford Road and was one of a family of eight. Prior to her marriage she had been an employee of Lever Bros of Port Sunlight, probably on the production line of the soap factory.

At that time the area was remote and transport almost non-existent. It must have been a lonely life for my mother, as work on farms was dawn to dusk and probably seven days a week. Little can be gleaned of their first few years of marriage except that in August 1916 my elder brother was born. At the same time my father was conscripted and sent to France where he served in the Cheshire Regiment, probably with the (then horse drawn) artillery. I still have in my possession their marriage certificate together with a receipt dated 28 July 1912 for, 'One Ladies diamond and ruby ring', priced at £2 2s 0d. This would have been the equivalent of at least two week's wages so one must presume that Tom (my father) had been careful with his money. For some time I had been puzzled as to why, in such hard times and with limited transport the pair had travelled to Liverpool to purchase the ring. I then realised that until 1930 there was still a pier in Rock Ferry with regular sailings to Liverpool Pier Head.

Rock Ferry pier was then adjacent to Bedford Road and so, nearly 100 years ago it was quicker to travel to Liverpool than it is today!

Rock Ferry Pier.

Farm worker's tied cottages may conjure up an idyllic country existence today but at that time were mostly a very primitive form of accommodation. They were likely to have had a large garden with a pig sty but very little else. In this area such cottages would have had no internal sanitation, only an external water tap and of course no electricity or gas. Oil lamps were used for lighting with only a little wood or coal, (a luxury to some) for heating and cooking. This then was my mother's life until 1919, a Spartan existence with a pittance of an income from the army, a child under three years old and with the nearest railway station at Spital being some two miles away. On my father's return to civilian life, he resumed his employment at Claremont Farm and worked under the strict supervision of Lennox the farm bailiff. Lennox his wife and their eight children lived in a corrugated bungalow. This accommodation would have had no superior features than my parent's cottage and life must have been pretty tough for the assorted children.

Tom starts a haulage business – the state of the nation and Clatterbridge 'spike'.

Sometime between 1919 and my birth in 1921, my father set up in business as a haulage contractor by firstly buying one horse with his small army gratuity.

He employed his younger brother George to look after the animal to enable him (Tom) to keep his job, for reasons of security - and of course the cottage also. Work for this 'one horse team' was provided by Lever Bros of Port Sunlight. The facilitator for this arrangement was one Sammy Smith, a horseman employed by Lever Bros who had been stationed with my father in France during the War. On their return the two men kept in touch and indeed remained firm friends until they both died in the early 1960s. They are buried within a few yards of each other in the grounds of St Andrews Church, Bebington. Where the horse was stabled at this time isn't quite clear but unfortunately and within one year, the horse suddenly died. It was therefore just as well that Tom had hung on to his job.

The dealer who sold the horse (for, I think fifty guineas) would accept no responsibility for the loss but was moved sufficiently to re-pay four sovereigns and two half sovereigns, by way of compensation. Despite the hard years which followed, this bounty was kept by both my parents for the next two decades. I'm not sure how Tom overcame this difficulty in order to continue in haulage, but overcome it he did. By 1931 he had not one horse but about twelve, almost all of which were on contract to Lever Bros at their Port Sunlight soap factory which, despite the 1926 General Strike and the 1929 slump, continued to flourish.

In April 1925 Tom and Lilly had left Claremont Farm and Tom signed a one year lease (with an option to extend) for Richmond Farm in Townfield Lane, Bebington. The annual rent was £50, payable quarterly. The business must have expanded rapidly because by 6 August 1925 my father had signed another lease, with Viscount Leverhulme of Thornton Manor, for the tenancy of Beech Farm in Barnston, Wirral. The land available with this farm was 102.199 acres. Quite an achievement for a man who had left school at age ten or eleven and who as an adult had suffered severely during his war services.

At this point my own memory recall clicks in and I can remember many of the incidents which happened during the next fifteen years. By contrast to the rent of £50 for Richmond farm, that for Beech Farm was £260 per annum. My uncle George moved into the Bebington farmhouse and managed the day- to- day running of the Lever Bros contracts, which included the training of new employees as they were taken on.

Beech Farm boasted four generous bedrooms and many improvements to property and outbuildings had been carried out to a high standard. This was indeed a luxury for my mother after the era of Claremount cottage, however it was not all good news. Right next door to the farm was the Fox and Hounds pub, in fact both properties exist today and are thriving.

I don't really know much about Tom's life before he served in France but there was no doubt that since his return he had developed a habit of 'pubbing' which led to much discord in the home. This probably led to our stay in Barnston terminating at the end of the first year. During this time there were three incidents which I can remember with absolute clarity and will recount them before moving on.

Beech Farm was situated at the top of a steep hill and it was the custom of the scout movement to occupy one of our fields in which to hold their annual summer camp, for a period of two weeks each year. The summer of 1925 was notorious for a series of storms of heavy thunder and lightning. During one such outbreak, a scout was apparently carrying water taken from the stream in a bucket, when he was struck by a fork of lightning. I can't recall whether or not he was killed but I well remember his arrival and the subsequent upset at the camp. I well remember the arrival of the ambulance and the subsequent disruption and distress. I was therefore, at a very early age taught to respect the power of the elements.

The second incident occurred just a short time later when an aeroplane landed in a field in Thingwall, approximately two miles away. It wasn't a crash, just a forced landing which was not in the least unusual for those times. My elder brother and I visited the site just in time to watch the pilot and his passenger carry out remedial works. It was probably only one of many two seat open cockpit aircraft purchased cheaply after the Great War but to me at that time it represented another way of life, although I was too young to realise it at that time.

The third 'incident' was perhaps more of an illustration of differences across the time span from then to now. One Sunday evening we went to Higher Bebington to visit my uncle Jack and auntie Lena, my father's sister. Jack worked in local council offices and also assisted my parents with the accounts and other issues of administration of Tom's business. After a visit to The Travelers' Rest for liquid refreshment we were ready to set off back to Barnston. By now it was cold, dark and a bitter wind blew. Our mode of transport was two bicycles which were required to show lights after dark. The only available lights at that time were 'carbide'. These were filled with calcium carbide powder - when water was added this produced acetylene gas which in turn was ignited to provide a beam of light. This performance must have taken all of half an hour. To say that tempers were frayed would have been a gross understatement!

Eventually we set off for home. My father led the way with my ten year old brother on the cross bar (highly dangerous!), my mother followed him with me on a pillion behind her.

The shortest route of about three miles led us through Storeton. The road was steep, narrow and bumpy and the carbide lamps totally inadequate. Even now I retain recollections of trees and stone walls flashing past like monsters out of the gloom, which bore some comparison to later war-time sorties in Lancaster bombers. It was an experience I wouldn't want to repeat!

By late 1926 our family had moved back to Richmond Farm in Bebington. In 1927 we additionally took over the tenancy of the Rising Sun Farm in Clatterbridge which had some thirty acres of land. Rising Sun Farm was part of the Lancelyn-Green Estate (of Poulton, Spital). I was never able to discover what prompted the move from Barnston. It could have been the logistics of being too far from the Lever Bros factory but probably more likely, to the proximity of Beech Farm to the Fox and Hounds pub! During the duration of his stay in Barnston, Tom had been their most regular customer.

The General Strike of 1926 though of short duration, was the forerunner of many long - term problems. There were two prime ministers of that time, Stanley Baldwin (Tory) and the first Labour Party Prime Minister, Ramsey Mc Donald.

Rising Sun Farm at Clatterbridge

These two were highly criticised by both press and public but were not as much to blame as Lloyd-George, the leader of the coalition from 1916 to 1922. With a weak government Lloyd-George was involved in much poor decision making. This was to cause irreparable damage to the country's future economic policies such as those appertaining to the Irish problem of 1919 and the Indian unrest, (with Ghandi being the prime mover of those troubles).

Perhaps the worst result of Lloyd-Georges' flawed policies however was in allowing Georges Clemencau, the Prime Minister of France attempt to extract a level of reparation from Germany for its Great War crimes, to the point where in just a few short years the German economy came close to collapse. The American president, Woodrow-Wilson talked about a lasting peace but had no practical ideas whatsoever, with the results which we now know were catastrophic.

Back to the story, in 1927 our family was in residence at the Rising Sun Farm. The house was supposedly a former inn for the fettling of coach and horses travelling from Woodside to Chester and so was, and still is, built 'over the pavement' and therefore right up to the road.

Our nearest neighbour was the workhouse, commonly known as 'the spike' then a part of Clatterbridge Hospital. The hospital catered mostly for accidents and had two ambulances stationed there. The enclave included a maternity section and, not too far away a fever hospital, which had its own ambulance. The workhouse catered for the homeless, mostly distressed ex-soldiers who were allowed to stay for one night only.

I started my two mile trek to Thornton Hough Church School at 8.15 a.m. and would watch these men trundling along with their sole possessions strapped to their backs. They would often be wearing army greatcoats and boots and had the 'mandatory' 'billy can' strapped around their waist. The next port of call for them would be at least ten or fifteen miles away, probably at Upton by Chester. They would rely on the generosity of residents en route (if they were fortunate), for refreshments. This spectacle was to have a lasting effect on my attitude to life thereafter. In the mid-1950s my brother was cultivating a field opposite the old 'spike', when he discovered a parcel of rags under a hedgerow. On closer inspection this 'parcel' turned out to be the skeleton of a former inmate of the Clatterbridge Workhouse. The inquest recorded a verdict of 'Misadventure'. What hypocrisy! Today, in 2018 a fortune is spent on poppies in memory of 'heroes'.

CLATTERBRIDGE WORKHOUSE, c. 1908

The workhouse dates from 1836 when a site near the bridge over the Clatter was selected for its erection by the Wirral Board of Guardians. The building originally housed 130 inmates. Two women from Little Sutton were the first admissions.

In 1881 the workhouse had only one nurse. The Board of Guardians considered that she was underemployed so decided that she could be used on sewing duties also.

Over the years more land was purchased for additional buildings for the workhouse and infirmary. Following the First World War the Guardians concentrated on the hospital side of the institution and erected new wards for general and maternity patients. In 1930 the workhouse came under the control of Cheshire County Council and was re-developed as a hospital.

Tom expands his business – I 'inherit' piano lessons.

Despite the worsening economic crisis, Tom's haulage business flourished.
 He was awarded additional contracts for an associate of Lever Bros, Van den Bergh's Stork margarine works at Bromborough. These works would require at least an additional two, or three wagons per day with a further two on hire to local speculative builders. The later would have probably been Lloyds who were building mainly in the Spital and Port Sunlight areas.

 Among many relics from those days I found a cash receipt made out to Lily Davies of Rising Sun Farm for an upright piano and stool for the sum of £41 15s, a fortune in those days. The intention was for my elder brother Tom junior to learn to play. This he flatly refused to do, so at the age of seven I was sent to New Ferry (five miles away) every Saturday for an hour's tuition at a cost of 2s 6d, (twelve and a half pence). My piano lessons continued for seven years and to my eternal regret I just 'became none-musical' - if only! What a privilege and what an opportunity missed. We remained at Rising Sun Farm for the next two and a half years.

By 1930 the depression had damaged the country significantly and the Wirral was not to escape its share of suffering. Cammell-Laird shipbuilders would virtually close with just about 500 employees retained for maintenance duties etc. Shipbuilding and mining were two of the hardest hit industries in the country.

CHAPTER TWO

Lancelyn Farm and A Change Of Direction For Tom and His Family

We move to Poulton Lancelyn.

At this point in time we moved to Lancelyn Farm in Poulton, Spital. Lancelyn was a 100 odd acre 'mixed' farm which was part of the Lancelyn-Green estate. The tenancy of the Rising Sun Farm was retained and the stabling of the horses, by now numbering some twelve animals was split between the two farms. Unemployment had hit the families of both my father and mother. I well remember several of the drivers being uncles of mine and also one cousin, Jack Harford who was killed in action at Dunkirk in 1940.

Lancelyn Farm at Poulton Lancelyn

Lancelyn farmhouse was (and is) a three storey solid Edwardian building which had one quite unusual feature. Adjacent to the main farmhouse is a two-storey section which housed the dairy - nothing unusual in that. Above the dairy however and accessed by a set of narrow wooden steps, was a consecrated chapel complete with organ and pulpit! Before we moved to the farm, I attended Sunday school in this chapel.

For me the main benefit of our new location was that I would no longer have to walk the four-plus miles each day to Thornton Hough School. A small bus service had been inaugurated from Thornton Hough, which called at the surrounding villages for the benefit of the local children. I would leave home at 8 a.m. and walk for just under a mile to Raby Mere where I would be collected at 8.20. I was the first person on the bus which wound its way through lower Raby, Hargrave Lane, Raby village and finally Thornton Hough. Lancelyn farmhouse was an undoubted improvement on Rising Sun but was still some eighty years old. One upstairs room had been converted into a bathroom but there was only running water, no electricity or gas. The only sanitation was outside in the form of an earth type privy. There were a further three rooms on the second floor but these were unsafe due to an advanced woodworm infestation. Compared with many back-to-back estates covering the Wirral it was probably luxury in the extreme, despite being some three-quarters of a mile from the nearest (limited) public transport.

My younger brother had been born at the end of 1928 while we were still at Rising Sun and was less than three years old. It was my responsibility to ensure his safety during any spare time I had when not helping with jobs around the farm.

New projects on Merseyside and a jugful of cockles.

The (1929) slump was entering its third year and the stagnation was turning into a deeper economic crisis where unemployment was still increasing. The new 'joint-parties' government headed by Ramsey Mc Donald was desperate to slash outgoings. They introduced the hated 'means test' as a prequalification for 'dole' (unemployment benefit) and against which measure organised marches were carried out. These would often be led by jazz bands and mostly started peacefully. They would however often deteriorate into pre-organised riots and general disorder.

The government set up construction projects which were intended to alleviate some of the more serious areas of unemployment.

The first local project was the construction of a 'Mersey Tunnel', from Birkenhead to Liverpool. The tunnel was all of three and a half miles long and so it was 1935 before it could be completed. Local new council housing was starting to reduce some but by no means all, of the slums.

A new grammar school for boys and an identical one next door for girls, opened in late 1932 (in Bebington). A third project was the building of Speke Airport in Liverpool including new duel-carriageway access from the city centre. The plan was for Speke to replace Hooton Airfield as the official 'Liverpool Airport'. The opening date was 1938. All of these projects helped in a small way but for the majority of the unemployed it was as usual 'too little, too late'.

Many colourful characters called regularly at Lancelyn Farm. A fisherman from Parkgate riding a tricycle with an attached trailer, used to call twice weekly. Among his wares for sale were 'dabs' a white flat fish, small but delicious. For tuppence (less than 1p) we could purchase a pack of four or five fish carefully wrapped in newspaper. Then there would be cockles also locally caught, a jugful for just tuppence, this was Tom's favourite supper after a sojourn at either, The Rose and Crown in Bebington or The Seven Stars in Thornton Hough.

Raby Mere 1917

Raby Mere 1930

Then there was 'the onion man' - he would call two or three times each year and had large strings of onions slung about his person and from every conceivable projection on his bicycle. We never did discover his name or nationality. There were many others but with the passage of time one forgets their names and products.

While the time bomb was ticking away towards the next war, most folk were still trying to adjust their lives from the disruption caused by the Great War of 1914-1918. Tom's health had become a problem. Each Saturday before going to the pub, he would visit a 'quack' doctor in Grange Road, Birkenhead for 'consultation and observation'. He would regularly receive three bottles of medication for which he would pay the princely sum of 5s 0d (25p) and which he would take three times each day. At the time, I used to believe that his illness was psychological but now at the ripe old age of ninety-three, I am sure that he had had great difficulty in shutting out the years between 1916 and 1918 which he spent in France.

Michael Morpurgo, the author of the highly acclaimed book, *War Horse* is too young to have been around at the time of the Great War. His inspiration was discussions with veterans (who had) and also an oil painting left to his wife.

The painting showed artillery horses charging into barbed wire barriers while attacking the German lines. Morpurgo describes this as 'A very frightening and alarming painting, not the sort you would want to hang on a wall.' and added that it 'haunted' him. What then must it have been like for those who were actually there?

From 'soap and margarine', to milk and potatoes.

Things were, however about to change very suddenly. Both Lever Bros and the Stork Margarine Works finally decided to move with the times with regard to their haulage contracts. They had decided to transfer from utilising horse drawn transport to the modern motor lorry. Tom was offered the opportunity to change with them. For the first year he was offered a firm contract for three lorries for Port Sunlight (Lever Bros), a similar number for Stork and with a distinct possibility of 'doubling up' the following year.

I can clearly remember the visits made by representatives from local commercial garages which brought proposed vehicle specifications and terms of purchase. Driving tests were still three years away (1935) and all the offers included free instruction for the drivers. Uncle George one of Tom's younger brothers was to be transport manager and was offered some two weeks' tuition regarding the requisite administration etc. A done deal – or was it? Out of the blue Tom called the arrangements off. He was a horseman through and through and wanted no truck with lorries (excuse the pun). Decision made, now how to make a living in these desperate times. The Lever Bros company was extremely understanding and most of Tom's dozen or so staff were found jobs with either Levers or with Stork Margarine. Tom now needed to dispose of seven of his fourteen horses.

This was a problem because all over the country motor vehicles were replacing horses, so values were at an all-time low. On the positive side there were better returns to be made in North Wales and so there was still a demand for good shire-horses at the Wrexham auctions. By using the Wrexham facilities Tom was able to sell his beloved stock and received sufficient funds to invest in a herd of some twenty dairy cattle. Life would change forever - gone were the weekly cheques for transport. Our first consideration was to establish a monthly income from wholesale milk sales, then we would plan ahead for the potato season (normally seven to eight months), and also the annual wheat or barley harvests. In the meantime Tom had to self-finance wages and expenses out of what remained of the twelve years of profit from his haulage businesses.

Tom had some good fortune with his selection of staff. As cow-man he appointed one Frank Jones (Taffy), a Wrexham lad who came to England to find work. He married Violet Howerd, who was the hard working daughter of a small-scale farmer who had lost his farm due to building-land requirements. Frank had already worked for Tom over a period of a couple of years in the haulage business.

A 'tied' cottage went with the seven day a week job. This suited Frank well and he soon took up residence at 'Rose Cottage' in Dibbinsdale with Violet and their two daughters. Rose Cottage was a remote and primitive place, with water available but no sanitation, however that applied to most properties in the area at that time.

My elder brother assisted my father with the horse-work, ploughing, harrowing, harvesting and the like. Tom Peers from Neston was taken on as general labourer. Tom's background was in the building industry but he had become frustrated at being laid off (and thus unpaid) during inclement weather and also due to material shortages. Tom's wages as a labourer were £1 10s a week (£1.50) for a fifty-two hour week. Not a fortune but it was a regular position and one which he retained until the late 1940s.

Part of Lancelyn Farm dairy herd circa 1958

Last but certainly not least was my mother. Firstly there was the mountain of housework to be done with no modern appliances to assist her. Cooking was carried out on a cast iron 'range' incorporating an open fire and an oven and hot water system (which rarely functioned). In addition Lily had not only the dairy work to attend to but also had the poultry to look after.

The early farming years were harsh and Tom had many setbacks to overcome. He learnt that agriculture was being 'controlled' by both national and local government departments, mostly by officials who had no concept of the difference between urban and rural living.

No sooner had the new herd of cattle settled into Lancelyn Farm than fresh directives forced Tom to spend still more money, on alterations to shippons and to upgrading dairy utensils. These were to vastly higher specifications than had been the norm for centuries. There were of course other problems, purchase of the whole herd en bloc led to sickness and low milk productivity. It was to be some time before a healthy and high-yield herd was established at Lancelyn Farm, and no small thanks were due to Frank Jones.

We were now gradually integrating with the hamlet of Poulton – some twenty five adults (excluding residents of Poulton Hall, our landlord, Major Lancelyn-Green, his wife and four children) and slightly more teenagers than children.

At this time the farm opposite ours, Vinyard Farm, was run by Mr and Mrs Wareing, well established farmers. The Wareings had a prosperous milk round which covered the Port Sunlight area. Each morning at 8.30 prompt two milk carts and ponies left for their deliveries. One cart was driven by Mr Wareing himself and the other by Harold Donkin, his cowman. Donkin, his wife and daughter Dorothy, occupied one half of the tied cottage (see photo page 18) opposite Lancelyn Farm whilst Jack Williams (horseman), his wife and four children, occupied the other half.

Two cyclists accompanied the milk round riding carrier bikes. The milk was transported in ten-gallon churns to be measured out into customer's own jugs using pint and quart measures. The journey was repeated in the afternoon except for weekends when only one delivery was made.
I mention this to give some indication of just how primitive life was in the early 1930s.

In these early years our milk production averaged only between twenty-five and thirty gallons per day and was sold to a dairy in Rock Ferry.

That of course was before the advent of the Milk Marketing Board. This was one of the government's supposedly brainy ideas designed to control agriculture and simultaneously make profits. To achieve this they introduced quotas and directives regarding the distribution of this previously neglected product. Their mistake was as usual to allow urbanites to dictate to rural communities, but I digress so back to the story.

Surprisingly for such a small population two of the families in Poulton were Londoners. Mr Salter, his wife and their four sons lived in a semi-detached cottage situated at the rear of Poulton Hall. Mr and Mrs Jeffries and their two sons occupied a small remote cottage situated between Poulton and Spital. It appeared that the two fathers had served with Major Lancelyn-Green in his regiment during WW I. When the Major returned to his estate in 1919, he had brought the two families back with him. 'Jeff' (Mr Jeffries) was employed as the estate handyman, while Mr Salter was engaged as manager and general factotum of the Major's own farm, which probably measured fifty to sixty acres.

The estate gardener, known only as 'Bradshaw', resided with his wife in one of the cottages situated behind The Hall. Perched on the edge of Dibbinsdale was an old corrugated bungalow, similar to the one I mentioned earlier as the abode of Lennox the Claremont Farm Manager. This offering was occupied by Mr and Mrs Milton and their six children. Although Milton suffered ill health, he worked as the road and verge caretaker responsible for the mile long road to Spital.

We have already mentioned Frank (Taffy) Jones and family at Rose Cottage which leaves: Harry Aspinall and his wife who resided in the stone cottage and was gardener/handyman to the large mansion at the end of a long drive. The mansion was rented out to various families and today is part of the Poulton Institute.

Then there was Mort the gamekeeper and his wife who lived in the keeper's cottage adjacent to one of Tom's fields. Altogether the Morts had seven sons and two daughters, obviously over an extended period of time. His eldest son had served in WW I finally becoming a prisoner of war. Being of that persuasion he served in the RAF Auxiliary for two or three years in WW II. The two youngest sons, Les and Ron were conscripted for WW II. Since the keeper's cottage only had two bedrooms and no modern sanitation, one can only wonder where those still at home, were accommodated?

I will now relate a small incident, of little consequence maybe but

one that happened on Good Friday 1932, when I was ten years old. I inadvertently stepped on to a hidden plank which had a large nail protruding from it. I shouted for help and my father came to my aid. My mother improvised a temporary dressing and Tom harnessed the pony and trap and whistled me away to the local doctor. Dr Cowan had his home and surgery adjacent to St Andrews Church about two miles away. Despite it being a bank holiday I received immediate and first class attention.
As we left Tom asked for the bill (no NHS then!) to which the good doctor replied - 'Just drop off a bag of spuds when you're next passing'. The value of potatoes then would have been less than 3s 6d (17 ½ p) and illustrates the rapport between families in those hard times, and they certainly were hard.

   New Ferry and Bebington were enduring continued resentment regarding the increasingly harsh treatment of families due to the means-test and further reduction of the pittances of dole and pension payments. As often happens the protesting started off peacefully with marching and placard waving but became more intense as time went on.

   At about this time I witnessed the horrifying results of a fox visit. He forced his way into one of our chicken houses and killed all occupants by severing their necks; it was just sheer cruelty as not one had been eaten. Today's protesters at anti fox hunting demonstrations don't understand the way of life of the country. Apart from the expense of having to renew the poultry I would always remember the savagery without provocation. This was only one instance of the fox's cruelty to wildlife. Almost weekly while walking the fields I saw bodies of wild duck, pheasant and other birds destroyed for no reason whatsoever – the fox is aptly named.

   A decade later I met three more 'Foxes'. This time they were Lancaster Bombers and each disappeared with eight humans, none of whom would escape. They were:

LL 771   June 11 / 12 1944   LM 479 August 29 / 30 1944

NF 936   November 4 / 5 1944

   There was however a plus side to life in an English hamlet, most people would find time for a chat and light banter. Bonfire Nights, Halloween, etcetera would see people together and finding enjoyment in the simple pleasures. Even Mort the gamekeeper would stop to pass the time of day, despite his stern appearance.

After the airship disaster of 1931, travel of the future lay in ruins. Consequentially and shortly afterwards, a few entrepreneurs started mail and passenger flights on an ever increasing scale. One of the first places to benefit was Hooton Aerodrome situated on the edge of the river Mersey and about five miles from Lancelyn Farm. Until 1933, Hooton was the main airfield for the Liverpool and Wirral areas. During this period and for a short time afterwards, daily flights could be observed setting off for Ireland and other not too distant destinations. This new activity added interest to the area because, due to the close proximity of Hooton, the aircraft passed at a low altitude over Poulton.

CHAPTER THREE   Darkening Clouds over Europe

Wirral Grammar School and a future prime minister.

Elsewhere events were taking a more sinister turn. Germany was once again showing truculent aggression and there seemed to be unrest all around the world. At home Tom's demons seemed to be driving him more deeply into heavy drinking. With hindsight it is easy to understand this problem but at that time it made life at home most unpleasant. Lily, my mother had by this time become a strict Christian and a strong believer, which only added to the home complications.

The dreaded 'Eleven plus' examination took place in 1932. That was the year of the opening of Wirral Grammar School and there would be some ninety extra places available in the area. Due to this I managed to secure a scholarship from Thornton Hough Church School to Wirral Grammar. My mother was delighted. Tom however was furious. In his mind the increase in school leaving age *to fourteen years* was just too much but now I would be at school until I was at least sixteen years old! Lily however bravely ignored his moods.

Against this background I attended a brand new school which had probably been designed for 500 to 600 pupils - in its first year there were just 100 of us. Today the school accommodates 1,250 pupils. The headmaster was a Dr J.M. Moir B.Sc., a man of vision who ran the school with a rod of iron.

To compound my problems at home, the school had a half day on Wednesdays but to compensate we had to attend for studies on a Saturday, until 12.30 p.m. Worse still, one was expected to take part in school sports on both afternoons!

In effect the school week was six days with two to three hours homework each evening and at least three hours at weekends. Tom was furious – I can't say I felt too happy about it either.

The transition from a small church school with two rooms and three classes for children from five to eleven years of age, and with just three female teachers, to a huge grammar school with some fifteen teachers was difficult enough without the added animosity at home. On the positive side I was now allowed to cycle and travelled two and a half miles, each way to and from school, twice a day. Cycling was certainly an improvement on walking (and / or bussing). I came home at lunchtime because school lunches were 9d a day, (just over 3p).

Dr Moir was another Great War casualty and walked with a profound 'list to port' which was a complete contrast to his political leanings. Because the school was in its infancy, both he and the staff were in effect under-employed and consequently the lives of the early entrants were even more tightly controlled than would have been normal.

Fortunately in 1934 there was a welcome diversion in the shape of the seventeen year old Harold Wilson. Wilson had recently arrived in the Wirral area due to his father's change of employment. Immediately on arrival Wilson became the sole occupant of the sixth form. He received the undivided attention of both Dr Moir and the deputy headmaster Mr Norris, a historian. By 1936 Wilson (the future prime minister of Great Britain) departed for Oxford – Jesus College to be exact – with an exhibition in history.

Wilson's position as head boy was taken by a charismatic Bob Weighall, a good cricketer, a tremendous rugby player and all round athlete. Weighall later joined the RAF, rose to the rank of Air Commodore and on retirement became Secretary to the Board of The Rugby Football Union. For most of the remaining pupils, life was much more modest and for the forty-six members listed on the WW II memorial, much shorter.

We get a radio – Hitler becomes Chancellor of Germany.

At school, myself and a few others were in the minority in that our families did not own a new-fangled wireless (radio) set. In our instance due to both the expense and the fact that we did not have electricity connected at Lancelyn Farm. A couple living in straightened circumstances in nearby Bromborough, set up a service to supply accumulators for battery operated radio sets, so several of us in the village were soon 'on the air'.

The couple would call each week with a ready charged battery which they exchanged for the used one. The husband was obviously injured or disabled and stayed in the car which was one of the last Lanchesters made and probably an automatic. It was his wife who carried the heavy accumulator into the farmhouse and affected the exchange. It must have been a struggle to make such a venture pay but they were pleasant and being able to listen to the radio certainly made a difference to our lives.

At about the same time we began to receive delivery of daily newspapers. This was because the two elder Salter boys, Sam and Jim, became delivery boys for the newly opened newsagent in Bebington. This involved a four mile cycle ride twice a day (once on Sunday) plus of course the distance involved to actually deliver the papers. On weekdays they also had a five mile cycle journey for school. The boys were probably paid 2s 6d which most certainly would have contributed to the family finances.

Newspaper headlines indicated the tremendous financial and economic problems facing the country. In the background loomed additional foreign problems. In 1931 Ghandi had reappeared, this time exchanging his lawer's suite for a loin-cloth. He would attend meetings thus clad and also barefoot. Mussolini, (the Italian dictator) was also making demands in Abyssinia, while by 1933 Adolph Hitler had become the German Chancellor.

The first period at school was a forty-five minute current affairs programme chaired by the art master inappropriately named Mr Carpenter, whose parents were 'leading-lights' in London for the Salvation Army. Carpenter himself was a pacifist, so he ensured that we were kept fully abreast of the anti-war feelings so prevalent in the UK in the early 1930s. Feelings couldn't have been more clearly expressed than at the 1933 Fulham by-election. A pacifist candidate turned a former 14,000 Tory majority into a 4,000 plus victory for the Labour Party. Even the most ardent believer in a 'Great Britain' would have cause to have doubts about the future.

The hazards of rearing farm animals – Tom breaks his leg.

Back on the farm family life was also proving difficult. As previously mentioned purchasing a dairy herd en bloc was a hazardous affair. There were continual scares of bovine sickness and although in those days Foot and Mouth disease was not prolific, there was always the odd outbreak.

Whenever a cow became sick there was a requirement for a veterinary surgeon to visit the farm to confirm that it was not a contagious disease. One of the farms adjacent to Lancelyn reared a beef herd (unlike ours) which in 1934 became infected with anthrax, another deadly disease. This involved wholesale slaughter and burning on site of their entire herd, not very pleasant.

Additionally the local Bebington council began 'dawn raids'. These consisted of the sanitary inspector visiting the local dairy herds at six a.m. (milking time) to ensure that all the latest instructions regarding hygiene were being carried out. This applied to both the shippons and the dairy.

Our cowman, Frank (Taffy) Jones' views regarding these matters were unprintable! His pet hate however was 'the dossers', (mainly Irish) workers who visited the area at busy times such as harvest and potato picking. These workers would, if given a few day's work spend the night in a stable or loft, generally without permission. They would have no washing or other facilities and the authorities didn't seem to give a damn. These free-lancers would drink themselves comatose on a Saturday evening but would somehow smarten up for Sunday morning Mass. There would apparently be an 'all silver' collection at the church. The three penny 'joey' (just over 1p today) was then the smallest silver coin in circulation and was always in great demand.

In early 1934 Tom had a serious fall, this time when he was sober and was removed by ambulance to Clatterbridge where he was incarcerated for almost eight weeks. Visiting times were two hours on a Wednesday afternoon and the same on Sundays, with NO CHILDREN ALLOWED and rules and times being strictly enforced. I did however manage to peek through the ward window while my mother was with Tom. I would see him lying on his bed with his leg suspended in mid-air by a system of pulleys - it was apparently a very serious fracture.

Inevitably Tom's absence caused great problems to the routine of farm work, which waits for no one. By now my elder brother was competent to carry out most of the arable work. The problem however lay in providing support for Frank, who was coping alone with a seven day week carrying out all milking (twice a day) and cattle care duties. The decision was taken that I would have to do a couple of hours' work before attending school and a further two hours on my return in the evenings - and of course Saturday afternoons and Sundays! This was for me at least a tremendous shock and at the time seemed impossible.

A call from my mother at 5.45 a.m. was most unwelcome. I do have to say that working with Frank was a great experience. Although he was probably in his mid–thirties we managed to work well together and I thoroughly enjoyed hearing his experiences of working in Wales in the 1920s.

At this time milking machines did exist but their use was not yet mandatory, so in common with many other dairy farms we chose to milk by hand.
We milked some twenty or so head of cattle between the two of us and brought feed and water to each animal by hand. The cattle needed this food even when they could be taken out to pasture for grazing.

I struggled to maintain my schoolwork and consoled myself that it wouldn't last forever - indeed after seven or eight weeks Tom duly returned home. The downside was that his leg was in plaster and quite apart from being in agony he was barely able to walk.

Troubles come in twos, so it is said. Within days of Tom's return home there were visits from officials. The first demanded that a schedule of very expensive improvements be immediately carried out to the shippons. The second visit was from the Social Inspector. My grand-parents had retired and their 'wellbeing' had come under the scrutiny of the pensions' division. It had been decided that Tom's contribution was to be 5s 0d (25p) per week commencing – yes - immediately! Since a cash payment would have found its way into the till of The Rose and Crown, my mother decided that I would have to shop to purchase this value of groceries on my way home from school. Every Saturday lunchtime I did this and delivered the goods directly to my grandmother. Could life get any more difficult? Well yes, and it did.

When the time came for Tom to have his plaster removed it was revealed that the fractured parts had not knitted together as expected and that further surgery was required. Added to these woes my elder brother had been badly kicked by one of the horses in his charge. A resulting severe shoulder injury incapacitated him for some weeks and thus my mother, Taffy and I were pushed beyond our limits. Fortunately it was my six-week school holiday period, some uncles were able to help during the evenings and we received hired help from the Salter family. Thus it was that a crisis was narrowly averted.

Good farming practices at Lancelyn pay dividends – the geese 'police'

There was a plus side in that some three and a half to four years after

Tom's farming policy had been in operation, the quality and quantity of our arable products had risen by sixty to seventy per cent. When we took over the farm, the soil had been neglected for many years and was consequently of very poor quality. The ground had now responded well to regular treatment with cattle manure - our own of course. The improvements in the health of our dairy herd, aided by rearing our own livestock, gave hope for the future. Our milk yield had also improved and by now we were supplying the farm opposite, Vinyard, with 100% of our output, which certainly made life simpler.

It was just a matter of taking the milk tankards across the road, no transport costs and no dependence on the middleman (wholesaler).

My brother returned to work and Tom left hospital but was unable to walk without a crutch. He made his presence felt by interfering with our hastily arranged routine. This did not please my brother and friction soon became apparent. The flip side of Tom's accident meant that the 'demons' had subsided, but had not disappeared altogether. With transport provided by his friends, he gradually began attending livestock markets. The difference was that he would now return home by mid or late afternoon, which caused sighs of relief all round.

One of Tom's first new schemes was to enlarge the poultry section by introducing a flock of geese. They were constantly escaping from their pen in a small croft and would strut around the farmyard putting the fear of god into everyone, including me, who stood in their way. Despite our protests the flock remained a permanent feature of the farm, at least their presence discouraged burglars!

Tom was a very fair and indeed generous man and showed his appreciation of Frank Jones' contribution by allowing Frank full use of the six acres surrounding Rose Cottage. This land was (and still is) unfit for cultivation, as it frequently floods in the section adjacent to the Dibbin stream. It was however adequate to enable Frank to enlarge his own poultry section and to enable him to breed goats. You may wonder just how a man who worked almost all the daylight hours available and never had a day off or took a holiday, could possibly take on even more work.

It was symbolic of rural marriages that wives were just as hard working as their husbands. Violet Jones was no exception. Money was so scarce that constant work helped save one's sanity! For example Frank's wage in 1935, for a seven day week with just a couple of hour's break on a Saturday and maybe four or five on a Sunday, was just £2 plus free rent.

My father would pay say 5s (25p) above the going rate. This still didn't compare favourably with a factory worker on a forty-four hour week who received between £2 15s (£2.75) and £3 10s, (£3.50). It may be difficult today to appreciate the complete inequality between agricultural and industrial wages but this country has always had a history of encouraging cheap food. It took the Second World War to bring realism to government policy which only then encouraged the dying interest in agriculture.

The Milk Marketing Board force local changes – my brother takes a brief trip on a motorcycle.

Back to the mid-1930s – the outlook was bleak and still more interference by the Milk Marketing Board led to the retirement of the Warings of Vinyard Farm. The Warings were a couple who had devoted their lives to farming and charitable works within the community. Lord Leverhulme personally rewarded their efforts by building for them a new bungalow on his land at nearby Raby Mere. They left at a time when 'change' was the order of the day.

Vinyard Farm was taken over by Harold Donkin, the Waring's cow and dairyman. As no arable work was to be undertaken, Jack Williams, their horseman, left farming and took a council post in nearby Bromborough. Both families left the small white semi-detached cottage adjacent to the farm. Harold occupied Vinyard farmhouse while Jack and his family moved into a vacant house behind Poulton Hall. Immediate changes were made at Vinyard, the ponies and traps and the horses were dispensed with. In their place a second hand Morris Oxford and trailer arrived to handle the milk deliveries which could then be reduced to once daily.

Up and until this time, Harold had been the only person in our hamlet, except Major Green and his family, to own motorised transport. The old BSA motorcycle with its open cockpit type sidecar was purchased by my elder brother. There was no driving test back then, just a requirement to purchase a driving license for the sum of 5s (25p). With this document he was able to drive any two, or four wheeled vehicle of up to three tons weight. The motor-cycle was delivered into our farmyard. My brother kick-started the engine and engaged first gear. He travelled twenty yards before colliding with the main gate post - the side car was wrecked and the whole contraption disposed of without delay.

I particularly mention this incident to illustrate the complete lack of government controls designed to ensure safety on the roads during the transition from horse to motor power.

Eventually restrictions did come into force and from June 1935 it became mandatory to have passed a driving test prior to taking to the roads. Up and until the present time there have been only two exceptions - during WW II and during the 1957 Suez crisis when inspectors were appointed to administer the fuel rationing.
Segregation of driving licenses to cover motor-cycles, cars, heavy lorries (over two or three tons), imposition of speed limits and establishment of pedestrian crossings all followed later.

At about the same time as the change-over at Vinyard Farm, Major Green made the decision to retire from his farming activities and so Sam Salter took over as tenant farmer.
It was probably part of the agreement between them that Salter would have to supply fresh produce to The Hall, but otherwise he would have had a free hand on day to day management of the farm.

The hard lot of farmer's wives – religion and my aunt Annie.

Thus began a friendship between Salter and Tom which continued until Tom's death in 1961. Salter became a frequent visitor to Lancelyn Farm as well as a reliable drinking partner on market days. Mrs Salter played a role on the dairy side of the farm affairs. She could often be seen on shopping days walking to the bus stop (over a mile away), to return again much later heavily laden with shopping bags.

Feeding five males all with hearty appetites must have been very demanding. My mother continued to run not only the house but also attend to the ever increasing pressure from the dairy, essentially due to the almost monthly changes being instigated by the local sanitary inspector. Mother would also attend to the general farm administration although by then I was able to assist her from time to time.

Government grants and some deregulation of green belt areas led to increased activity regarding speculative building. The most successful local developer was Archie Bolton who over a period of several years developed most areas of Bebington and Higher Bebington. Archie was from a Methodist background and personally contributed to the cost of building 'Bethesda' a modern chapel located in the centre of Bebington village. He also purchased a large plot of land (from Lancelyn Estates) by Spital cross roads, on which he constructed a magnificent house, called 'Bethany', for his own occupation.

My mother became one of the most regular attendees at Bethesda on Tuesday afternoons. She and her sister (my aunt Annie) made worship their focal point of the week. At the week-ends my brothers and I would regularly attend Sunday school, but were not quite as enthusiastic about it as my mother.

Aunt Annie was a young widow. Her husband Willie, had worked at Cammel Lairds until about 1929-30 as a ship's cabinet maker. He had been laid off during the slump and had then (with help from Tom) started a poultry farm in Plymyard Avenue, Bromborough. Tragically he was killed instantly in a fall at Plymyard. He had been a good tradesman and a part time lay-preacher as well as a husband and so it was a tragic loss. After his death my aunt returned to work at Lever Bros, where she had worked before her marriage, but this time as an office cleaner.
She lived several miles away in Rock Ferry so getting to work involved a very early start. She had over a mile to walk before she could catch the train to Port Sunlight where she would have to start work at 6 a.m. prompt. She would work until 8 a.m., return home and repeat the process in the evening when she would work from 6 p.m. until 8 p.m.

Although Annie was childless herself, she would ensure that each of her seventeen nephews and nieces would receive a Christmas parcel costing at least 2s 6d, (12.5p). To achieve this, she would at the beginning of each year pay regular amounts into a 'sweet club'. Because the two sisters' religion was an essential part of their lives, the annual day trip in June of each year (usually to Llandudno, N. Wales) together with the Christmas party held at the chapel itself, were the highlights of their year.

Rearmament - hard times for the country.

1935 was an unsettling year both at home and across Europe. The dictators flexed their muscles and were in no mood for appeasement.
The unrest of the British public was becoming more difficult for the coalition government to contain. Many historians write that the 1929-31 financial crash was beginning to 'bottom-out', due in no small part to the decision to rearm. That may well have been the case in the Home-Counties and the Midlands. Here in the North-West however many were on and indeed beyond the poverty line. Companies and businesses were not slow to take advantage of this situation and indeed Bebington Borough Council was among the worst offenders.

As a result of long term unemployment and malnutrition, many workers were physically unable to return to heavy manual work. Two of my uncles died in their early thirties!

Lever Bros had a high standard of commitment to their employees, however some of their subsidiaries were less understanding.

Ice cream manufacturers and distributors were also based in Port Sunlight and employed labour (many were ex-servicemen) for as little as £1 a week and commission on sales. For this pittance they would be expected to peddle a tri-cycle delivery cart with the words 'Stop me and buy one' emblazoned on the side. Their hours were from 10 a.m. or 10.30 a.m. until dark for either six or seven days a week.

Then there was the Lever's Cattle Cake Factory close by. They ran a three shift system over a seven night period - not only poorly paid but universally known as the 'sweat shop'.

Some of the antics of the Bebington Borough Council were even more outrageous. Apprentices in most trades were taken on straight from school at fourteen years of age and on reaching twenty-one when they were due to receive a full wage, were dismissed without explanation. Little wonder then that in Poulton, Major Green was forced to employ an assistant gamekeeper in an endeavor to contain the increasing occasions of poaching. Local residents had to start locking doors and keeping an eye out for opportunist thieves – something they were not accustomed to in country areas.

In order to help out her sisters, my mother would often detail me, on a Friday evening, to cycle to Port Sunlight and meet my Aunt Annie.
I would be carrying a parcel of eggs, vegetables and occasionally a rabbit, prepared for the oven I might add. As four of the five sisters lived in the same road in Rock Ferry, these items could easily be distributed to alleviate in some part, the families' 'bread line' existence.

CHAPTER FOUR
War Looms Closer – I Become A Full-Time Farmer

Hitler breaks the Versailles Treaty.

By October 1935, 'Il Duce' of Italy (Mussolini) finally lost patience with negotiations and his troops stormed Abyssinia. The English election was in November 1935 and this time produced a victory for the Tories over Labour by 387 seats to 150. Once again Stanley Baldwin became prime minister. In early 1936 Hitler occupied the Rhineland in contravention to the Versailles Armistice Agreement.

Once more the League of Nations seemed hopeless and would not intervene.

King George V died in January 1936 and his eldest son became King Edward VIII. Unknown to most people in this country but common knowledge in 'The States', Edward was deeply involved with the twice married, Mrs Wallis Simpson. Britain was torn between her alliances with other countries (Austria and Czechoslovakia), and the risk involved in joining forces with the most feared dictator of all – Stalin of Russia. 'Friendly Uncle Joe', he was not! France's foreign secretary, Pierre Laval was secretly in league with Mussolini. He was thus indirectly involved with the Civil War in Spain where General Franco successfully overthrew a legally elected government, with a little help from Hitler and Mussolini.

The USA, in the shape of President Roosevelt attempted to intervene in negotiations but his proposed suggestions were not even considered by the nations concerned. Little wonder then that Hitler chose this moment to announce his intention to extend Germany's boundaries to incorporate millions of German speaking subjects.

By December 1936 Edward VIII had abdicated and was succeeded by his brother, the Duke of York, who became George VI. By May 1937 Stanley Baldwin had resigned and was replaced by Neville Chamberlain. Within six months Eden resigned, to be replaced by Lord Halifax as Foreign Secretary. The country had had three monarchs within a year, three prime ministers in under two years and three foreign secretaries within two and a half years. There had also been little cohesion between each prime minister and their respective foreign secretaries.

Unemployment was still unacceptably high and little action appeared to be being taken to bring the situation under control. This period was also formative for me personally. I was due to leave school by the summer of 1938 and the prospects were far from rosy. Vacancies were few and applicants many. I sat exams for a Merchant Navy scholarship. Although I had passed the exams I was deemed to be outside the qualifying percentage and advised to re-sit for a scholarship in six months' time.

It was at this point that matters were taken out of my hands. My elder brother, who was now the mainstay of the farm and thus a large contributor to the family income, rowed with Tom and changed his occupation. As my father had little faith in higher education he now wanted me to replace my brother on the farm. Having already spent four years trying to study and simultaneously working many hours each week during term time, and full time during school holidays, I was far from enthusiastic - however there seemed to be little alternative.

I 'exchange shoes for wellingtons'.

So it was that in August 1938 I commenced my apprenticeship as a potential farmer. As was to be expected the general comment was that, 'A grammar school education didn't do him much good'. In the short term this may have seemed true but I did feel privileged to have experienced those early years at Wirral Grammar School, though at the time they seemed far from enjoyable. Joining the farm at that time meant that I would experience the rigours of the harvest with its 'dawn to dusk' operations. For the first time I needed to study the farmer's worst enemy, the elements.
August 1938 was not a month for good weather. Despite many setbacks the oat and wheat fields did get cut, the sheaves were 'stooked' and left to settle. They were finally collected and formed into rectangular stacks some ten to twelve metres high. Without an elevator all this had to be done in the primitive style which consisted of manhandling from one wagon to another. Extra labour had had to be brought in to assist with this back-breaking and dusty work. Finally the stacks were completed and their tops protected from inclement weather by having a thatched 'roof' - laid by Tom himself. Then in late autumn the thresher would arrive. The power unit was similar to a steam roller.

The sheaves of corn were projected into a large hopper and via a series of cogs and wheels until the ears of corn were segregated from the stalks. The corn ended up in sacks at the front of the machine while the stalks (chaff) ended up at the rear of the contraption. Hence the expression - 'separating the wheat from the chaff'. Once again hired labour was required and because of the amount of dust produced by the threshing process, ample quantities of tea, cordial (and occasionally something stronger!), were in constant demand.

The day started at 6 a.m. for the thresher driver. He would cycle to the farm and light the coal fire which produced the steam, this directly propelled the belt which drove the thresher itself. This all took some two to two and a half hours. The labour arrived at 8.30 a.m. and only then could the day's work commence. On a medium sized farm such as Lancelyn, the whole operation took three to four days providing there were not too many snags. If the belt should break, the whole machine would grind to a standstill until it was either repaired or replaced. Dairy herds are of course unconcerned with such seasonal distractions and the cows still needed milking twice a day. Thus in addition to the threshing operation the usual farm routine still had to be maintained.

With the harvesting finally complete, the corn dealers arrived to evaluate the quality and quantity of the final product, prices were negotiated and deliveries arranged

It was now time to start ploughing in order to beat the first frosts, and the annual cycle would start all over again. Once the cold weather made it impossible to cultivate the ground, the dreaded hedging and ditching, all carried out by hand, began. In this part of Cheshire most fields were comparatively small in acreage. At Lancelyn we had two fields of fourteen acres each but the others were mostly between six and ten acres in area. Each field was surrounded by four hedges and four ditches. That's a lot of work! Today, many farm fields have had the hedges grubbed out to make life easier for tractors and the more modern machinery. A team of horses would struggle to haul a single plough along while modern tractors make light work of double treble or even four 'tines'. This drastic reduction of natural habitat explains why our wild life has suffered so much in the last century or so. Many familiar birds of my youth such as skylarks, corncrakes and so many others are virtually extinct.

In autumn 1938, Prime Minister Neville Chamberlain returned from Munich to Heston Airfield waving a piece of paper indicating that there would be - 'Peace in our time'. This was the signal for recruitment, but by the back door. This meant The Territorials for the army and the Volunteer Reserve for the RAF.

A school colleague asked me to join him and enlist as a dispatch rider in the Royal Army Service Corps (RASC). Due to my work on the farm I was unable to make the interview that week and by the following week all vacancies had been filled. Len Barlow, my friend, did join up and by 1940 was on his way to Egypt where he remained until VE day 1945. Fate had determined a very different course for me.

The winter of 1938-39 passed uneventfully. On the farm the main potato season was long gone but the overflow crop had been stored in a 'hog'. This was a purpose made triangular- shaped mound, with the crop adequately protected by layers of soil and straw in order to survive the frosts. We were therefore able to supply our customers on a twice weekly basis until the end of February 1939. Thus we created a welcome additional cash flow to supplement the monthly cheque from the Milk Marketing Board.

There were now only a few months remaining before the early cropping Aran Pilots would be ready for lifting. The last peacetime spring arrived and work was hectic.

Crop rotation ensured a healthy yield of potatoes, turnips and mangolds, (a large type of beet used for cattle food), in the fields of last year's corn harvest. The 1938 potato fields were sown with clover for the first half of the year, to be followed by wheat, barley and oats. There was never a dull moment.

Rabbits and goats - a 'farm too far'.

At about this time I purchased my first gun, a double barrelled BSA twelve bore. While ploughing one day I was approached by Mort, the estate game keeper. He was traditionally clad in deer stalker, tweeds, long thick knee high stockings and very heavy boots. Mort was normally a taciturn man, grumpy even. I was somewhat surprised therefore at the friendly manner in which he offered instruction in the use of what could be a very dangerous weapon. Mort would always carry his gun in the 'broken' position i.e. with the stock detached from the barrel, while he was not actually using the gun. Tenants were allowed to shoot both rabbit and hare within their own grounds but not, of course pheasant, partridge or other game. Mort also introduced me to the art of deflection shooting which stood me in good stead in my next profession.

Talking of rabbits brings me back to Frank Jones, our cowman. Now he was a great rabbit hunter but not with either guns or traps which were used by most farmers in an endeavor to contain the numerous warrens on the estate. Taffy's method was to use nets and ferrets, a vile, smelly (and dangerous) weasel-like animal trained specifically to hunt rabbits. Frank's interest was not purely environmental. Each rabbit was worth at least 1s 0d (5p) and were much sought after by folk with medicinal problems, due to their low saturated fat content.

Frank's small herd of goats was steadily increasing and by now his wife Violet had built up a number of selected clients who, mainly due to medical conditions required goat's milk.

The potato planting season was now over and it was a rush to get on with sowing the spring crops. The lighter nights meant longer working hours and life seemed a continual race against time.

The dark and ominous threat of war was never far away. During May the new conscription law was introduced to the effect that all males of twenty years of age would be required to join the services for a period of six months. The Poulton hamlet saw one of its inhabitants caught in the net.

This was George Williams, son of Jack Williams, the ex-horseman of Vinyard Farm. George had worked for a short time for my father but then he left to be an ambulance driver at the 'Fever Section' of the local (Clatterbridge) hospital. Oddly enough, out of barracks these conscripts did not wear uniform. Instead they were kitted out in a cheap tweed jacket, grey flannels and a French style blue beret. I wonder who received a knighthood for thinking that one up!

Once again there were threatening noises coming from Germany, this time relating to the Polish part of Danzig. There was little to be gleaned from the press on this subject and I found that due to pressure of work I had insufficient time to follow matters as closely as I would have liked.

Our biggest problem was trying to cope efficiently with two separate farms which were separated by other farmer's fields. To exacerbate matters Tom would refuse to be drawn into anything connected with mechanical plant or transport. Today it would be referred to as a 'logistical problem'. Back then we just called it 'a farm too far'. I did however manage to obtain a small concession - instead of travelling with carts and wagons each day to work at the Rising Sun Farm, I arranged for a spare set of these to be left permanently at Rising Sun. That way I could take the shorter (but too steep for horses *and* wagons) route via Raby Mere and Thornton Common Road, to Clatterbridge. This way was three-quarters of a mile shorter and very useful in the evening at 'knocking off' time. It also helped Tom Peers our labourer who cycled in each day from Neston. He was now able to start and finish his day at Clatterbridge, thus saving him a round trip of four miles.

I was also successful in making arrangements with Mr Ashcroft our neighbouring farmer on the Spital side to use his elevator at harvest time. This would hoist both hay and corn into stacks thus saving labour. Unfortunately it was a bit antiquated and lacked engine power. To compensate, it required a horse walking in circles to propel the elevator's mechanism.

Britain declares war on Germany – Life changes forever.

It was essential to make all the economies possible because the farm's finances were extremely tight. As I mentioned earlier Tom's social contribution to his parent's upkeep was 5s 0d a week. They were now out of a home and had to be re-located to Rising Sun Cottage (rent free of course!) Not content with these 'freebies', my grandfather would plunder our potato crops and decamp to The Rose and Crown for the rest of the day, whenever the opportunity presented itself.

The distant families in Rock Ferry were still dependent on the Friday night largesse dispensed by my mother, via her sister Annie. In addition to the previous contributions there would be a brown envelope probably containing a 10s 0d note (50p). These donations together with increasing deductions made by the Milk Marketing Board from the monthly milk cheque, left a very slender margin of profit.

My weekly wage was 10s 0d plus a little overtime. The balance would go to my over stressed and over worked mother. Changes would have to be made - but what? The RAF was still advertising for Volunteer Reserves but I had little time to offer. I then read that applicants were invited to apply for pilot training as non-commissioned officers. 'Worth a try', I thought, so off went my application – I received no reply.

Meanwhile Hitler's demands persisted, then came the bombshell. On 23 August 1939 Russia signed a non-aggression pact with Germany. The next day, in anticipation of immediate war, the passing of the Emergency Powers Act signified that at last the country appreciated the seriousness of the situation. In the early hours of 1 September 1938, German troops invaded Poland.

At 9a.m. on Sunday 3 September an ultimatum was issued to Hitler for an immediate withdrawal from Polish territory – giving him just two hours to comply. By 11a.m and as no reply had been received, we heard the prime minister declare that - 'A state of war now exists between our two countries'.

Before elaborating on the events which followed the government's Defence of the Realm Act, I would like to remind people of a 'behind the scenes' act often overshadowed by other international happenings. 'Kindly Uncle Joe', Stalin, extracted his price for his alliance with Hitler by invading a neutral Finland in a ferocious unprovoked battle of attrition. The Finns put up a tremendous fight against a powerful regime but finally had to accept defeat. The invasion started on 30 November 1939 and ended in the Moscow Peace Treaty on 13 March 1940. The Finns were forced to cede over 10% of their territory and almost a third of their economy. They did however retain their sovereignty and enhance their international reputation.

Now back to this country, after the issue of the DoR Act some 1.5 million people were evacuated from the cities, mostly London. Gas masks, civilian for the use of, were issued and air raid shelters provided.

There were black out orders issued for both property and vehicles and ARP (Air Raid Precautions) Wardens were appointed. Auxiliary Fire Service personnel were recruited. The Women's Voluntary Service was established initially in support of the ARP, in reality they spread themselves far and wide to great effect. In September 1939 a British Expeditionary Force was sent to France.

Only one evacuee arrived at Poulton. He was a nephew of Mr Salter, from London. A wave of sympathy was extended to Mrs Salter, a small lady already coping with five males, and as sometimes quoted six men is over half a football team! Somehow Mrs Salter took it in her stride. 'Jeff', the other Londoner, in addition to his estate duties took on the position of part-time ARP Warden for the area.

I enrol for aircrew training – the government demand more food from farmers.

September is the start of the busiest time in the calendar year in mixed farming. At the outbreak of war we were just commencing the corn harvest. As soon as the crops were gathered the potato picking season started. Despite the war there was no shortage of casual labour on which the success of the season depended. It was at this time that we received a slight bonus.

British Summer Time normally ended during September but was now extended through the winter. The following summer would witness the introduction of Double British Summer Time. This gave valuable extra daylight hours in which to complete outside work. Once the farm routine returned to normal, I managed to visit the RAF recruiting office in Chester where I enrolled for aircrew training. Of course I did not divulge this to anyone except Taffy, who thought I needed my head examining – maybe he was right.

Ration books were now being issued for all the civilian population. Since the country imported over fifty per cent of all its food, plans were soon underway to increase home production. From this point we were inundated with correspondence from the 'Agg. and Fish', the Ministry for Agriculture and Fisheries.

October passed without communication from the RAF. This month was also extremely busy on the farm. The main crop of potatoes had to be lifted and 'hogged' and as previously outlined, there was much ploughing to be completed before the first frosts.

At about this time I noticed that yet another new tenant had taken occupation at Mere Brook House in Thornton Common Road. Through the 'grape vine' I heard that it was the ex-owner of a small fleet of private aircraft. This fleet had operated (pre-war) out of Hooton Airfield. The new tenants were a certain Frank Davison and his wife Ann, the RAF had now taken control of the airfield.

Any thoughts the neighbourhood may have entertained that a nearby RAF station would improve our safety in the event of German air raids were quickly dispelled. The crack No 610 squadron had already been moved southwards. Coastal Command replaced 610 Sqn as Hooton was to be used as a base for anti-U-boat operations.
The Tiger Moth flew from the newly named Hooton Park on daily patrols along the coast. Their only aids were flare pistols and carrier pigeons! A few Anson aircraft and the latest Westland Lysanders also carried out these patrols. Needless to say there were no reports of submerged U-Boats and later, the airfield was passed on to Training Command.

Back to the Davisons. I would occasionally see Mrs Davison driving her 'governess' cart which could be readily identified by the large steps at the rear. She appeared to alternate the horses between a 'grey' and a 'chestnut'. Whichever horse she was using, there was always a large dog on board. Although the lady and her husband were experienced pilots, there had been no vacancy for either of them in the RAF in any flying capacity. While Frank ran his parents' sand and gravel company in North Wales, his wife was trying to earn a living out of the five acres of land which accompanied the tenancy of 'The Mere Brook'.

Early November saw the annual visit of the thresher. Shortly afterwards I received an invitation for an interview and examination in accordance with my 'aircrew' application. I was fortunate to be able to conceal this letter from my parents and with the passage of time have forgotten the excuse which I made to explain my absence.

And so to the first Christmas of WW II. Very little had happened to date in the combat war. The words 'phoney war' now used to describe this period was certainly not in use then. Headline news was the war at sea and the sinking by U-boats of merchant shipping carrying important goods, not the least of which was food. These acts further motivated the government in its pursuit of harassing the farming community to increase productivity of both milk and arable crops. I returned from my successful attestation selection only to be told that it would be some months before I would be required for service.

Horses with 'claws' on their hooves – the severe winter of 1939-40.

Once more I clambered onto the treadmill of a seven day per week routine. It was a bitter winter, one of the coldest that I can remember. A shortage of supplies intensified the severity of rationing and Frank Jones and I spent what little free time we had, catching rabbits. After just a few months of war, the rabbit fur itself now had a value. Wrapped up well, we were probably warmer outside, than inside our respective homes.

Christmas of any year was a busy time at the farm. Both the geese-flock and the many cockerels reared for the festivities, had to be killed, plucked and 'dressed' for our potential customers.
One of the many memories I took with me after my 'call-up' was of Tom after a bout of over-celebrating at the Chester Christmas Fair. He was chasing the reluctant geese around the farmyard with feathers flying and the angry geese snarling and honking – none of us would attempt this job.

Over the festive season itself the weather was somewhat milder but as the calendar turned to 1940 there was a complete change. One of the worst blizzards I had ever encountered blew in from the east. By the middle of January everything almost came to a standstill – but not quite. Somehow public transport operated on a restricted basis and woe betide anyone who failed to arrive for work on the farm. Tom Peers our labourer, on pay of £1 10s per week, was unable to cycle the seven miles from his home in Neston. He would walk three-quarters of a mile to his local rail station, and travel on the country line via Willaston and Hooton to alight at Bromborough. He would then travel the last mile on foot and so arrived for work at 9 a.m. rather than 7.30 a.m. On his arrival, he and I were dispatched to the potato 'hog' to prepare the Friday market deliveries against almost impossible odds.

A fire was lit and somehow before dark, the potatoes were released (undamaged!). Tom Peers would then reverse his earlier journey to get home. He continued in this fashion until the roads became passable after some seven days. Due to the inclemency of the weather most producers almost doubled the going rate of 3s 6d (22.5p), for a cwt of potatoes, but not Tom, who would not allow one penny to be added to his usual charges.

Delivery under these weather conditions was a frightening experience. The horses were taken to the smithy, (blacksmith's workshop) where projecting screws were fitted to their metal shoes. It required three horses rather than the usual two, to thus shod, trek the ten to twelve mile return journey to Birkenhead to supply our customers.

I particularly mention this because in the winters of 2009 and 2010, which had much less intensive snowstorms, both public transport and many private vehicles came to a complete standstill - this after seventy years of so-called progress. The weather in February 1940 was a slight improvement over that of January. Life was however still hard and the hours long. This gave me very little time to reflect over the reason why my call-up papers had still not arrived.

CHAPTER FIVE

'Called Up' For the RAF – My First Home Leave

I join the RAF – breaking the news to Tom and Lilly – 'a change of sons' - spring 1940.

The last of gamekeeper Mort's sons still at home, Les and Ron, were conscripted into the army so now three of the hamlet's population were in uniform. In the spring my own papers finally arrived. I won't go into the ensuing row with the furious Tom. Suffice it to say that I was so chastened by his anger and my mother's distress, that the memory of it is as strong now as it was seventy years ago.

My eldest brother had long since regretted his decision to leave the farm and returned to take my place. Although at the age of twenty-three he was within 'call up' criteria, because he re-joined Tom at the farm, he once again worked within a 'reserved' occupation and therefore was not required for compulsory service. Ironically the situation was really a 'change of sons'. In fact Tom junior fully contributed to the war effort between his essential occupation and the mandatory home-guard duties he later performed.

An exhausting journey home - the 'horse with wings' - November 1940.

I returned to the farm from RAF Ansty, ten miles north-east of Coventry on 24 November. This was my first leave since joining the RAF in the spring of 1940. The journey home had been long and tedious. Travelling cross country even in the twenty-first century by public transport leaves much to be desired. To a teenage airman, carrying full equipment in back packs and kitbags and additionally overloaded with flying clothes was trying, to say the least. It was almost 22.00 hrs before I struggled onto the platform at Chester station.

I was fully expecting to find myself marooned until the morning 'milk train' to The Wirral arrived. To my amazement there was a train about to depart from platform one for Woodside (Birkenhead) station. With the first smile of the day on my face, I boarded the train with all my luggage still intact. I found myself amongst a party of RAF and WAAF (Woman's Auxiliary Air Force) personnel returning to their unit at Hooton Park. The company was welcome and we soon started the circa half hour journey. There had however been an earlier air raid on Merseyside, and on arrival at Hooton Station there ensued the inevitable conversation between train crew and station management. The outcome was that due to 'line difficulties' ahead, the journey would terminate right there i.e. at Hooton. Fortunately for me some of the forces party were billeted well away from the RAF station and proceeded to show me a short cut to Plymyard Avenue in Bromborough. They also gave me welcome assistance with my luggage. We finally parted company and as if the journey itself was not a sufficient challenge, the road was unmade. It had large potholes, dangerous at any time but with a 'black out' in force absolutely horrendous. I was more than glad to arrive at Lancelyn Farm at about 02.30 hrs but not so pleased at having to 'knock up' the inhabitants, which took a bit of courage. Surprisingly Tom answered the door with the remark - 'Am I pleased to see you'. At the unearthly time of 06.00 hrs I found out *why*. Woken from a deep sleep I discovered that I was required to take one of Tom's (now only five) shire horses to Hooton Station. We were then to entrain via Chester to the Wrexham horse sale, as he was surplus to requirements. The train was due to leave Hooton Station just before 09.00 hrs.

After having dressed and taken a hurried breakfast, I left the farm in total darkness with the animal in tow. It was only later that I realised that he was not from one of the regular teams I had been familiar with a year ago. Fuddled by tiredness I didn't give the matter another thought. By the time we reached Raby Mere some fifteen or twenty minutes later, I decided to give my legs and body a rest. Using the low wall surrounding the mere as a stepping stone, I clambered onto the horse's broad back. Fortunately there was a horsecloth covering his upper parts which avoided any damage to my No 1 'Blues' (best uniform). The horse didn't seem to object to its uninvited rider and proceeded to obey all the signals I issued to him via the bridle.

It was in this fashion that the journey proceeded, past Bromborough Golf Club, left at Hargrave Lane (a well-known lovers tryst) and into Benty Heath Lane. This was a very exclusive road to have as one's address in 1940 when all dozen or so houses had chauffeurs, gardeners and very likely other servants.

Despite my weariness I realised that it was only twelve months ago that I had traversed this road, albeit in the opposite direction. On that occasion I was returning in a horse and cart from the Hooton Christmas Fair, with an unsold goose. I had taken six geese altogether but only five had been sold. As I passed one of the large houses in Benty Heath Lane I saw Len Taylor, one of the inhabitants of the white cottage of Vinyard Farm, working in the garden. A quick word with his 'governor' and he collected the goose which was honking its disapproval at being taken away. I however was very relieved to receive the princely sum of 12s 6d (62.5p) to pass on to Tom. Now, twelve months later Len was serving in the Navy.

Back to the story – at last we were at Hooton Station where I escorted the horse down the sidings to the waiting, pre-booked horse box. These boxes were mostly used for the transportation of racing horses, the carriage being an elaborate contraption. The horse entered through a bottom-hinged door in the far end which doubled-up as a ramp, from the ground to the floor of the box. Once inside, the animal faced a manger filled with food and would then be strapped by its halter to the side of the carriage. The groom, me in this case, entered the other end of the box by a conventional door to sit on a long bench seat. A metal grill fixed to the manger enabled the groom to keep an eye on the animal's well-being.

After a twelve mile trip we changed trains at Chester for the Paddington train, whose route was via Wrexham where we alighted. The station was of course as far away from the auction premises as was possible. The journey was accomplished without incident and I noticed that the horse had a label attached to its flank bearing the number 'nineteen'. This was of interest for two reasons, firstly it would be my age in just a few week time and secondly it would mean that the start of the sale was imminent and that I could have the remainder of the day off (Tom's largess)! However, where was Tom? He was supposed to have met me on arrival at the auction. With the horse safely stabled I could visit the local taverns and eventually located him drinking with his pals. I acquainted him with the sale number. He gave me 1s 0d (5p) to arrange for one of the hostlers to ribbon the horse's mane and tail. This was done and I was most relieved when Tom arrived to escort the horse around the show ring. It comprised a large circle of straw bales with the auctioneer's rostrum at the far side. Eventually it was Tom's turn and farmer and horse paraded around the area watched by some twenty-five to thirty taciturn, hard bitten dealers.

Starting the sale of Tom's horse, the auctioneer waved his gavel and bellowed – 'A lovely gelding, 16.8 hands – well-disciplined and attended, do I hear thirty guineas?'

To emphasise the question he thumped the rostrum with his gavel - it was almost the last thing he ever did! The horse reared its full 16.8 hand height fearsomely onto its hind haunches and careered around the circle. Tom, still clinging onto the halter, left the ground. Within seconds the crowd disappeared and I might add I was at their head. Tom however had not qualified many years ago as a teamsman without accruing a wealth of experience in the handling of recalcitrant horses. Within a few seconds he was not only quite sober but fully in charge of both horse and situation. The auctioneer never heard any bids let alone the one for thirty guineas. There was no option, the animal would have to be taken back to the farm – but how!

One Vic Crutchley, a pal of Tom's (and also the owner of a large Packard 'Limo'), discovered that the horse box which brought us here earlier was still available. It was immediately re booked for a return journey to Hooton. Tom was nonchalant about the situation and instructed me to take the horse back to Wrexham Station. Once the animal had been safely ensconced in the box, I was to ring the farm to advise them regarding the time of arrival and then I could have the rest of the day to myself! Things however did not go as planned. Now I was fully aware of the huge animal's antics the journey back to the station was far more terrifying than any Tiger Moth aerobatic manoeuvre I had experienced. I haven't yet told you that the horse's name was 'Johnnie', but some wag seeing an airman leading a horse, re named him 'Pegasus'. I continued, keeping a wary distance between myself and Pegasus.

Yet another wag thought the country to be on the verge of capitulation if the *air* force was reduced to using *horses*. Fortunately for me neither civilian nor military police was in evidence. Not so fortunate was the situation we encountered on reaching the Goods Yard. With the ramp of the horse box ready to receive Pegasus, I attempted to lead him in. The stubborn animal had other ideas and refused to move from mother earth.

In every difficult situation however bizarre there appears one (or more) individuals who attempt to take command. Number one arrived moments after Pegasus' mutiny. He turned the horse away from the horse box and attempted to reverse him in. No success! The do-gooder quickly departed muttering, to be followed by another who decided to place his coat over the horse's bridle – again no movement.

The third intervention came in the shape of a railway worker who insisted that a feed bag was required so off he trotted to secure a bag of food. I remembered an Irish saying that, 'A dog is your friend whether you feed it or not but a horse is your friend if you feed it, I felt a glimmer of hope. This was soon dashed on the fellow's return. The horse wasn't falling for this one either!

By now successive trains had arrived and departed and I felt in need of divine help. A seasoned looking chap came along, heard the story, patted the horse gently on its front flanks, whispered a few words which I couldn't hear and HALLELUJAH the animal almost leapt into the box. On enquiring, I learned that that after hearing about the other attempts to move the horse, 'our man' suspected Pegasus could have been brought up in Wales and so spoke to him in Welsh. He explained that the horse was used to the softer intonation of commands given in the Welsh language and that if he could be handled by a Welsh- speaking horseman, then we would probably have no further trouble.

By this time a train was imminent. There was no time to telephone the farm so I leapt into the cabin and we proceeded to reverse the outward journey. We duly arrived back in Hooton some ten hours after the morning departure. Here I was met by my outraged elder brother who had been dispatched by my bewildered mother to find me and of course Pegasus!

The following day I related this tale to Taffy who, when he had finished laughing, translated some 'horse commands' into Welsh, to which Pegasus responded admirably. As a result the animal remained at Lancelyn Farm until the change-over to mechanical horses (tractors) and furthermore maintained an excellent behavioural record.

The Luftwaffe attempt to destroy Merseyside.

I was no stranger to air raids but will admit to being horrified at the bombing intensity on Liverpool, Birkenhead and the surrounding areas. After London, this North-West port (Liverpool) had been targeted more often than any other UK town or city. The raids had first commenced in August 1940. One of the first buildings to be hit was part of Wirral Grammar School.

Unlike Coventry, which had been a one-off concentrated raid, Merseyside seemed to receive the unwelcome visitors over long-delayed periods each night. Our deterrent, flak and night fighters which were completely out of their depth, was virtually non- existent and the enemy bombers could fly over this country at will.

The seven nights of my leave were no exception and, on the third night I think, disaster almost decimated Lancelyn Farm. Shortly after midnight a 'swoosh' of bombs was heard and felt. Shelters were not thought to be necessary in the country so we could only wait and hope. By daylight we received a visit from a visibly shaken 'Jeff', the ARP warden, who advised us that a bomb had fallen some 250 yards away, fortunately in a field but only a mere fifty yards from Jeff's cottage. Already dressed I started to walk to the scene when I suddenly realised that the field behind the farmhouse was virtually black with unexploded incendiary bombs. Later in the day I discovered that the second of a 'stick' of three bombs, each probably 500 kg, had dropped right in front of 'Bethany' the home of the builder Archie Bolton. The third bomb had scored a direct hit on two houses in Fielden Rd (off Church Rd), in Bebington.

When I later applied my newly acquired knowledge of trajectories, velocities and the like, I realised that had the bombs been released a miniscule of a second earlier, the probability was that both Poulton Hall and Lancelyn Farm would have been decimated.

It was just five weeks ago that Uncle Ned (my father's elder brother) had been killed, when his home in the north-end of Birkenhead received a direct hit from a bomb, during a similarly heavy raid over that area. One might have said that the war was taking a serious and sinister turn. It had only been in March 1940 that the then prime-minister publically declared that, 'Hitler had missed the bus'. So much for the predictions of prime ministers!

During my period of leave, the Luftwaffe had visited Merseyside every night and virtually without loss of aircraft. Apart from bad weather the air raids continued for a further six months, until the end of May in fact. Bombs fell on Eastham, Spital and Bromborough, all within a mile or so of Lancelyn Farm but the near misses of that November night in 1940 were fortunately not repeated.

Extract from Merseyside at War by Rodney Whitworth.

'At 7.03 p.m. on 28 November 1940 a purple warning was issued from Defence HQ and sirens sounded at 7.33 p.m. Within a few minutes it was realised that this was no ordinary raid. Wave after wave of bombers headed up the Mersey dropping both incendiary and HE (high explosive) bombs. For the first time the area's population would experience the devastation and terror of landmines. These were naval mines dropped by parachute to act as blast bombs and were capable of demolishing whole streets of houses. A further heavy attack which occurred on the 29 November was both the longest and the most severe to date - the cost in terms of lives and damage was also the most severe to date. An Air Ministry communique laconically issued a statement as follows –

" There was considerable enemy air activity over the country during the night of 28 – 29 November. A large number of bombs were dropped on

The Liverpool Blitz

'They that sow the wind shall reap the whirlwind'

Hosea chapter 8; verse 7

various districts but the main weight of the attack was directed against the North-West of England and particularly against Merseyside."

The Nazi press described it rather more graphically, and for once they were right. Huge fires in Liverpool are reported by our returning bombers from a large scale raid throughout the night. Mile high fires are reported throughout the area of Merseyside covering - grain elevators, oil mills, docks and oil depots and aircraft factories"

The Nazi report did not however mention the destruction of a large air raid shelter at The Junior Technical School in Dunning Road. Sixty of those trapped were rescued alive but in excess of 180 were killed in that incident alone.'

I take a trip to 'theatre land'

This then was the state of the country when I made a last trip to the 'fleshpots' of Birkenhead. As I alighted at the bus stop in Argyle Street a blank space now existed where previously the famous theatre had stood. It was hard to believe that, less than a year ago I had visited the Argyle to hear 'Private' Donald Peers singing the popular songs of that time, 'By a babbling brook I sit for hours … midst the showers…' I recalled the supporting act, Wilson, Keppel and Betty. They were a trio both made up and dressed in eastern fashion whose routine consisted of a half shuffle - half dance across a sand coated stage. Their hand and body movements were full of Egyptian imagery popularised by the discovery of Tutankhamun's tomb. The stage set was painted with depictions of pyramids and Pharaohs. Hilarious! Today no doubt they would be placed under close arrest and the audience branded as racists.

Utterly dejected at not seeing one familiar face, I returned home on the next available bus which deposited me at Spital Crossroads from where I walked the final three-quarters of a mile to Lancelyn Farm. At this point the air raid sirens commenced their soulless wail and searchlights lit up the sky. No longer were we fighting for freedom, from now on it was to be a battle for very survival itself.

I spent the remainder of that evening by a roaring family fire listening to the wireless (radio), something that had been non-existent in my service life so far. I can't recall the actual programmes but it would probably have been Jack Warner with his 'blue pencil' monologues, during which he would read out fictitious letters to and from home which the official censor had 'doctored' with a blue pencil.

Or perhaps it could have been Tommy Handley with the ITMA, ('It's that man again') show, the title reflecting Hitler's territorial claims. The show included Mrs Mop with her catchphrase, 'Can I do yer now, sir?' and a character named 'Dick the Diver' who stated that he was, 'Going down now, sir'. Daytime was spent helping the hard pressed family at work. Thus ended my last home leave for quite some time.

On a lighter note it was on this leave that I continued my earlier conversations with Ann Davison, the new resident of Mere Brook House. During an exchange of experiences I discovered that during the eight years or so of her flying career she had amassed over 1,000 flying hours. Up and until that time I had been full of self- importance at having achieved something less than 100 training hours in the air.

Anne and Frank Davison were noted adventurers. Their 'Mere – Brook' smallholding later made the headlines in all the national newspapers in the summer of 1949. They had taken their seventy foot boat Reliance out of the harbour at Fleetwood knowing that there was a distress warrant due to be issued on it. Some three weeks later they ended up near Newlyn, shipwrecked. Frank drowned but Ann survived and wrote a book 'Last Voyage' describing her experiences, which not only paid off their debts but enabled her to purchase a twenty-three foot boat in which she would become the first woman to sail across the Atlantic, single handed, in 1952. That boat the 'Felicity Ann' was kept near New York for many years.

After an abortive attempt at restoration in Alaska, Felicity Ann was donated to the North West School of Wooden Boatbuilding at Port Hadlock, Washington State. In 2017 the NWSWB handed the completed boat over to the Community Boat Project. In 2018, with a female captain and all female crew the Felicity Ann will tour the inland marine waters of Washington and British Colombia (the Salish Sea) as an 'on the water' training platform for women, youth and the community. I'm sure that Ann Davison would approve. Second hand copies of her books 'Last Voyage' and 'My Ship is so small', (which describes her solo Atlantic crossing) are still available and are both riveting reads!

In late October 2017 a Blue Plaque was installed at Mere Brook House – some sixty five years after the completion of her amazing feat. I could be cynical regarding the delay but let's say better late than never.

Vandalism and violence visit the countryside.

Although Part One virtually finishes here, there are a couple of incidents which occurred in 1943 which I shall recount.

Shortly after the hay harvest in the early summer, two boys aged ten and eleven entered Lancelyn Farm stack yard and succeeded in setting fire to one of the hay stacks. As they were escaping Frank Jones caught them and the police were informed. The stack could not be saved.

Before the end of the summer of that same year, Tom was attacked by a gang of youths when he reprimanded them for trespassing.

I mention these incidents as an indication of how quickly social conduct can collapse without strict discipline being in force – due to the absence of a strong father figure, perhaps? Were these people the forerunners of today's feral youth?

I was reliably informed that after the near bombing of 'Bethany', the home of builder Archie Bolton, that the property was offered for sale at around £1,000.

CHAPTER 6   Epilogue to Part One

Tom died on 30 December 1961, just a few weeks before his seventy-second birthday. A few days before Christmas of that year he arose as usual before 6 a.m. to assist with the milking of his herd of twenty- five dairy cows. Even although a milking machine had been installed for over a decade, Tom insisted that a few cows had to be milked by hand... He came into the kitchen for breakfast at 8 a.m. and just keeled over losing both speech and muscle movement. Tom was quickly transferred to nearby Clatterbridge Hospital, failed to respond to treatment and passed away peacefully about ten days later.

A year later, the tenancy of Lancelyn Farm was transferred to a neighbouring farmer and animals and implements were quickly disposed of at an auction. Due to the kindness of the Lancelyn - Green family, my mother was permitted to stay in the farmhouse for a peppercorn rent, where she remained peacefully until the summer of 1976. After her death she was buried at St Andrews Church in Bebington, with Tom; they are just yards away from Sammy Smith and family - so ends an era.

Auntie Annie died in 1964 and among the many documents rescued from the farmhouse, I discovered her will. She left an almost unbelievable (for those days) sum of £2,500. Annie had been a widow for some thirty-five years and earned an income from working of not even £2 a week. The people of that age saved because it was always the spectre of poverty and debt which kept them living a life of thrift but without being mean.

In stark contrast Frank Field, Labour M.P. for Birkenhead berates the present 'benefits system' which he maintains allows so many people to lurch through life without making any effort or contribution to their own well-being.

Frank (Taffy) Jones disposed of his goats and poultry shortly after WW II and firstly managed his own green-grocery business. Later he took over the tenancy of a small farm in North-Wales, (back to his roots). As far as I am aware the venture was successful but he and his wife suffered the tragic loss of their son, (born in 1943) in a motor-cycle accident.

Rose Cottage in Dibbinsdale, the abode of Frank and his family while working at Lancelyn Farm, has recently had a major re build. It now sports a sparkling solar panel roof!

Harold Donkin who had taken over Vinyard Farm before the war was not so fortunate. In the early 1950s the farm and business went into liquidation and Harold became a driver in a funeral director's business. Unfortunately Harold had a penchant for liquid lunches. One day he parked his hearse outside The Seven Stars, a local pub in Thornton Hough. On his return – no hearse! This was long before the days when anything which stood still was deemed to become the property of the beholder. I think he finished his days as a Verger, probably at Bromborough.

George Williams who had been the militia boy of the village and Ron Mort, the youngest of the gamekeeper's family both returned to Poulton after the war, but sadly both would die in their very early forties. By contrast, Mrs Salter, the 'football team' mother, went on to reach over 100 years of age.

'Bethany' which as you will remember was the home of Archie Bolton until 1940 when it was bombed, had two other houses built on its extensive grounds. In about 2004, developers offered an undisclosed sum (but rumoured to be in excess of £2.5m), for the purchase of these properties, to enable a development of flats to be built in their place. Rightly, in my view, the local council vetoed the proposal. The developers then approached the office of the deputy prime-minister, John Prescott who overturned the veto and gave permission for the development to proceed. Today on that same spot there stands a conglomeration of buildings with vehicles parked in every available space proudly proclaiming itself as –

'POULTON MANOR'

Whenever possible I take a diversionary route to avoid this eye-sore. Ashcroft's Farm no longer exists, its fields converted into modern suburbia. Jeff's cottage has long ceased to be, as has Mort the gamekeeper's cottage.

The 'tied' cottages of Vinyard Farm which in my early days housed the Williams' family of six and the Donkin's family of three was converted some years ago into a single country cottage. Hooton Park was vacated by the R.A.F in 1957. At that time Manchester's Ringway Airport (less than forty miles away) was developing swiftly. Entrepreneurs of the air showed little interest in Hooton. In the early sixties a part of the site became a Vauhall Motors car factory, essentially an overflow from their Luton base. (Editors note: Hooton later became a centre for Wartime Memorabilia Exchanges as Ron found out. See page 204.) Speke Airfield returned to commercial flying but struggled to attract major airlines. Speke's name was changed to John Lennon International Airport in 2001. In reality (at the time of writing) it is a base for both Easyjet and Ryanair, for their 'no frills' mainly European flights.

My younger brother, seven years my junior died suddenly in 2008 and many of the documents used in this story were found in the attic of his house. Among said papers was an envelope (dated 1957) containing several large professionally taken photographs of Tom's current dairy herd. The envelope was addressed to one 'T.Williamson' who at the time was Lever's cattle food representative for the Cheshire area. It is likely that the photographs had been taken on the instructions of Lever's as a promotional initiative.

We also reclaimed a brown Rexine, simulated leather, three piece suite and amazingly also the receipt, dated 1928 - for the sum of £12! With just the cushions replaced it now does sterling service providing comfortable seating in a pine cabin with a wood burning stove, used by my son.

PART TWO   TAKING TO THE AIR

CHAPTER 7

Farmer's Fields and Classrooms

Padgate – we encounter Dick Turpin!

We had just three weeks' basic training and inoculations at Padgate, Cheshire. A new camp at Ludlow, Shropshire was only just in the process of being developed into a permanent site. This was to become 'home' to 350 aircrew volunteers. The mood of the men was mutinous at our overall treatment at Padgate but in particular at the rate of pay. While under training the rate of daily pay was to have been 2s 0d (10p!) payable fortnightly in arrears. On the first pay day we found that 4s 0d (equal to two day's pay) had been deducted for 'barrack room damages'. On our exhortations of:

'But we haven't damaged the barrack room!'
- the response was:
'Maybe not but the intake before you lot did.'

   Like myself most of us had obligations to meet and would give half of our pay to our parents. It would mean having to survive on just 10s 0d a fortnight (50p).
Most of us had given up reserved occupations to join the forces so felt justified in our annoyance, however much worse was to follow.

   The country was in chaos, 345,000 troops had just suffered a humiliating escape from France - an invasion seemed imminent so the expectations of a band of less than 400 untrained airmen must have seemed of little consequence to 'the powers that be'. A new prime minister manipulating a coalition cabinet had more important matters on his agenda than the unjustified levying of 'barrack room damages'.

Ludlow and a massive 'culture' shock.

   On the other hand, to the party of men marching from Ludlow station wearing full equipment and carrying all their worldly possessions on their backs, the three mile march along the main Shrewsbury to Hereford road seemed interminable. Finally, and on the command of 'Left wheel!' from the corporal in charge, we turned into a field which was to be our home for some weeks.

The scene which unfolded before us was incomprehensible. An empty field of some thirty or forty acres with about forty 'bell' tents, un-erected and just strewn carelessly about on the ground. Some wag called out - 'At least they can't charge barrack room damages here.' He was however wrong and these wholly unreasonable charges continued to be levied for a further four or five months.

Our immediate problem was to erect the tents. We formed groups of eight to do this. When all our kit and personal possessions were stacked inside, there was hardly room for eight airmen. We erected tripods outside the tent awnings for ablutions then moved on to erect the marquee which was to serve as a dining room - when the trestle tables and chairs finally arrived, some ten days later! We then commenced to put up the field kitchen and water purifier (incomplete naturally). Finally we built a screen in preparation for an excavator to create 'instant latrines'. Yes you've probably guessed, the excavator was several days late, so spades became the order of the day.

By the end of that first weekend it was apparent that the complex was doomed and the view was widely held that we would be posted to our respective aircrew training units – wrong again. On the Monday a warrant officer (discipline) arrived - he was little more than a monster. Working rosters were established and we were drilled very early in the morning and again, very late in the evening. There were daily kit inspections and roll calls at least three times per day. Charges were instigated for the slightest indiscretion.

Construction work commenced immediately with road making and hard landscaping being formed around the dining areas. This work was mostly carried out by ourselves under supervision from a handful of construction workers. We then received the disturbing news that two of our group had been attacked and badly beaten by a passing army unit. There had been rumours of 'bad blood', between the Dunkirk survivors and the RAF. The army wrongly believed that the RAF had, through absenteeism, not supported the evacuation adequately. Some thirty members of the military police were drafted in to ensure tight security. Of what, one may ask? The final indignity was that an FFI, (free from infection) inspection was conducted in the field beyond the tented area. The whole unit lined up in 'open order', the front row two paces forward and the rear two paces behind. The medical officer, and the warrant officer, holding his regimental cane, would on the command 'balls to the left', march down the ranks (all trousers having been already dropped to the ground).

On reaching one end and on the command 'balls to the right', the MO and WO would inspect the next row. The warrant officer would continually use his swagger stick to ensure the inspection was carried out to the full. Words cannot adequately describe the indignity of such a public inspection carried out in the open air over a period of some two hours.

Ludlow - Saved by a scythe.

Poor quality food and lack of general hygiene coupled with inadequate toilet facilities, rapidly took their toll. Almost nightly ambulances removed airmen vomiting and stricken with dysentery, to mention only two ailments.

There was a call for volunteers to scythe the overgrown grass surrounding the various permanent buildings which were to be used as an administration block. Several people including myself stood forward to offer themselves as fit for this task. Following a close inspection of the ancient and decrepit tools available, the others withdrew shaking their heads. As the middle son of a struggling farmer, I quickly realised that scything duties could alter my daily routine of drill, equipment inspections and interminable roll-calls.

With the help of Reg Cosham, one of my tent crew and a resourceful cockney, I commenced re setting the blades, adjusting the 'toe' and 'heel' and extensively honing what were essentially medieval agricultural instruments. We then set to work and managed to create the impression of having carried out a good day's labour. In reality we found time to attend to the fire and ovens in the kitchen and soon had a supply of tea, basic food and a little comfort. Our efforts must have impressed because further work was offered, and gratefully accepted, to enable us to remain off the 'general duties' list. During this time, the health and moral of the unit was going rapidly downhill with no apparent efforts being made to resolve the issues. We were all now convinced that this was a 'ministerial' project aiming to prove that a new camp could be established at negligible cost - no doubt resulting in a knighthood for the instigator.

The project thus lurched into its fifth week, the list of casualties increasing daily – then it happened. As he called the early morning parade to attention, 'the monster' whose soubriquet had now become 'suicide', suddenly became stricken with the dreaded lurgy and staggered off towards the nearest set of latrines clutching his nether regions. Fortunately he failed to make it and collapsed into an uncontrollable spasm, later to be removed by ambulance.

With amazing decorum the unit remained civilized and respectful. This event gave us the opportunity to demand of the flight sergeant who took over the parade, that firm and drastic action be instigated forthwith. Our requests bore fruit and the following day the unit was declared 'disbanded' and all personnel were posted to their respective units.

Newquay - professional training at last.

I well remember the administrative NCO reciting his chapter and verse to us:
> 'Some of you his educated.'
> 'Some of you hisn't.'
> 'Some of you are posted to Torkway.'
> 'Some of you are posted to Newkway.'

Being of the Newquay contingent, I relinquished my trusty scythe to assist with the dismantling of the tents. The whole unit packed kitbags and haversacks containing our belongings, including water bottles, gas masks and tin hats, to march to the local station. Two days later we found ourselves at the railway station, situated off Cliff Road in Newquay. We were the fresh intake using the once sought after hotels facing the Town Beach and Newquay Bay.

I believe this was known as No 1 ITW (Initial Training Wing). This was a circa fifteen week course designed to further establish our fitness for aircrew training. As expected the training was tough and difficult but this time both professionally administered and rewarding. Reveille was at 05.30 hrs with lights out at 22.00 hrs prompt. Movement between classrooms was always 'on the march' at 140 paces per minute, by comparison the army marched at 110 to 120 paces. In view of some of today's whinging student's high opinion of the difficulty of their study regime, I think it is worth recording a resume of our curriculum:

Half hour PT daily before breakfast.
One hour drilling daily.
One and a half hour rifle drill weekly.
A seven to ten mile cross country run, fortnightly on a Saturday, followed by night manoeuvres against the local defence volunteers.
On the intermediate Saturdays there would be night manoeuvres against army recruits from the area, later to be called, the Home Guard.
Monthly visits to the rifle range for rifle, revolver and machine gun (only one available) practice.
Clay pigeon shooting was used to practice deflection shots.

**The New Recruit
Spring 1940**

There would be at least two visits during the duration of the course, to the harbour for Survival Ditching Practice. This entailed jumping from the harbor's edge at high tide, a twenty to twenty five foot drop into the (usually choppy) sea. There we had to immediately inflate our 'Mae Wests' which were inflatable collar /vests, and swim fifty yards to an upturned dingy. We then had to right the dingy, clamber in, clamber out and turn it over again. This was followed by a swim back to shore to climb the many, many steps up to the headland. Guard duties were conducted on a rota basis – each airman usually served one night in every ten. This comprised being on duty from immediately after our evening meal to breakfast time the next morning.

No weapons were provided... So much for the physical side...Theory consisted of: Six one hour lessons per week on navigation, (advanced geometry and practical maths).Four one hour lessons per week on meteorology. Weekly lessons on RAF law, the theory of flight, the internal combustion engine, gas hygiene and aircraft recognition. Competence in Morse code - send and receive at ten words per minute was obligatory, as was signaling using the Aldis lamp at eight words per minute. 'Armaments' comprised about four hours per week. This entailed stripping all weapons for stoppages, breach blockages etcetera, including doing so while blindfolded.The standard phrase was; 'On compression of the trigger, the bullet nips smartly down the barrel hotly pursued by the gases'.

Worried that we had too much spare time, one evening per fortnight was reserved for housewifery: darning socks, sewing on loose buttons and repairing tears. Oh! I nearly forgot – burnishing of boots until they shone and the application of 'blanco' to all webbing equipment.

Newquay - Study by the sea.

As the weather warmed up some of us would take study books down to the Fistral beach to do a quiet hour's work after supper, always remembering that 'lights out' was at 22.00 hrs sharp! It was our good fortune that until this time, closing off of all beaches in preparation for the invasion had not yet been implemented. At the end of the course we would anxiously await notification of our passes (or failures) and our subsequent postings.

I was relieved to receive my posting to EFTS (Elementary Flying Training School) at RAF Ansty – some ten miles north-east of Coventry - as a pilot u/t (under training). The eagerly awaited seven day's leave had been cancelled, but the thought of actually arriving at a flying training station after almost six months of general training, helped lessen the disappointment.

Just prior to leaving Newquay, out came the housewifery sets to sow on to our tunic sleeves the much coveted 'propeller'. This signified the rank of leading aircraftsman (equivalent to lance-corporal in the army). There was also a most welcome pay rise to 4s 0p (20p per day) and an additional 3s 6p a day flying pay, a total of 37.5p per day. There were NO barrack room damage deductions. There were always deductions for some reason but never on the scale of those which had been imposed at Padgate and Ludlow.

Our weekend departure to Newquay railway station consisted of a contingent of immaculate airmen marching at 140 paces per minute, fully in step and with full webbing kit on our backs. What a difference to the 'rabble' band which had arrived just four months earlier and a credit to the Newquay Initial Training Wing.

At the station the special train due to take us as far as St Austell arrived fully laden with our replacements for the next course. This was a moment of particular satisfaction to us all.

Disembarking at St Austell we had a long wait for the arrival of the 'Great Western' train from Penzance, which would take us to Bristol for a further change of train. When it arrived it was already almost fully loaded – someone remarked that it was going to be a long journey – how right he was! When we finally arrived at Bristol, we discovered the impact on the city (and railway), of a heavy air raid carried out during the previous evening. With it came the realisation that Britain was fighting a war **alone**, and furthermore, one for which she was completely unprepared. It was to be several more months before radar equipped night fighters would do battle with the Luftwaffe. A similar period of time would also elapse before searchlights and anti-aircraft batteries would coordinate their efforts, in order to offer some measure of protection to our cities. Meanwhile the enemy could, with minimum effort, carry out devastating raids across Britain with minimal losses to themselves. A very sobering thought.

CHAPTER 8   RAF ANSTY – Flying At Last!

Don't mention the food – I did but I think I got away with it!

We arrived at No 10 EFTS (Elementary Flying Training School) located at Ansty just ten miles east of Coventry, in mid-September 1940.

Too many accounts of EFTSs already exist and so despite the fact that my stay at Ansty was one of the most pleasant and memorable experiences of my service life, I shall keep the account of this period of training as brief as possible.

Ansty was a pre-war private flying club which was hastily requisitioned by the RAF in 1939. Most of both maintenance and flying staff were civilians and so there was little need for the NAAFI (services canteen). There was however a Red Shield Club run by the Salvation Army. This was much appreciated by both us pupils and the few regular staffers.

The training aircraft were the DH 82 Tiger Moths - the most popular of the initial training planes at that time. They were bi-planes with two open cockpits. They featured a Gosport Tube for air to air communications but with no provision for air to ground communications! The pupil sat in the rear cockpit, the instructor in the front. The pupil placed both feet on the rudder pedals, which steered the aircraft. To the left was the throttle lever which controlled the power to the Gypsy Moth engine.

One's hands were placed on the central joy stick which controlled ailerons (a moving part of the wings) and enabled the aircraft to be steered. The instrument panel boasted an asi (air speed indicator), a compass and a 'climb and descent' indicator.

Finally there was an 'artificial horizon' indicator which showed whether the wings were level or tilted to port or starboard. Not as complicated as it may sound and certainly not complicated at all compared with training aircraft of today.

On arrival we were issued with flying equipment. This comprised, a one piece flying suit (Sidcot), fleece lined suede flying boots and three pairs of gloves. These were a pair each of silk, wool, and leather gauntlets. There was also a leather helmet with headphones and microphone and we would have three sets of underwear, comprising long sleeved vests and Long Johns. Last but not least we exchanged our service issue boots for regular lace-up black shoes. This last was in no way for the airman's comfort but to protect the fuselage of the aircraft while entering and exiting. To most of us this was a relief, however there was certainly an air of nostalgia associated with parting with the boots. For almost six months they had been polished and buffed and were always sparkling. Ground lessons were held in classrooms to which we were required to march, but as individuals now. Our lessons included, navigation, meteorology, armaments - maps and charts, aircraft recognition and photography, to mention just a few.

The food was appalling and the accommodation primitive but the atmosphere was fantastic. The Battle of Britain was now approaching its peak and the threat of an invasion. (Sea Lion) was imminent. This meant that in addition to our studies we undertook regular guard duties and fire-picket patrols. It was during this period that I was first called on to issue the command - 'Halt, who goes there!' - and wait for the valid password in response. Guard duties consisted of two hours on, and four hours off spent in the guard room. One of the airmen I shared duties with was a LAC 'Doc' Davison, and, yes he really was a qualified MD.

'Skirts' and golf clubs.

I remembered 'Doc' from Newquay where he had been in a different flight from mine. It was rumoured that on an afternoon designated for sport, he had been observed by a wing commander (Admin.) from an upper window of HQ at the Hotel Bella Vista. Doc was walking nonchalantly along the pavement dressed in a kilt and carrying a small set of golf clubs over one shoulder. The livid CO ordered a corporal to make haste and pursue and arrest the offender. Fortunately for Davison the NCO in question was in charge of the doctor's flight and was quite aware of this airman's occasional oddities. The NCO quickly found a bicycle and armed with a pair of regulation slacks, caught up with Doc and they duly exchanged the kilt for uniform trousers. Also the golf clubs were immediately made to disappear. No doubt a monetary donation was made to the NCOs favourite charity! The corporal eventually returned to the HQ explaining that despite a thorough search of the area, the miscreant had not been discovered. No doubt leaving the senior officer with the belief that it was his own sanity which was questionable.

Intruders in the camp – we feel sheepish.

One night Doc and I were patrolling the airfield at Ansty. Due to equipment shortages, one of the guards would be armed with a .303 Lee Enfield rifle and the second man would carry a torch. On this particular night I was detailed to carry the torch. We were patrolling an area behind the parked Tiger Moths in absolute pitch darkness. Suddenly we were both alerted to sounds of movement a short distance away. I shouted out the command – 'Halt, who goes there!' I repeated it twice – no response. Doc exclaimed, 'Shine the bloody torch at him!' That was easier said than done, when it eventually did operate only a pencil thin beam was visible. It was just sufficient to illuminate the intruders – several sheep from an adjacent field had strayed through the hedge - in search no doubt of lusher grass. Just as well the invasion was indefinitely postponed.

Life continued with both ground and air training so one had little time to think about the future. There was one further incident which occurred during our stay at Ansty which I think is worth recording. I have already mentioned the atrocious food. On one occasion our lunch was mutton stew which smelt awful. Despite this one u/t pilot was so hungry that not only did he eat his own portion but both mine and that of the chap on his right!

Cooking (the books?)

Shortly afterwards, a corporal cook who actually owned a car, when few could afford bikes, was about to leave camp. He was stopped by the military police who carried out a routine search of his vehicle. The results must have been positive because the car was impounded and the corporal placed under arrest. We all expected him to be charged and receive his well-deserved punishment – wrong. After some days the man was released, promoted to sergeant and reputedly sent post-haste to the Outer Hebrides. Whatever the truth, there was certainly no improvement in the quality of what came out of our cookhouse and the Red Shield continued to be the main source of our dietary existence. For this reason I have always felt grateful to the 'Sally' Army and on return to civilian life always made an effort to contribute to that charity whenever possible.

As the course approached completion, the ranks of u/t pilots was diminishing by the week. There were a few accidents but most of the students were eliminated for inadequate flying or groundwork performances. Only twenty out of circa thirty students, received 'passes' at the end of our Ansty stay. The course duration was originally fifteen weeks but was shortened due to the Coventry blitz.

By the end of November we had gone from, for most of us, stepping inside an aeroplane for the first time, to having circa ninety hours flying time after having gone solo. Included within this total were thirty hours of night flying. Towards the end of the course we were looking forward to moving on to secondary flying training school, with an expectation of starting bombing operations in the second half of 1941 – it was not to be. We now found ourselves staring at an overseas posting.

PART THREE   BOUND FOR THE US of A

CHAPTER 9   Crossing the North Atlantic
– Encounters with the U- Boats

Not exactly a cruise!

By the end of 1940 Britain had for six months, struggled for survival without allies and with just a little help from the United States, mainly in the form of Lend-Lease arrangements. These however required guaranteed funding by the UK.

   The London Blitz was still at full force but even more importantly, the U-boat carnage of our merchant shipping was reaching an unacceptable level. The US offered some assistance with help to train RAF u/t pilots to handle flying-boats, at their naval base at Pensecola in Florida.
A small party of trainees, at that time located at a 'holding unit' in Lancashire, found themselves released to join a convoy bound for North America to participate in the said scheme. Among these recruits were some twenty men who had recently passed the first stage of flying training at RAF Anstey EFTS. I was one of those airmen.

   Following an all night train journey to Greenock, the weary and hungry airmen disembarked to view a harrowing scene. There were stormy seas, high winds and black clouds within which seemed to be ships of all sizes and types.
Preparation was being made for an Atlantic crossing. Naval frigates (escort vessels) were darting to and fro bellowing constant instructions through loud-hailers. In other words we were joining a convoy for the crossing.

The *City of Benares* tragedy.

It was inevitable that the thoughts of many of us dwelt on the fate of the *City of Benares* which was torpedoed during a convoy crossing just a few months ago, while carrying many school children who were being evacuated to Canada for the duration of the war. On Friday 13 September 1940 the Ellerman Lines flag ship the *City of Benares,* just four years old, left Liverpool bound for Quebec and Montreal. It was a magnificent vessel of over 11,000 tons. The evacuees were joined by not only teachers, doctors and clergymen but also by a film crew. It was the intention of their director Alice Grierson, to make a documentary film of the ninety child evacuees for the National Film Board of Canada. There were other adults and children on board as private passengers.

The C o B was also the 'commodore' ship for convoy OB - 213 consisting of some nineteen smaller and slower vessels.

By 17 September, while about 400 miles into the journey, the principal escort vessel, HMS Winchelsea and two sloops departed to escort an eastbound convoy. This left convoy OB – 213 unprotected. Due to appalling weather and Force 8 winds, the passengers stayed in their cabins. Shortly after midnight on 18 September the German U-boat U-48, having failed on two earlier attempts, scored a direct hit on the *C of B*. A terrific explosion was heard as the torpedo ripped through the ship below the cabin area. Quickly the stricken vessel keeled over and those able enough took to the lifeboats. Out of the total of circa 406 persons on board c256 were killed including seventy-seven of the ninety evacuees. It was many hours before HMS Hurricane reached the scene to rescue survivors - this did not improve the survival rate at all – major blunders had been made. The official overseas evacuation scheme was cancelled and it was decided that all future convoys were to be accompanied by rescue escorts

The War Crimes Commission was forced to accept the Captain of U-48's later explanation that there was no way that he could have known that the *C of B* carried children. Little wonder that the embarkees of our vessel all kept their thoughts to themselves.

Our own fraught journey across the North Atlantic.

Because the US was at that time a neutral country, it was necessary for the UK contingent to be issued with civilian clothes ready for our arrival. In addition to kit-bags, full back-packs, steel helmets and gas masks, we therefore had to cope with manhandling our bulky 'civvies' packages onto the passenger ferry. As the ferry neared our vessel, we could see that she gave the appearance of having overstayed her years of service - by at least a decade.

Once aboard, we were swiftly allocated accommodation in the bowels of the ship - certainly well below the Plimsoll line and issued with hammocks. Almost as quickly we were given our tasks for the duration of the voyage - mine were to be kitchen duties. Within hours of boarding, the anchor was raised and thus began the worst few weeks of not only my life, but I suspect the lives of all the other occupants of our cramped billets.
Once the convoy of some thirty odd ships, reached the south-west coast of Ireland, the freezing sea spray over the bow and decks together with the buffeting waves, literally hurled the ship about like a toy in a bathtub.

The U-boats commence their carnage of the convoy.

The convoy was supposed to achieve a rate of progress of seven knots per hour but even this speed was virtually unobtainable. Shortly after we left the coast of Ireland, the U- boats commenced their attacks... Meanwhile seasickness pole-axed the airmen but somehow we kept reporting for duties - just. I shall always remember the heroic sailors, working in appalling conditions for miniscule pay. Should these same men suffer the misfortune to be aboard a vessel sunk by the U-boats, then 'the powers that be' ensured that their pay was immediately suspended.

After I would say, four day's sailing, the air-cover provided by the planes of Coastal Command exceeded the limit of their range. Despite the appalling weather the U-boats continued their attacks. To those of us confined below decks the noise of the gunfire was petrifying, but to those on deck (i.e. the gun layers), the sight of burning allied ships would have been even more terrifying. Eventually the attacks subsided, probably due to the adverse weather. About one third of the convoy had been set on fire and sunk.

There could be little hope for survivors in the freezing waters... Apparently the lost ships had been stragglers and the naval escorts now made their presence felt. They tightened up the cordon and somehow managed to increase the overall speed of the convoy. Discipline on board was rigorous and frequent lifebuoy practices were held, despite being restricted by weather conditions on deck. During the twenty odd day voyage, there were two further U-boat attacks but the ferocity of that first attack was not repeated.

Despite storms, fog and freezing ice the journey finally came to an end. On entering New York Harbour, and for the first time since leaving behind the coast of Ireland we finally knew where we were! The airmen, hung-over from constant sea-sickness queued up at the purser's office to exchange sterling for the US dollar – then incredibly $4 to the pound. The dollar notes looked like monopoly money – the cents, dimes and quarters almost pathetic. Seventy-five years later our own decimal currency is almost as worthless.

Preparing for disembarkation, the airmen would with both hilarity and incredulity don their civilian clothing issue. This consisted of, a cheap tweed jacket and even cheaper grey flannels, topped by a ludicrous French style black beret. A blue shirt with two detachable collars, black tie and RAF issue black shoes completed the attire. This dress mode was similar to the original militia call-up issue.

CHAPTER 10 We Step on to US Soil – Jackson Field Academy

UK training counts for nothing! - we become k(ay)dets.

We disembarked and were transported to Grand Central Station but had many hours of waiting before our train arrived. This took us to Atlanta via Washington DC, Virginia and the Carolinas, (whatever happened to Pensicola?). From the station, Greyhound buses took the by-now disheveled airmen to a nearby Army Air Corps base where, surprise, surprise, no one seemed to have the least idea of who we were. A few weeks later nine airmen myself included were posted to Jackson Field Academy, today better known as the Hartsfield Jackson International Airport. This is now one of the busiest airports in the world. Then it was home to several hundred trainee pilots in Uncle Sam's US of A, Army Air Corps. It was here that the nine men were informed that from this point onwards they would become k(ay)dets and would swear allegiance to rules, laws and discipline as enforced by the United States of America. From now on we would no longer queue but 'stand in line' – no longer eat lunch or dinner but 'have chow'.

'De-merits' would be awarded for even the slightest infringement of rules. At the end of the week those de-merits would be totted up and appropriate fatigue duties allocated. I was immediately awarded six de-merits for failing to answer immediately to the call for Kaydet Daveees, a name which would stay with me for the remainder of my service with Uncle Sam. There was worse to come. Our previous service at RAF Ansty EFTS was totally disregarded and there were to be three categories of pilot training.

The one custom which was not changed was the RAF salute – longest way up, shortest way down – compared to 'Uncle Sam's' arm straight up to the forehead and straight down again. We immediately commenced a fifteen hour day at Primary Flying School where we flew the Boing Stearman 75. This was similar to the Tiger Moth we had trained on at RAF Ansty. The Stearman was fitted with a 220 hp Continental Radial Engine capable of a maximum speed of 120 mph and a range of 400 miles.

Discipline and PE training were also different. 'Left-face' and 'about face' instead of left or right turn, 'tay-hup' for attention and 'hup' two-three instead of left-right, left etc. 'Callisthenics' replaced PE and was instituted on every possible occasion. All marching was carried out at 'double' time.

The Stearman 75 (P17 'Kaydet')

The airfield was mostly occupied by civilians including the flying instructors, aircraft maintenance crews and most of the catering staff,

   The u/t pilots were split into two classes, upper and lower with a course duration of some twelve weeks. The upper course was responsible for discipline on the ground thus a cabal was formed consisting of a kaydet captain leading some ten or twelve kaydet lootenants who 24/7 would harass the unfortunate victims of the 'lower' class. It was both masochistic and vindictive, with extra special demonization of the British who were frankly tolerated but not really accepted. The course syllabus comprised some 100 hours on the Stearman and similar on the link trainer, the forerunner of today's flight simulator. Additionally we covered in depth, maintenance engineering, armaments, theory of bombs, navigation, signals, use of service equipment etc. Oh I almost forgot: Army Air Corps history and regulations.

   The flying training was repetition of what we had covered at EFTS Ansty as far as spins, rolls and aerobatics. Here however we would be taught to, 'jus yo all fly by the seat of your pants' - by pilots who had not only flown in WW I but also had been the pioneers of air mail and transport, from the early 1920s.

   Navigation was also entirely different to anything we had previously experienced due to the vast expanse of the open plains.

Most important however was the notice one had to take of what appeared to be just a small cloud in the far distance. Flying would be cancelled because it could often turn out to be a 'twister', a small hurricane with a velocity of up to or even above 100 mph!

Another difference was our uniform. We were now kitted out in fine cloth khaki twill. So, having joined the RAF as 'Brylcreem' boys' we had now become 'brown jobs'! A further difference between the AAC and the RAF was pay. Before leaving England we had been briefed by an Air Commodore to act as ambassadors for our country. He had obviously never tried to exist in 'the States' on $1 50c a day. By contrast the majority of the US pupils had their own luxury cars and so for them at least, transport was never a problem

We however, on the very odd occasion that we were able to leave the station had to rely on public transport. We then had the shattering experience of observing two tiers of travelers waiting to board the coaches, 'Whites' at the front end and 'Blacks' at the rear. History books tell us that Atlanta was the birth place of Martin Luther King, one of the great orators of his time. It's little wonder he became the champion of his race!

The 'chow' was excellent, the accommodation, of superior quality and the discipline acceptable - just. Slowly the course hit the highlights in the flying programme - interspersed of course with de merits in abundance and the Captain Kaydet, was nicknamed 'Der Kapitan' by the Ansty tyrants. Apart from the Lootenants rushing around to provoke students (similar to traffic wardens today), we also were forced to suffer as much humiliation as possible from our course leader, one George Moore III. Despite supreme efforts on our part to cooperate in every way possible, the demented maniac would always discover a way to ensure that everyone's day was ruined.

Chris Cockshot and I become firm friends.

Fortunately for me it was about this time that I became friendly with Chris Cockshot, a bluff North Yorkshire lad. We had first met at Newquay ITW and again at EFTS Ansty. As our surnames were alphabetically consecutive, we shared much flying and classroom instruction in the same sections. Chris's outlook on the world was constantly optimistic. He always took the lead when it came to improving the quality of life and took advantage of any opportunity to relieve the humdrum of routine. On one of the rare chances we had to leave the camp for twenty-four hours, we hitch-hiked some fifty miles to watch a special showing of Glen Miller and his band – an event which I shall never forget.

News from home was sparse and it was difficult to discover how Britain was surviving. This of course changed when Germany declared war on Russia. Apart from being good news for the British Parliament and the people, it alerted the USA to how dangerous the situation would become if Germany overcame the Russians.

At about this point the 'upper' class moved onto the next stage of training. We would become that part of the hierarchy and new recruits took our place. This time the intake included a much larger influx of RAF.

Cross-country trips of circa two hours duration were now a prominent part of our flying training. The 220hp radial engine which powered the Stearman proved itself to be a very reliable piece of engineering. This was more than could be said of the temperament of a few of the instructors. There were check-tests every fifteen hours of solo flying and these were indeed TESTING. It went something like this:

'Kaydet, do yo HEER, watch your airspeed!' Or:
'Hey MISTER, watch your wing tips.' Then:
'MISTER which way's the field (airfield).'

Before one could reply, a throaty roar:
'Do yo HEER! Keep that head turning Mister.'
Or suddenly the engine would stop:
'HEY Mister, what yo gonna do?'
Again before one could reply, he would bellow:
'That's ANOTHER '75' lost!'

The Stearman was model 75. The motor would be quickly restarted and utter silence would follow until touchdown on the airfield. The instructor disembarked and strode off. I was left wondering whether I was still a u/t pilot or ready for the CHOP – I never encountered this fellow again.

The heat and with it the corresponding humidity increased in intensity and the light weight summer attire was much appreciated by the RAF. Our 'Blighty' issue of tropical kit remained in our kitbags.

The news of the war at home was sketchy but of much concern to our small RAF contingent - Germany was still advancing on Russia, the Middle East forces were again on the retreat. My mind returned to the autumn of 1938 when the then prime minister, Neville Chamberlain returned from Berlin waving his white incantation –'Peace in our time' – was that only three years ago? I recalled how I almost joined up as a despatch rider (recounted in Chapter one – Life in Rural Britain). At this point my pal from home, Len Barlow, had been in Egypt for some fifteen months. On reflection I was grateful for my, so far, good fortune.

The course was now some ten days behind programme due to an over loaded 'skedule'. Now both the flying syllabus and ground studies were intensified until finally the course completion was achieved. Several of the trainees were allocated to give an 'on stage' Constructive Instruction (pep) Talk to the lower class. I found myself as one of the named speakers. The much rehearsed speech concluded smoothly. As I walked to return to my seat, an arm appeared from nowhere and a voice hissed - 'Hey Scouse! What part of "the Pool", (Liverpool) do you come from?' So much for my rehearsal!

Next, we moved from training on bi-planes to a sleek low winged monoplane. This was also fitted with a fixed undercarriage and was powered by a single Pratt and Whitney 440 hp radial engine.
The Vultee Valiant boasted a perspex canopy (no more open cockpits). The Valiant was also equipped with radio, intercom, and wing flaps to reduce the landing speed and was known as the BT 13.

The Vultee Valiant BT13

There was also a change of instructors - AAC lootenants who were designated to initiate students in the art of flying these 'ships', to the satisfaction of the 'great' United States Army Air Corps. No other way was acceptable and within just a few weeks many students were 'washed-out' and returned to base.

Those of us spared this early demise, needed all the determination possible, to maintain our ambition to complete a course imposing such a rigorous and exacting level of authoritarian control. Here Chris was a valiant support to me and his continued optimism and enthusiasm was an inspiration. His help with classroom study was indispensable.

Once past the solo stage, the u/t pilot then spent many hours 'blind flying'. Accompanied by another kaydet, the 'artificial horizon' and 'direction indicator' instruments were blacked out. One kaydet flew the aircraft and the other dealt with navigation etcetera. After some fifteen lessons of two hours plus, duration, the two kaydets reversed.
These exercises were repeated over and over again and were not my favourite way of flying. It was a relief to eventually return to cross country and navigation trips. A little night flying was introduced to break the monotony. On the ground we were reintroduced to clay pigeon shooting but here known as 'Skeet Targets'.

Time to choose – fighters or bombers?

It was at this time that a visiting full colonel interviewed us to discuss the next stage of our training programme. The options were –'Persoot' ships (single engine fighters) or the twin engine Bombardment ships. This was for me a hazardous confrontation. All one's achievements, and of course demerits, would be in front of the colonel. When he asked for my thoughts on the matter I was much more concerned with 'staying the course'. With this in mind I thought that twin engines could be the easier decision and said I favoured Bombardment ships. Fortunately this must have already been in the colonel's mind as he reduced his former offensive tirade somewhat and suggested that I increase my ground test marks. He also made notes to the flying instructors regarding the need to improve my co-ordination during formation flying. The interview ended there. Time marched on and finally we moved on to the third and final stage of training:

Advanced flying – 'let down' by a weak undercarriage.

The single engine contingent was allocated the North America AT 6 Harvard. The remainder of us was split between the Curtiss AT9 and the Cessna AT 17 with two Jacobs 220hp engines. Chris and I were fortunate to remain together to train on the Cessna. This aircraft was fitted with, retractable undercarriage, beam approach facilities, cross-feed fuel tanks and constant-speed propellers, to name just a few advantages it had over the Stearman. In reality neither of the twin-engine planes was really up to the job and there were many problems, not least of which was a weak undercarriage. Within a few months both aircraft would be replaced by the Beechcraft AT 10. Unfortunately this would happen long after Chris and myself had finally been dismissed from the roll of u/t pilots and sent post-haste to Monkton, New Brunswick, Canada.

Back to the present – as flying proceeded apace so did the reigning cabal, an intake of 'West Point' graduates who exercised complete control of the lower class, our status once more. The problem was slightly alleviated when alternate times for flying training were allocated – upper in the mornings, lower in the afternoons, alternating weekly. Once the whole course had achieved solo flying with the Cessna, single occupancy of the aircraft ceased. Apart from check tests two cadets flew in tandem, one as pilot and the other would act as co-pilot/navigator. This took some of the thrill out of being in control. It did have some advantages in that one was able to learn the more advanced techniques required from us.

The Cessna AT 17 Advanced Trainer

(Note the spindly undercarriage)

Time was ticking away and for the first time since arriving in the USA, the RAF contingent, now very reduced in numbers began to see light at the end of the tunnel – that is until tragedy struck! Chris and I had been briefed to fly a two and a half hour cross country trip during which many landmarks were to be located and observed. Chris was normally well above average at carrying out this sort of exercise. Today however he appeared to be off form and several detours were made which added some thirty minutes to the schedule. Acting as pilot, I was also having an off day and had difficulty locating the landing strip. By the time I had recognised the strip, we were far too low. Instead of opening up the power and making another approach I attempted to land the aircraft. The result was that after much bucking and bouncing the undercarriage buckled under the strain…

CHAPTER 11   Transferred to Canada

Hanging about in Moncton.

Within twenty-four hours we two ex-cadets, now relieved of all our US kit were heading on a four day train journey to Moncton. To add to our misery we were both victims of theft.

We lost much government-issue equipment, (the value of which was deducted from future pay) and additionally many personal items acquired during our US visit.

Winter was now approaching and Moncton, a transit camp, was stretched to its limit. The incoming troops from the UK were held up from starting flying training due to poor weather conditions. On the other hand, the airmen now trained were delayed from commencing their return journey home, due to heavy losses to allied merchant shipping by German U-boats.

There were now some dozen or so 'washed-out' pilots from the USA whose documents had not yet been received by the Canadian authorities. As a result we were allocated menial duties at the large camp hospital. Shift work was imposed and a further indignity was added to our tasks. Twenty-four hour surveillance of several mental patients - many were French Air Force personnel – was required.

Then there was - Pearl Harbour. Two or three days passed during which time the German U-boats attacked US shipping along the well illuminated coast of Florida and the US failed to declare was on Germany. Finally it was left to Adolf Hitler to declare that Germany was now at war with the United States. So much for the British PM's optimism that the US of A would come to the Allies' assistance.

Back at Moncton, the morale of the unwanted ex u/t pilots deteriorated and it was late spring before some recognition of our plight was investigated. To be fair to Churchill and indeed to Roosevelt also, the scenario they faced was still devastating. The fiasco in the Middle East was ongoing – Bomber Command had all but disintegrated and a new commander with a different strategy was urgently needed. Malta, so important to the Allies was virtually marooned.

Boredom and frustration were the biggest enemy of ex-pilots in Canada. Most became involved in the heavy gambling schools in the camp. Dice, cards and lotteries to name but three and the constant radio with its many advertisements. Local gossip and chat became almost unbearable. Announcements would advise that:

'Last night the Royal Canadian Air Force carried out heavy raids on Germany - and the Royal Air Force also took part.'

Little wonder that the British airmen confined to Moncton felt divorced from reality.

It was the spring of 1942 before a committee sat to investigate the men's future in other aircrew categories. At that time there were only two options available, re-muster as either air gunners or observers. (The categories of flight engineer and bomb-aimer did not exist at that time.)

Posted to Jarvis (Ontario) – bombing, gunnery and air navigation training.

Four airmen, myself, Chris, 'Brummie' Clark and 'Timber' Woods headed initially for a refresher course at RAF Hamilton Air Navigation School. It had been almost six months since we had last flown. We therefore spent the next three months at RCAF No 1 Bombing, and Gunnery School. Initially we flew the Bollingbroke, the Canadian version of the Bristol Blenheim IV. We then proceeded to RAF No 31 Air Navigation School at Port Albert, Goderich where we flew in the sturdy Anson for a further five months.

No 1 B & G School was based at Jarvis Ontario, the nearest town being Hamilton, some sixty miles east. We worked long days (as in the US) but were entitled to a forty-eight hour break every twelve days. During these breaks I visited such places as the Bell Aero Cobra aircraft factory, downtown Detroit and many others. We always hitch-hiked and used small cafes and hostels to enable us to live within our tight budgets. I would never cease to be amazed at the high standard of cleanliness of eating establishments and the quality of low-cost food. Never did I visit any café without having a glass of iced water placed before me, something that rarely happens within these shores even today.

The last day of our course finally arrived. I stepped out of the Anson 4 B flown by F/O Gardener at 0400 hours, after a two and a half hour night navigation exercise. I returned to the dormitory, changed into 'best-blues' and arrived at the graduation ceremony at 09.00 hours, there to discover my course result of 78.6% (a pass required 55%).

By 09.45 hrs, twenty-five remaining pupils gathered on the parade ground, to be presented with a coveted 'O' brevet and three sergeant's stripes. Promulgation of this promotion was to be processed by 09.00 hrs on the following day. Meanwhile the remainder of the day was spent obtaining clearance certificates from the various sections and a mandatory but routine medical check.

I receive a shock and fail an eye test.

Imagine my horror to be advised that I had failed both day and night eye tests miserably. 'Timber' Woods had also failed his E.N.T (ear, nose and throat) tests. Immediately the two of us were stripped of both brevet and stripes and sent without delay to the main RAF hospital in Toronto. I was fully aware that if I arrived at Toronto as an LAC, (leading aircraftsman) I could wave goodbye to my promotion. Together with 'Timber' (who only reluctantly agreed), we altered our passes and travelled as NCO s. Two days later I was examined by several medicos. They were all sympathetic but confirmed there had been a rapid reduction in the quality of my vision over the previous year.

Finally a squadron leader MD, my last hope, issued a medical certificate to the effect that I was suffering from severe fatigue, but need not at that time wear spectacles. 'Timber' Woods was a borderline case but also managed a reprieve. When I arrived back at Port Albert, there were problems with a RCAF corporal concerning my rank of sergeant, when of course I was by now an LAC again!

Matters were getting tricky when in walked the original Flt/ Lt. MO who immediately addressed me as 'Sergeant' and who was delighted that the matter had been resolved. Unfortunately, our course had already returned to Monkton to await repatriation to the UK. I would therefore have to wait for the next course before promulgation of rank and title.

A tourist visit to Niagara Falls and New York.

The top cadet of the course had been an LAC, Ron Coulter. He had received a commission and was remaining at Port Albert as an instructor. Before starting the post, he was planning to travel to New York where he had an uncle who was a museum curator. Ron invited me to join him at the RAF club, Adastra House in New York, and I said, 'Maybe'. Forty-eight hours later I hitch-hiked to Niagara Falls, passed into the US of A again, and then boarded an evening train for the eight hour journey to New York.

We arrived at Grand Central Station at the still unearthly hour of 06.00hrs. An American civilian whom I had met on the journey insisted on taking me to the bar and buying me a Bourbon. There followed seven days of sight-seeing. During this period I visited or viewed – Jack Dempsey's Bar, Louis Armstrong's Band, The Empire State Building, The Stage Door Canteen and The Andrew Sisters. All of these at little cost to ourselves, thanks to the benevolence bequeathed to us by Adastra House and the City of New York.

On the due date I arrived at Monkton to discover to my horror that my old course, including Chris, had already departed for the UK. Perhaps things were indeed beginning to move forward and we could enter the war on a more active basis. Sure enough, within ten days or so, several hundred airmen entrained for Halifax Nova Scotia – HALLELUJAH – homeward bound at last!

A speedy trip back to 'Blighty'.

The train travelled almost directly to the docks and there were roars of approval when the three funneled *Queen Mary* was observed berthed alongside the magnificent wharf. The RAF contingent was the first party to board this massive floating city. As days went by, the arrival of mostly American troops together with a few Canadian Army personnel, filled the ship to its absolute capacity. Articles concerning the two '*Queens*', *Mary* and *Elizabeth*, written after the war quoted 16,000 - 17,000 passengers on an average Atlantic trip. At this time however, there was estimated to be somewhere in excess of 19,000 troops aboard. Perhaps a few lines will explain how this number was achieved.

This liner operated a 'hot-bed' system. We had twenty-four hours in a cabin, with an alternate twenty-four hours on deck, each included two meals per day. Breakfast was from 06.00 hrs until midday, with dinner from approximately 15.00 hrs until 21.00 hrs. All passengers displayed a coloured label to denote their designated hours of eating. As the liner was victualed by the US, there was a large PX store which sold cigarettes as well as many items in short supply in the UK. During opening hours there were long queues with waiting times in excess of four to five hours.

Most troops arranged relays of personnel to alleviate the long wait, however once at the service counter there was no limit to the amount of purchases any individual could buy. It was probably four days later before this mighty vessel upped anchor on its solo journey across the North Atlantic. As its cruising speed was well in excess of twenty-five knots, there was little risk of U-boat attacks.

Nevertheless continual change of course took place. With my new found knowledge of navigation I plotted our course to be well north of the Azores. Lying in the open air on the alternate nights of accommodation, we felt the decks quiver as the engine revs increased. Because the journey was completed in just under four days, we calculated that speeds in excess of thirty knots had been achieved.

The *Queen Mary* anchored some three miles off Gurock on the east coast of Scotland.

Then the massive task began to disembark, not only the passengers but also their luggage and the much needed supplies for Britain. Far too little coverage has ever been given to the contribution these two '*Queens*' and their absolutely fabulous Merchant Navy crews, made to the war effort, (for the whole of the war in the case of the *Queen Mary*). The *Elizabeth*, completed by 1940, sailed to the 'States' for conversion to a troop carrier and was available by late 1940.

PART FOUR   HOME ONCE MORE
- AND ADVANCED FLYING TRAINING

CHAPTER 12   Slow Progress to an Operational Training Unit

Back on UK soil – home leave on The Wirral.

Eventually the RAF contingent disembarked and were grateful to the (volunteer) ladies waiting on the quayside distributing lashings of hot tea. We took the train to Harrogate in N. Yorkshire and were allocated rooms at the Majestic Hotel, where we were welcomed by the Station Commander, John William Maxwell ('Max') Aitken, DSO, DFC. Harrogate was a UK reception centre consisting of a few hotels catering for aircrew returning from overseas.

While already enjoying a distinguished career as a pilot, Aitken, a modest man and the son of Lord Beaverbrook the newspaper mogul, ensured that his entourage made our short stay as pleasant as possible. We were granted seven day's leave during which we caught up with local news and discovered just how much the country had changed during our absence. Very little of the damage caused by the Luftwaffe Blitz of 1940-41 had yet been repaired but the streets had changed.

The influx of American troops was obvious as was the Canadian Army, to a lesser degree and Australian Air Force blue was also prevalent, together with smatterings of other nation's uniforms.

At home on The Wirral I heard of the demise of several school friends, and also a few neighbours. Ron Speakman with whom I had attended the Church School in Thornton Hough and later Wirral Grammar School, had been killed in 1942 while flying as an RAF observer. His father was Resident Engineer at Clatterbridge Hospital and Workhouse and resided within the campus.

Ron Moon had been killed while flying on pilot duties in the Fleet Air Arm. Both were a loss to their country. Ron Moon's sister was married to Philip Lever, son of Lord Leverhulme and on the death of Philip's father, she became the last Lady Leverhulme. Ron was a very affable personality and although I didn't know him well, I missed his presence in the area.

We become squaddies

Back from leave we received devastating news. There were now insufficient vacancies at training bases for the RAF. This was largely due to excessive demand as a result of prioritized requirements from the re-named US Air Force. The whole new intake of RAF observers was to be transferred, for some three months, to the Army Assault Course at Whitley Bay. It seemed incomprehensible after all those years of intensive training for our flying brevet and stripes, that for seven days a week and sixteen hours a day, we would wear khaki denims to cover these items. As a further snub we, as sergeants, were placed under control of army lance-corporals! With no disrespect to these fellows we felt utter despair. I remembered my father's words when I had announced my intention to join the 'forces'. He had just walked away and said – 'You'll learn.' How right he was.

Day after day we tackled obstacle courses, clambered up rope ladders and forded virtually every local stream and river. There were simulated battlefields where we were required, with bayonets attached to rifles, to attack the 'enemy' (sand bags). It was only the blessed comradeship, i.e. we were all in it together, which kept our spirits from plummeting.

We were originally billeted in tents, as the weather worsened we were allocated requisitioned terraced houses. Rumours were rife – the much vaunted 'second-front' was about to materialise - or Uncle Joe (Stalin) needs help. 'If it's us', we thought, 'heaven help him'! The latest rumour had it that Hitler was about to launch his secret weapon. In the event it was nothing of the sort.

Bomber Command was now off-loading its faithful Wellingtons. The Whitleys had already been phased out and the Stirlings fell well short of expectation. Add to all this, the fact that the Halifaxes were underperforming and the picture was not a pretty one! The Canadians, who were increasing proportionately in numbers compared to the RAF were allocated their own No 6 Group and the Australians had created several independent squadrons. At this point it should be remembered that over 10,500 Canadians serving in Bomber Command would be killed.

One of our airmen is missing.

On the fourth Sunday of training, a formal church parade was held in the town. The lance-corporal in charge commenced the roll call - one airman, Tommy Crane, had without warning gone AWOL (and who could blame him!).

When the name 'Crane' was called no one answered but for some reason, possibly because the next four airmen were called 'Davies', the lance-corporal didn't notice. At the end of the roll call the L/Cpl had ticked fifty names but only had forty-nine men! In a fury he decided it must have been a 'Davies', who was the missing man.

The roll-call was undertaken once more but this time each man, on answering his name, was ordered to stand on the other side of the road. When the name 'Crane' was called, yet again no one answered. The L/Cpl was so convinced of a missing 'Davies' that he failed to notice for a second time! At this point in the proceedings an officer arrived and asked: 'All present and correct'? The L/Cpl had no option but to answer: 'Yes Sir', otherwise he would have been in deep trouble himself. He conducted the church parade faultlessly. After the parade however and convinced that he was being deliberately deceived, he marched us to the stores where we were issued with full haversacks. We were then forced to drill-march for several hours. After each hour the L/Cpl demanded the name of the miscreant.

No one was prepared to cover for Tommy Crane but neither would anybody break silence. It was late afternoon when we were finally dismissed, having missed both lunch and dinner. Many airmen queued to help construct the finest apple-pie bed - made with the sheets folded so that the legs cannot be accommodated. He was lucky to get away with just this. However Sgt T. Crane was not exactly 'flavour of the month' for some considerable time afterwards.

After many weeks of training at the Army Assault Course, thirty vacancies suddenly appeared for bomb-aiming and navigation training. The course was to be held at No 2 AFU (Affiliated Flying Unit) at Millom, Cumbria. I became one of the successful applicants. And back to doing what we were paid for!

28 Operational Training Unit (OTU), Wymeswold.

By the end of the six-week course, twenty-seven of the thirty men on the course including myself were posted to No 10 OTU at Abingdon and just three to 28 OTU, Wymeswold, Leicestershire.

I was standing at the rear of a group of observers watching a high profile game of 'crap'. I was personally engrossed in as much as one of the participants was in debt to me for the sum of £4 - a week's wages! I was then approached by a tearful colleague.

The reason for his misery was that he was one of the three airmen who were to be posted to Wymeswold. The other two were one Paddy C. and a Jock Mc. who, our friend found unbearable as prospective colleagues. You will understand, I'm sure that at that time my mind was more concerned with the outcome of the crap game. I casually commented that I was prepared to exchange places, should the orderly office agree to the change.

He disappeared immediately to return some twenty minutes later and jubilantly announce that the change had been officially recognised. Firstly - I received all of my outstanding loan PLUS £1 as the participant had struck a 'roll'. Secondly – and even more fortuitous, No 10 OTU flew Whitleys and then Halifax and very few of the twenty-seven aircrew posted there survived their tour of operations. Thirdly – on arrival at Wymeswold the very first person I met was my loyal friend from the 'States and Canada, Chris Cockshot.

Crewing up for 'heavy' bombers – training accidents take their toll.

Some 100 assorted NCO aircrew (non-commissioned officers), arrived at Wymeswold for the purpose of 'crewing-up'. Most of the intake were members of the Royal Canadian Air Force but there was a smattering of Royal Australian Air Force and some RAF aircrew. The RAF proportion included most if not all the wireless operators/air-gunners and just a handful of pilots and bomb-aimers. The weather was appalling - continuous rain and cold.

The dominion influx was finding it difficult to adjust to accommodation without central heating and double glazing! The crewing-up involved no external supervision and it was up to each individual to find and join other appropriate members, in order to form a complete crew. The procedure lasted just a couple of days.

The Australians tended to crew together and the Canadians formed as many complete crews as possible, the remainder joining the RAF aircrew as noted. One sergeant RAF pilot Peter, (call me 'Pancho') Hyland was in fact an Argentinian and proudly wore the words ARGENTINA below the RAF eagle on his tunic. His crew included an RAF (Northern Ireland) bomb aimer, one Tommy Crane who you will remember from the 'Whitley Bay fiasco'! Pancho Hyland's air-gunners and navigator were Canadian.

The crew I chose was led by Flight-Sergeant F. G. James. He had previously been at another OTU at the beginning of the year but had crashed and had only just returned to flying. In addition to myself, the crew comprised:

Sgt 'Titch' Taylor from Leicester   wireless operator/air-gunner.

Sgt Jim Coleman from Saskatoon   navigator.

Sgt George Williams from Alberta   rear gunner

Sgt Eric Smith from British Columbia   mid-upper gunner.

Accident to F.G. James, pilot.

Fred James did his pilot training in Georgia, USA in 1941 and received not only his RAF pilot's wings but also the coveted USA silver wings. He was allocated to Bomber Command in 1942, initially as a Wellington Captain. On the night of 9 December 1942, while returning to base in appalling conditions after a night operation, his aircraft failed to clear high ground by just seven feet. The result was disastrous – two crew members killed outright - two others severely injured. Fred himself was hurled through the cockpit canopy suffering severe injuries which would leave him in a critical condition for a considerable period of time. A subsequent court of enquiry absolved Fred James of any blame, proportioning the onus of responsibility on:

'Poor navigation compounded by adverse weather conditions.'

After just ten months, Fred arrived at 28 OTU Wymeswold to assemble crew replacements, having, against all odds, finally received medical approval to return to operational flying. This accident is mentioned as it relates specifically to Fred's 'martinetish' style of crew command some time later.

Walt Reif's struggle to join Bomber Command – 'Lucky' Johnny Webb.

Within the Canadian contingent there were two airmen (not at that time known to each other) who had in fact been born in Germany. One, a bomb-aimer became a naturalised Canadian, while the other, Sgt Walt Reif, a pilot became a naturalized American. The American Army Corps refused his application to join, so he crossed the border into Canada and joined the RCAF.

Although the James' and Reif's crews became friendly, it was fully sixty years before I became aware of this.

Once the crewing-up procedure had been completed, two crews each shared one Nissen hut. The crew of Flt/ Sgt James shared with four Australians, one English RAF bod and 'Lucky' Johnny Webb. Webb, claimed to be an American who had flown as a **pilot** during the Spanish civil war and was now a Sgt MUG (mid-upper gunner) in the RAF.

Snow started to fall in early December that year (1943) and much flying time was lost. The crews however, were heavily involved with the task of clearing snow from the runways - not the most popular task but it had to be done.

By the beginning of 1944 the unit had moved to Castle Donington, now better known as East Midlands Airport. A Canadian crew attempted a daylight landing in a snowstorm, the plane landed heavily, ran off the runway and burst into flames. The Vickers Wellington which they were flying needed constant care in bad weather. The whole crew was incarcerated within the burning aircraft and a deep gloom spread over the entire airfield. The 'grim reaper' however wasted very little time before orchestrating the next tragedy, which this time took place at night. The Australian crew who shared our billet failed to become airborne and their Wellington crashed, literally a few hundred yards from the billets. Once more the plane burst into flames and despite heroic efforts by the off-duty crews, little help could be rendered.

The reader will recall of course that one of the unfortunate crew was none other than 'lucky' Johnny Webb. Only the previous week the local newspaper ran an article concerning Webb and his amazing escapades in Spain. The article concluded by commenting just how fortunate his crew was to have 'Lucky' Johnny Webb on board.

This prompted one of our crew to postulate as to how L J W was going to get out of this one! At about this time a lorry carrying ATS personnel home from a dance drew to a halt and its occupants advised that they had seen a parachute open - this despite the fact that the Wellington hadn't actually left the runway! It was well after 04.00 hrs before the off-duty crews, including our own, retired to their billets after searching for the supposed parachutist. For the James' crew it was yet another sobering thought as they entered their Nissen hut. It would have probably been about 07.00 hrs when suddenly all the lights were switched on and Johnny Webb's voice was heard shouting, 'Wakey – Wakey'.

His Australian pilot had unofficially allowed L J W to have the night off.

That fateful night's flying programme had been for 'circuits and bumps' with no real need for a mid-upper gunner. In due course Webb was charged with 'Absence from Duty' and duly received just fourteen days 'jankers' (confined to camp). As the rest of his crew had perished, it was not a bad deal in exchange for a life! The appalling weather was again affecting the whole of the country and indeed the continent also.

On the night of 16/17 December 1943, almost 500 Lancasters and ten Mosquitos carried out a raid on Berlin. Twenty-five Lancasters (5%) were lost, mainly to the Luftwaffe. This however was only part of the story as a further THIRTY planes were lost back in England due to low cloud and perverse weather. Bomber Command records are confusing but certainly 148 aircrew had been killed, many more injured and at least six missing presumed lost at sea.

Before Christmas, two further large raids were carried out by the main-force. Frankfurt on 20/21 December (6.5% losses), then Berlin again on 23/24 December with slightly lower losses, but with many crashes on the return journey

Percentage losses.

You will have noticed that I have started to quote percentage losses for main force bombing raids - and there will be more to come. After five minutes of reading percentages my eyes go blurred – after ten minutes I fall asleep and drop the book I was reading! There can be no better source to explain the relevance (and indeed importance) of these figures than the Commander-in-Chief of Bomber Command, Sir Arthur Harris, and I quote from his book, Bomber Offensive, Pen & Sword, (p105/106.)

'In the attack …13 aircraft were missing … a loss rate of **five and a half percent** …However if this casualty rate had continued as an average for any length of time it would largely, if not entirely have prevented the expansion of the Command, or as an alternative would have prevented the Command from operating at the fullest intensity of which it was capable.

There were two occasions during the later offensive when the losses were for a considerable period **more than five percent** of the total operational sorties of the Command, and on each occasion expansion was extremely small, while operational intensity was comparatively low – if it had not been, the Command would have contracted instead of expanding.

At the height of the offensive we were getting not much more than 200 aircraft a month from production, and it was only by unremitting effort and ingenuity that we kept our monthly casualty rate below that figure. We were working throughout the war with an extremely small margin for error and unless this is clearly realised it will be impossible to understand the nature of the prolonged battle we had to fight.'

So, and solely in the context of war, a raid with losses of say **below five percent** was 'acceptable' and casualty rates of **over five percent** (especially if sustained on a regular basis) indicated that progress of the bombing campaign was at best standing still, and at worst going backwards. I would like you to please remember this as you read on.

Training increases in intensity.

The effect of the heavy operational losses on the training stations such as 28 OTU, was to highlight the importance of navigation skills and crew co-operation. Classroom skills assisted in the battle against 'Issac', (RAF term for weather).

Some of our flying was carried out in Airspeed Oxfords, whose best attribute was that of being only just less antiquated than the Avro Anson. This aircraft was ideal for exercises which had been quickly introduced as a serious part of the bomb-aimer's curriculum. At this time most RAF bomb-aimers were 'washed-out' pilots with massive 'chips on their shoulders', and I was no exception.

Most of the intake coped reasonably well with daylight flying. However at night, especially on long cross-country trips of between five and six and a half hours duration, many began to fall by the wayside, especially as new stricter rules for navigation began to take effect. Some crews were sent for special training with others being split up for re-training.

***The Original Four* get together.**

As the course progressed our own crew formed a friendly association with the crews of the Argentinian, 'Pancho' Hyland, Walt Reif and Pilot Officer Gover. Incidentally P/O Gover's bomb-aimer was one Chris Cockshot! I shall refer to the James, Gover, Hyland and Reif crews as *The Original Four* as we follow their (and our) progress through advanced training and operations. These four crews successfully completed the course which included two 'Nickel' raids. These were leaflet drops over France.

Normally only one trip would be required but because of poor visibility the first trip was declared 'abortive'. Nickel raids were also used as 'diversions' for main force bomber raids.

The main bomber force, meanwhile was continuing its assault on Berlin, with the odd trip to Magdeburg, Stettin and Brunswick. **All** of these raids **involved unsustainable losses** and from all accounts were not even achieving the desired results.

The crews anxiously awaited their postings for the next stage of training, converting to Halifax four engine aircraft, at a Heavy Conversion Unit (HCU). As they did so our Canadian mid-upper gunner one Sgt Eric Smith, fractured his wrist. He was given the options of either, following us a few weeks later, or re-crewing with another pilot when the injury had healed. He confided to me that he disliked the authoritarian attitude of our pilot and decided to grasp this opportunity to change crews. Unfortunately he made the wrong decision and shortly after returning to flying, joined a (mostly) Canadian crew. He was to be killed in action on his first operation, just after his nineteenth birthday. What a debt this country owes to those heroic Dominion airmen who so unselfishly gave their lives to serve the 'Mother' country.

A Spitfire pilot sacrifices his life.

The remainder of the James' crew found ourselves posted, not to an HCU but to yet another transit camp, this time at Lindholm, Lincolnshire. This was due to a prolonged 'snarl up' in training due to bad weather. As Lindholm was already 'choc-a-bloc', seven day's leave was granted and I spent a few days in Wrexham, North Wales.

On the first morning of my leave, I borrowed a neighbour's bicycle and set off to a local shop located some two miles east of Wrexham, to exchange ration coupons for food. On my way there I heard the distinctive sound of a Rolls-Royce Merlin engine screaming in a steep dive. Looking towards Wrexham I saw a Spitfire heading for the centre of the town. Just when it appeared that it would immediately crash, the aircraft levelled out for a few seconds before finally crashing into a hillock near the Wrexham / Hope road, at Bradley less than half a mile from where I stood.

I forgot all thoughts of shopping and pedaled furiously to the crash site. I left my bicycle by a fence. There was no need to lock it up in those days and in any case there would have been no materials to spare from the war effort.

I clambered over the fence and up the hillock but all that was left of the Spitfire was one rubber tyre (still burning), a few bits of fuselage and a large hole in the ground. This was obviously where the engine and pilot would have come to rest.

There was no doubt in my mind that the Spitfire pilot had forfeited any chance to bail-out in an endeavour to save the lives of the residents of Wrexham. After a brief prayer I was about to return to the bike when suddenly an overweight 'plod' (policeman) came puffing up the hill. Before I could speak he removed his notebook from his tunic pocket and demanded: 'Are you the pilot of this aeroplane?' My comment was, and is, unprintable.

There is I believe, a plaque on this site to commemorate the accident, although I have never returned to the area.

The remainder of my leave was restless – The Spitfire incident had rekindled memories of the past three years or so and which were best forgotten. Memories of that winter crossing of the Atlantic to the 'States' and the carnage of the convoy perpetrated by German U-boats. Memories of taking part in funeral services at US training stations - during which we did however carry out impeccably the performance of 'The Slow March'. These and other incidents were recalled and the worrying fact was that apart from during the ocean crossings, 'I' had not yet fired a shot in anger.

The thought that my leave would shortly end and I would return to yet another transit camp did little to lift my spirits. The return to Lindholme meant yet more 'square bashing' and class room training, but no flying!

CHAPTER 13

Heavy Conversion Unit and Lancaster Finishing School

HCU – Blyton, Lincolnshire.

Within two days of arriving at Lindholme, the five remaining members of the James' crew reported to HCU No 1662 at Blyton. Blyton, unlike Castle Donington, was a large and foreboding place with little or no personality. It was here that we would 'convert' from flying twin engine aircraft to those having four engines. Due to a shortage of Lancasters our conversion was to be carried out using the Halifax 'Twos and fives'. As might have been expected, the poorest performers of the whole series.

A hiccup in the training routine occurred at this point. The pilot Fred James, had had recurring medical issues from his December 1942 accident and was sent off for a couple of weeks for further investigation. When he was finally given the 'all clear', his overdue commission was promulgated and he was given ten day's leave to arrange supply of uniforms etcetera. His promotion was due to a recent No 1 Group ruling that all pilots of four engine aircraft had to be commissioned officers.

Meanwhile Bomber Command was suffering heavy casualties on raids to Berlin –Magdeburgh – Leipzig – Stuttgart – Schweinfort – Augsburg – Frankfurt – The Rhur and finally on 30/31 March, Nuremburg. The loss of ninety-six aircraft was announced on the radio but in fact the actual total was over 110 (10.1%) when crashes over the UK were included. To those of us in 'the pipeline' this didn't suggest an inspiring future. It was indeed fortunate that there were not more 'Nuremburgs'.

During the respite from training, Jim Coleman (navigator) and I were dispatched to RAF Lindholme for a three week intensive course in advanced navigation.

On our return we discovered that there had been two new additions to our crew. The new engineer was Bill Orr (Paddy), a volatile chap from Northern Ireland - Belfast in fact. The mid-upper gunner replacement was one Sgt A N Other, and No I haven't forgotten his name! Neither of these chaps appeared as motivated as the founder members were and there were to be many problems over the next six weeks as a result.

The biggest surprise (and shock) was to discover that although he wore the 'E' (engineer) flight brevet and sergeant's stripes, Bill had not only never flown but had NEVER BEEN INSIDE ANY AIRCRAFT WHATSOEVER. All his training had been at St Athan, South Wales, in aircraft 'mock-ups'. Worse still all the instruction had been given in Lancaster 'mock-ups'. Paddy therefore had absolutely no idea where any vital equipment i.e. fuel taps, were located in the Halifax we were flying!! Sgt A N Other's only interest appeared to be in birds but not the feathered variety!

It soon became obvious that the newcomers were not fitting into the strict crew structure, both on and off duty. The original four remaining crew used this time by flying with other crews and engaging in navigational, ground gunnery and link trainer practice Not so the two newest members who disappeared at any opportunity. There was little the rest of us could do so we decided to wait for the return of, the now, Pilot Officer James and let the captain make a decision.

Unfortunately Fred, now ensconced away from his crew in the officer's mess, seemed too distant to appreciate the problems that were manifesting themselves on an almost daily basis. The crisis came to a head when the newcomers 'adopted' a lost puppy and smuggled it on board a Halifax training flight. Fortunately the ceiling height for the trip was below 10,000ft or oxygen would have been required...

Later, back at the very basic Nissen hut a fight broke out between myself and Sgt A N Other. At the same time Jim Coleman (navigator) and Paddy Orr also engaged in fisticuffs. This was at the time when nearly every flight resulted in a 'return to base' with faulty aircraft. My own logbook indicates many instances of these occurrences.

Blyton itself was a pretty poor station with little or no facilities for relaxation during the short off-duty hours. There was however one plus point regarding training in the Halifax. This was that the navigator, wireless-operator and bomb-aimer were all accommodated in the nose-section. All three therefore worked in unison resulting in good co-ordination and a very high standard of performance. This was highlighted when the crew took part in 'Bull's Eye' exercises. These consisted of flying over France, without leaflets this time. We were creating diversions for the main bomber-force and paving the way for the much talked about 'second front'.

At this time all leave was cancelled but I did enjoy a few hours flying as co-pilot on the duel controls. It was also noticeable that flight times were being increased. At Castle Donington, the average cross country trip was of four to five hours duration. Similar exercises at Blyton varied between six and seven hours. The crew was now ready for the 'real thing', - except for the problem with the two newcomers.

There was only one crash during our time at Blyton, although the station had experienced a long list of crashes during the twelve months of its existence. They had lost thirty five aircraft and experienced many other mishaps.

The final flight took place on 19 May, 1944. Its duration was over six hours and once again I managed to get some 'duel' hours at the controls.

The last lap – Lancaster Finishing School, Helmswell.

The crew now moved to No 1 LFS at Helmswell. This was a pre-war station and for the first time the crew relished in the luxury of decent accommodation. The six of us shared a pre-war 'married quarters' house.

Had it not been for Paddy's nightly rants concerning the tragedy of the Irish Potato Famine and the continued unruly behaviour of A N Other, it would have been idyllic. As the pilot was now in separate accommodation, the original four aircrew had little time to speak their minds. In today's jargon we certainly 'hit the ground running'.

Lancaster familiarisation training began almost before we had time to unpack our kitbags. This was followed by 'circuits and bumps' and there was no doubt that the effect of flying such a superior aircraft reflected in the wellbeing of the four 'old timers'. Within ten days the training was over. No 1662 HCU and No 1 LFS were training centres for 1 Group, Bomber Command and crews completing the course could expect to be posted to any one of a dozen or so squadrons which formed No 1 Group. Notice of an immediate posting confirmed that the crew was to report to Ludford Magna, situated approximately eighteen miles east of Lincoln and twelve miles west of Louth. Ludford Magna was home to No 101 squadron.

PART FIVE

OPERATIONAL - AT LAST!

CHAPTER 14

The First Three Weeks of the Invasion.

At the end of March 1944, preparations were in hand to launch the second front, code name 'Overlord'. At this point the control of Bomber Command was handed over to General Eisenhower, the Supreme Commander. Air Marshal Harris however was allowed to concentrate on the oil refineries and cities of Germany whenever the force was free from 'Second Front' commitments. Harris was (rightly) cautious with regard to his forces' ability to carry out concentrated attacks on small targets in France - airfields, marshalling yards, and docks, not to mention 'front line' bombing activities – without causing too many unnecessary deaths to the resident population.

In order to increase the probability of accuracy, the main bomber force was split into smaller sections, which would carry out several raids of say 100 – 300 bombers each, all on the same night.

In addition to normal 1 Group bombing responsibilities, '101' was also a 'special duties' squadron. Their Lancasters carried an eighth (German speaking) crew member trained to operate the electronic 'jamming' equipment carried on board each aircraft. The system was code named 'Airborne Cigar' or ABC for short. The special operator would tune into the Luftwaffe's ground control frequencies and 'jam' them before they could alert their night-fighters regarding the location of the RAF bombers.

The initial trial of the equipment by 101 Sqn from June 1943, proved successful. From October 1943, 101 Sqn ABC aircraft flew with all Bomber Command main force attacks. 101 often bombed more than one target on any one night, however the downside was that the enemy could track the signals ABC aircraft were broadcasting. Consequently 101 Sqn suffered higher percentage losses than any other Bomber Command squadron during this period of WW II. In order to operate the ABC equipment, our crew collected nineteen year old Keith Gosling who settled into crew life exceptionally well. The arrival of the James' crew at Ludford, our fourth and final destination, was pleasant enough.

The accommodation and messes were well run. We were however back to sleeping in Nissen huts, with two crews to each and ablutions a good distance away. We also had to cross a MAIN road to access the flight area and administrative headquarters. The big difference however was that Ludford was a one squadron unit (rare) with some 2,500 personnel. 101 Squadron stood out as a well organised 'fighting unit' with dedicated maintenance / ground crews and a caring attitude from the headquarters administrative staff.

George Taylor (Titch), our English wireless operator, was bowled over by our reception. His youthful enthusiasm must have washed over Jim Coleman, the Canadian navigator, who remarked favourably on the squadron's cheerful atmosphere. Jim's standard comment regarding life in England was normally: 'Why don't you cut the barrage balloons loose, let the island sink – then we can all go home'!

George Williams, our rear gunner, had a different 'take' on things and enjoyed the conviviality of the local taverns. George was not a heavy drinker at all but coming from the wilds of Alberta, he just enjoyed pubs, company and the fact that these places were open until 22.00 hrs. The tiny village of Ludford Magna boasted two public houses, the Black Horse and the White Heart. Additionally when the squadron was on 'Stand Down', Liberty buses were laid on to transport airmen to and from Louth, some twelve miles east of Ludford.

These occasions were music to George's ears, one of his first comments was: 'Gonna kind of like this place'. For me this would be my eighteenth posting in four years of service. I remained unsettled regarding the continuing problem of Sgt AN Other and now to a lesser extent, Paddy Orr. How would they cope when under pressure from the eventual confrontation with enemy fire – something we couldn't train for?

Fred remained 'bunkered' in the officer's quarters and we would only meet for flying programmes and other training matters. This had become a problem for most crews, following the ruling that pilots had to be commissioned officers. I read somewhere that the Americans ensured that at the very least, the whole crew would eat together. I was also quite sure that Fred was still troubled by his earlier injuries.

Our crew was allotted to 'A' flight - the Flight Commander was Squadron Leader Thompson. The only unpleasant aspect was that news quickly circulated, to the effect that all operations to French targets would count for just 'one-third' of an operation!

The thought of having to carry out ninety trips, rather than thirty to complete our first tour was 'mind-boggling'. It did however seem appropriate that the aircraft allotted to Fred's crew was F- Fox (formally F- Freddie), LL-751.

Hard on the heels of this unwelcome news, were the reports of casualties sustained on the Mailly-le-Camp raid. This targeted Wehrmacht barracks close to the village of Mailly-le-Camp. Forty-two Lancasters out of a force of c 348 were shot down – 11.6% loss. 101 sqn however lost four out of fifteen aircraft, a staggering 26.6% loss! Amazingly there were NO French casualties, but the losses were not a good omen for new crews such as ourselves. Fortunately for us, we were still carrying out familiarisation flights in order to learn landmarks!

Over the next two weeks, our crew continued to carry out a heavy schedule of pre-operational flying. We also had to learn how to cooperate with the special duties operator Keith Gosling, who had joined the crew at this time, regarding any interface with the operation of the ABC jamming equipment. The reader will recall my mentioning that during our spell at 28 OTU and on through HCU Blyton and LFS Helmswell, we became friendly with the crews of 'Pancho' Hyland, Walt Reif and P/O Gover,(*The Original Four*). Imagine our delight to find that these three crews had also been posted to 101 Sqn at Ludford. It was not pure co-incidence, although there were another twelve 1 Group squadrons they could have been posted to. As mentioned, 101 Sqn's exceptional losses, and its key role as a 'special duties' Sqn, demanded replacement crews as a matter of priority.

The crews of Walt Reif and Pancho Hyland, joined 'B' and 'C' Flights respectively. P/O Gover's crew joined us in 'A' Flight. This meant that Chris Cockshot and I could reminisce over our times in America and Canada. 'Brummy' Clark and 'Timber' Woods had been with Chris and myself at Moncton (Canada) transit camp. Chris told me that he had seen Brummy's Halifax dive into the ground at the Heavy Conversion Unit and had also heard of the demise of Timber Woods. But, best not dwell on the dreary past – here's to the dismal future!

Heavy losses over France – 1/3 rule scrapped.

On 07 / 08 May, fifty-eight Lancasters took part in a raid on Salbris, there were no French casualties but seven aircraft were lost – over 12%. A few other raids with over 8% loss of the main force were sufficient for the 'one-third' rule to be scrapped – for the present anyway!

05 / 06 June 1944 – 'The Second Front' - ABC jamming operations, France, Belgium and Holland.

The night of 05 June saw the squadron flying over Luftwaffe bases, jamming as many transmissions from ground controllers to enemy fighters as possible. To the crews involved at that time it seemed to be an unusual trip. As they returned to base shortly after dawn on 06 June, it was apparent that something was afoot. Looking down through the bomb bay I saw that the whole of the English Channel was awash with shipping, of all shapes and sizes. We reported this fact at briefing after our return to base. At breakfast shortly afterwards, we all heard the long awaited news of the start of the Second Front. Despite the long, eight and a half hour flight over the open jaws of enemy fighter bases, only one of twenty 101 aircraft was lost.

From this date until the end of June, 101 squadron was on full standby, twenty-four hours a day and Battle Orders were issued, and often cancelled, several times each day.

Bomber Command War Diaries, **(Middlebrook and Everitt) stated that:**

'The Bomber Command crews who took part in the historic weeks to come – and survived – would never forget them!'

06/07 June – Operations Acheres - Aborted by Bomber Command.

We were part of many aircraft bombing ahead of the Normandy landing sites. Our particular target was obscured by cloud and the raid was abandoned.

Almost inevitably, circa three hundred civilians were killed on other communication targets, which were bombed during these raids. We had a weary trip back to base after the first of seven abortive trips. In this instance however it was not our responsibility.

07 / 08 June – Operations Versailles – Railway targets.

On this night we flew G-George, weather conditions were still poor but accurate bombing took place. It is likely that fewer civilians were killed.

Bomber Command still suffered a loss of twenty eight planes out of a total of 330 which had been detailed to bomb a total of four railway targets - they were shot down by the Luftwaffe, (8.3%)

11 / 12 June – The Gover Crew – The first of *The Original Four* to be lost.

Five days after 'D' day, our crew was in the flight changing room when I heard Chris Cockshot cheerfully call out: 'Coming with us tonight'? I responded with: 'No, just another cross country'. Chris took off in Lancaster LL 751 F-Fox together with the rest of P/O Gover's crew, for Evreux in France. The aircraft failed to return. Bizarrely this was the same F – Fox that we had been allocated when we first joined the squadron. It was another two and a half months before confirmation was received that the whole crew had been killed. Until that time I had fully expected Chris to arrive back at the station, having bailed out and escaped to England, Chris was that sort of person – but no, never again would we two have in depth discussions over a steaming mug of cocoa... Furthermore, it was sadly ironic that the losses for these (four in total) railway targets were less than 2%.

12 / 13 June – Operations Gelsenkirchen.

This target, a synthetic oil plant, was the first German target for our crew. Bad weather and smoke from the earlier part of the raid caused target identification problems but eventually the bombs were dropped and a safe return made to base at Ludford. Of a total of 300 aircraft bombing this target, seventeen Lancasters were lost – almost 8%.

Daylight raids commence.

The first daylight raids commenced on 14 June, the first for Bomber Command since 1942. Because of the 'special duties' responsibilities of 101, the squadron did not participate at this stage. Raids were now taking place night and day, weather permitting - much of the activity was front-line troop support.

Bomber Command War Diaries **stated that:**

'Never had the planners, air-crews and ground crews worked so hard and continuously on such a diverse range of targets.'

The Archery Club.

In common with most RAF stations, Ludford Magna was many miles from the nearest town, which in this case was Louth, twelve miles away to the east.

Due to this fact, card games, billiards and crap (Canadian dice) were the main pastimes of stand-by crews. During this period gambling became prevalent, obsessive even. Many senior ground staff, NCOs who became embroiled in this mania, often found that their fortnightly pay disappeared in just one evening. Personally, I was not averse to a flutter but being a non-smoker found the contaminated atmosphere of the mess claustrophobic. I therefore took to visiting the archery club whenever possible. The main problem was, that the current handful of members only had a station life of three to four weeks and thus membership of the club gave one an enhanced 'chop' reputation. The other crew members suggested I would be better employed doing crosswords or jigsaw puzzles.

21 / 22 June – Operations Wesselring - Aborted before Take Off.

We were bound for another synthetic oil plant and due to take-off at 22.30 hrs. In view of recent heavy losses, the operational height was raised to 12,000 ft. We were warned that the target would be heavily defended and that there would also be considerable Luftwaffe activity.

Our plane for the night was E-Easy, a battle weary 'old timer'. Departure was on time and 'Easy' was to be the last aircraft to take off. We taxied out on to the perimeter behind D-Dog. Its pilot was a new 'driver' on his first operational sortie, he seemed to have trouble with his sense of direction, and he ran off the runway and became bogged down in wet grass. At this point because radio silence had to be maintained at all times, the 'Dog' crew should have fired a distress signal, using the Very pistol kept in the aircraft for this or similar situations. This they failed to do. It was some time before the rescue backup arrived to give assistance. Meanwhile Easy, unable to proceed, had to remain behind. Not knowing the full extent of the problem, all four Merlins were left ticking over.

As the obstruction ahead was being moved, a vehicle containing Wing Commander Alexander arrived. He told us to take off as soon as possible and to catch up with the other five 101 aircraft, which had by now been airborne for some fifteen minutes, by short circuiting the first rendezvous point. Eventually we arrived at the take off point. All the usual checks were made –brakes fully on, throttles 'through the gate' (max. power) – then, brakes released. The plane should now have leapt forward like a stone from a catapult. It was not to be, at the point of no return the speed was less than seventy mph, so the power was switched off and the brakes applied. The heavily loaded plane was brought to a halt just at the end of the runway, we then commenced the trek back to dispersal to await the inevitable post mortem.

The Wing Commander and Chief Engineering Officer were far from pleased, for that matter the crew was less than ecstatic. It could however have been far worse. As a point of interest, taking off involved lifting approximately thirty tons of aircraft comprising - a fuselage built from ten tons of aluminium, four Merlin engines, three turrets, ammunition etcetera, plus 2154 gallons of fuel and a 12,000lbs bomb load! Crashing during take-off normally had only one result and very few crew members ever survived.

The raid itself was a complete disaster, Bomber Command losses were 27.5% whilst 101 lost two out of five aircraft (40%) with one of the three returning planes crashing short of the runway with several crew casualties.

22 June – Operations Rheims - Concerted attacks by the Luftwaffe.

Breakfast in the sergeant's mess on this day was a subdued affair. The previous evening 133 Lancasters from Nos 1 and 5 Groups, had been detailed to bomb the synthetic oil plants at Wesselring. Intercepted by the Luftwaffe, thirty-seven Lancasters (two from 101) failed to return, a loss rate of 27.8%. We had lost six aircraft so far this month and at lunch time the 'Battle Orders' for the evening were posted in the mess, with ten crews named for operations. Pilot Officer James and crew were on the list. The pre flying meal was at 19.00 hrs with briefing at 20.30 hrs. Sighs of relief greeted the news at briefing that the target was to be Reims railway marshalling yards. The predicted flight time was five hours and forty minutes with take-off at 22.45 hrs. Operational height would be 8,000 ft and the aircraft was LM 369 I-Item.

All crews were warned that only accurate bombing would be tolerated and that bombs were NOT to be dropped until the target was correctly identified.

There was obviously the concern for French civilians but also the important Notre-Dame de Reims Cathedral, (where kings of France were crowned) had been heavily damaged by German artillery, throughout WW I. It had only re opened in 1938. Reims was also one of the major commercial centres of the Champagne wine growing region . . .

We changed into flying gear in the crew room, carefully leaving all monies and personal belongings in our respective lockers. The crew bus had us out at dispersal by approximately 21.45 hrs, the time until take off was occupied with pre-flight checks and the usual banter with the ground crews.

We were aware of our inexperience, probably paid an excessive amount of care to every detail and performed the usual rituals with lucky charms. Mine was a silk scarf, a gaudy affair given to me by a maiden aunt some years previously. Inscribed on the scarf, were drawings of bombs to represent each of the three raids which we had so far survived. I recall that Paddy, the flight engineer, had his lucky rabbit's foot. The weather was inclement, drizzle and a cold wind and it came as a relief when we finally climbed into the aircraft, some thirty minutes before take-off.

At last the signal from a green Very pistol was given for start-up and immediately the air became alive with the roar of forty-eight Rolls Royce Merlins, from around the dispersals. We taxied out in the gathering dusk, each heavily laden plane waddling towards the main runway and carrying approximately 12,000 lbs of general purpose bombs. Eventually it became I-Item's turn to take-off - a final pre-flight check - then brakes locked and full power applied to all four Merlins. Finally the green light for take-off – brakes released and we were screaming down the runway, throttles 'through the gate' (maximum power). We were all conscious of the thirty or so station personnel standing by the duty pilot's caravan, all waving us off – then airborne. Wheels up at 500ft and then at 1000 ft throttling back on power to circle the 'drome, gaining height and watching carefully for other aircraft – easier said than done.

We then set course for the east, estimated flying time to the target, two hours and forty five minutes. The weather was deteriorating and ground visibility was poor but we could feel the turbulence of other planes in the vicinity. After some thirty minutes into the flight, I picked up a visual ground fix and passed it to the navigator, Jim Coleman. This helped him to confirm his estimated GEE (radar) position. I passed on a further fix when we crossed the enemy coast and which confirmed us to be some fifteen miles off track. A slight compass adjustment and we were well into enemy night-fighter territory – all eyes are alert. Bombing was scheduled for 01.30 hrs, being a fairly new crew we were in the last wave of bombing

The cloud was rather thick and the approach to the target quite difficult. The coloured target indicators dropped by Pathfinder Force were almost invisible. I was consciously aware of briefing instructions so had to utter the dreaded words: **'Go around again'**. Groans from some of the crew and a Canadian voice calls: 'This is "injun" (Indian) country, let's get outa here'!

The pilot complied with my instructions and began to execute the manoeuvre. Fifteen minutes later I had the target in the bomb-sight graticule – perfect!

'Bombs gone!'

Bomb doors closed and a further two minutes straight and level flying, to ensure an accurate photo flash, this was in order to record exactly where the bombs had fallen. The pilot dips the starboard wing down to ensure a rapid departure from the target area.

Now free of the flak of the target area, it must surely be a fast and safe trip back to Ludford Magna? Suddenly the rear gunner shouts: 'Corkscrew port – GO', (direction to the pilot to start diving and turning.). Almost at the same time the plane is shuddering violently. The rear gunner commences firing and bullets can be heard and felt, striking the fuselage – an accurate attack by the Luftwaffe! At the same time the port wing caught fire. In fact, first it was the port outer then the port inner engines on fire. At this point some twenty searchlights pin-point our position and we receive a second attack by another fighter. Our aircraft hurtles down to earth at a rapid rate of knots. The pilot's instruction to prepare to abandon the aircraft seems to be superfluous, as the 'G' force was horrendous.

The next few minutes were a blank for me. Lying prone in the nose, I had hit my head on the bomb-sight and additionally the lead from my helmet to the crew intercom had become disconnected. By the time I had come to and sorted myself out, a third fighter attack had been carried out and the situation was indeed precarious. The fires in the two engines had almost been eliminated, by the engineer rapidly switching the fuel from the port tank to the starboard. Only the two starboard Merlins were now functioning. We were however still covered by many searchlights and when the engineer shouted: 'Dive Skip, for Christ's sake dive'! - the pilot said: 'We're already down to 650 ft', - this height calculated from sea level, probably rooftop height where we were! This was borne out by the fact that we received no further attacks and after maybe fifteen or twenty minutes in searchlights, we were out of range and flew into the darkness. Since the port inner engine now feathered, housed the generator which drove most of the instruments, we were virtually flying blind. Taking stock of the situation we decided to try, subject to no further interruptions by the natives, to attempt to keep going in a westerly direction and head for home.

Fred James later said that we were under prolonged attack and searchlight conning for a good twenty minutes during which time violent evasive action had to be continually taken. When he heard tracer fire rip into the bomb aimer's compartment he thought that I'd been '…reduced to a bloody pulp'. Fortunately this was not the case.

Slowly the pilot and engineer coaxed the, now, two engined Lancaster up to about 1,500 ft. The two men ably bore the full responsibility for the safety of the other six crew members. After a further thirty minutes, when the airspeed was probably about 145 mph, I obtained a visual sighting of the French coast. Le Havre was to my starboard, indicating that we were heading for the English Channel, instead of the intended route over the North Sea. Suddenly coastal guns opened up, we had no option but to fly directly through the flak. We emerged with some further damage but shortly after were engulfed in the safety of darkness. The biggest worry now was not being fired at by the Royal Navy - motto: 'Shoot first . . .'

Situation critical.

It was now essential that we should be able to send out a 'Mayday' call on 'Darkie', a scrambled line to be used exclusively for RAF emergency use. We were successful in this and the call was answered by Thorney Island, a Coastal Command Station in the vicinity of Portsmouth. Our request for an emergency landing was refused at first and we were given instructions and a bearing to fly to Woodbridge, some 100 miles north. Desperately short of fuel and with one of the remaining starboard motors now overheating, the pilot demanded we be given permission to land.

Finally a decision was given that, 'Yes' we could land but only on the grass to the left of the runway. This was because there was another emergency being acted out, just ahead of us on the main runway. A Mosquito without an air-speed indicator was being talked down by another 'Mossie'. We were by now tuned into the Thorney Island airwaves and heard the whole tragic episode through our intercoms. As the stricken aircraft landed it veered out of control, finally crashing into the sea wall. The pilot was taken to hospital in Winchester but died later the same day. I shall return to this episode later in the book - and indeed some sixty years later in time!

Now it was the Lancaster's turn. I elected to stay in the nose and with a 'birds eye' view of the run-in, guided the pilot through both the outer, 1,000 ft and inner, 500 ft beacons. The pilot throttled the two remaining engines right back, ready to land as soon as we reached the perimeter. At this point I returned to the main fuselage and joined the wireless-operator, navigator, and special duties officer at the crash landing position, just aft of the 'main-spar' The plane touched down as planned beyond the boundary and made almost a 'three point landing' - the tail wheel touching down simultaneously with the main wheels.

Almost immediately the aircraft performed a 'ground loop' and turned through almost 360 degrees to port. Fortunately being on grass cushioned the impact damage considerably. The engines were switched off immediately and the uninjured crew made a beeline to the rear fuselage exit, to the tune of the fire engine sirens and blood wagon (ambulance) bells, both of which raced towards us.

Eventually a crew bus collected eight weary men shortly after 04.15 hrs - by this time it was almost dawn. We were taken for the usual post operation de-briefing, by a lack lustre intelligence officer. His main aim seemed to be to return to his rudely interrupted sleep with the minimum of delay. A signal was sent to our base at Ludford, to advise that we were all safe - and to request that an aircraft be sent to transport us back 'home'. At this point the two officers, the pilot and special duties officer, were taken to their mess, while the six NCOs were taken to the sergeant's mess. As it was over ten hours since we had last eaten, we protested that we needed sustenance. It was to no avail, the kitchens were closed. Worse news, there were no beds available either, so we settled into the mess anti-room and, using parachutes as makeshift pillows tried to get some sleep.

Despite the fact that it was over twenty-two hours from yesterday's reveille, the adrenalin was still coursing and we six NCOs ended up chattering amongst ourselves. 'Ah well', said one crew member, 'four down only twenty six more (ops.) to go.' For six of the eight crew this would, eventually, become fact but not for the other two. The mid-upper gunner, would never fly again and P/O Keith Gosling our special duties operator, flew with another crew and was killed on 21 July.

Finally and without getting any sleep, it was 07.30 hrs and time for breakfast. We trooped into the mess in time for the first air-raid siren of the day and there were to be a further six or seven that Friday alone. This of course was the first week of the V-I flying bombs, most of which were routed over this section of the south coast bound for London, Southampton or Portsmouth.

After breakfast we were called to see the senior engineering officer, who took great delight in showing us a 0.5 calibre bullet extracted from the port front tyre of our Lancaster. This of course explained the reason for the 'ground loop'. Incidentally LM 369 was so badly damaged, that it was eventually SOC (struck off charge). There was still no sign of a relief plane from Ludford and we shuffled around trying to borrow razors etcetera, to try to smarten up.

This was a bit difficult as we were still in flying kit, boots, polo neck sweaters, plus outer kit - helmets, gloves etcetera not to mention the parachutes – all chargeable items if lost!

Going back to the mess just before lunch, I saw a familiar face from six years earlier, a fellow Old Wirralian (Wirral Grammar School), now a petty officer pilot in the Fleet Air Arm. This was Mike Vickars and we had been in form VB together. We were a bit distant at first then became friendlier and started to yarn over times past - the future was taboo. In fact, did we have a future? For me, yes but sadly Mike would be posted as 'missing', from his ship in the Far East. Later I discovered that Mike was not one of the forty-two Old Wirralians killed, so I had to suppose that he was safe.

There was still no sign of a plane from Ludford Magna and so in the afternoon, I enjoyed an illicit flight in Mike's Barracuda – exhilarating!

A post mortem and the 'long haul' back to base.

It was now Saturday morning on 24 June, we had more air-raid warnings, then the bitter blow - all Ludford's aircraft were on stand-by and we must travel back to base by train. At least we had managed to obtain spare beds for the night and felt somewhat rested. Then came further bad news, to the effect that despite three successive attacks by enemy aircraft, our mid-upper guns had never been fired in return! The general opinion had to be that the gunner had 'froze', or in modern parlance had 'bottled out'. It spoke volumes for the courage and devotion to duty of the rear-gunner, George Williams that we had managed to survive.

The officialdom of RAF internal documentation now showed its perverse side. When the crew finally collected all their possessions – parachutes, Mae Wests, helmets, maps and personal equipment relevant to each individual crew member's function, we boarded a transport vehicle to be taken to the rail station at Havant. On arrival at the guard room we were told that we were 'improperly dressed' and ordered to return to the equipment centre to collect shoes (to replace flying boots) and caps (to replace helmets). We were urgently needed back at Ludford Magna who were now desperately short of operational aircrew, VI's were descending hourly and yet in spite of this, RAF bureaucracy decided to add a further (wholly unnecessary) three hours on to our journey time - unbelievable! It took most of the morning to queue at the equipment section for caps, shoes, etc, to ensure a respectable appearance for the return journey.

Then there was a further hour at accounts for a travel warrant and allowance. The reader will remember that we had had to leave all our money at base before take-off. The allowance subsistence was one shilling per airman (5p today), so we requested a subsidiary payment from our fortnightly pay. This took a further hour or so, consequently we did not leave the station until well after midday.

We finally arrived at Havant Station for the London train, loaded with the aforesaid helmets, goggles, flying boots etcetera, to find the train not only running one and a half hours late but also crammed full.

It was standing room only in the corridor for the whole of the journey to London. We crossed London, from Waterloo to Kings Cross partly by tube and partly by walking and immediately encountered the havoc and damage caused by the 'Doodle Bugs' (V-I s). The tube stations had been commandeered by the local residents and all of us received many cheers and good wishes from the people of London – because of our flying gear we had been recognised as 'combatant air-crew'.

Once we arrived at Kings Cross, the two officers were met by porters and swiftly transported to the First Class section of the train. We remaining six staggered along the platform and it appeared that the whole population was endeavouring to board this north-bound train. Apart from troops, many civilians were evacuating from the new 'Terror Bombs'. It was with great difficulty that we managed to find room in a corridor for ourselves and equipment. It was a slow and tedious journey to Lincoln. Transport from Lincoln to Ludford was finally arranged and we arrived back at 22.30 hrs - almost forty eight hours after take-off, on 22 June.

Postscript to Operations Rheims.

As noted, Sgt A N Other the mid upper gunner, had not once fired his guns to assist the rear-gunner, George Williams, to hold off the three concerted fighter attacks we suffered. He was not seen again. We did not acquire a permanent MUG until mid-September. Until that time, on each trip we would have one of the 'odd bods' awaiting trips to complete their tours.

The events of that evening however did have a profound effect on Paddy Orr, the flight engineer. While he didn't exactly become a paragon of virtue, in the air he became a first class airman and valued crew member. On the ground however he was still truculent and resented authority. These were issues which would not come to a head until he had finished his tour of operations, as you will read later . . .

The Strange Happenings of Sunday 25 June.

By 10.00 hrs, the 'Battle Order' for that evening had been posted in the mess and once again P/O James and crew were detailed to fly. At 13.00 hrs however this order was cancelled. I went over to the flight section to spend an hour on the link trainer, the forerunner of today's flight simulator.

I was however, intercepted by the deputy flight commander and ordered to fly with one Flt Sgt 'X'. This was to be an 'air and instrument flight test' in Lancaster Z-Zebra.

The pilot's own crew was unavailable and we took off with myself acting as engineer cum navigator, together with a wireless operator and rear gunner. The test lasted one and a half hours and permission to land was requested at 17.50 hrs. At this point I advised the skipper that a wind had risen and that the current short runway should be changed by flying control.

The pilot decided that this was not necessary and commenced the landing procedure. 'Zebra' hit the runway at about ninety-five mph (too fast), bounced some thirty feet into the air, touched down again and then careered off the runway and across the grass. From here we charged through the dispersal area, only narrowly missing Lancasters T-Tare and U-Uncle, flattened some ground crew huts, crossed the perimeter and ended up through the outer railings. As we came to a halt all engines were cut, fuel switched off and we four aircrew swiftly put as much distance as possible between ourselves and the wrecked aircraft. Fortunately the plane did not catch fire, but two crashes in three days did not actually fill me with a rosy view of life expectancy!

During this whole episode the pilot had not spoken and indeed was still uncommunicative during the walk back to the flight section - until however we were approached by an aircraftsman of tender years. He was almost in tears, as he related that his bicycle had been inside one of the corrugated storage sheds, which Z-Zebra had flattened. Without breaking stride the pilot barked: 'Thank the good Lord that you weren't riding it then'. No – these weren't his exact words!

A summary of evidence was ordered into both the pilot's and my own involvement, with a view to whether there had been any negligence on our part – it was eventually cancelled. Early in July our crew enjoyed seven day's leave. On our return Flt Sgt 'X' had left the squadron . . .

Zebra was eventually repaired only to be one of three 101 Sqn aircraft lost over Stettin on the night of 29 August 1944. All three crews were killed.

27 / 28 June – Operations Varies.

We were detailed to bomb railway marshalling yards from a height of 14,000 ft. We flew L- Love, encountered medium flak and recorded a total flight time of just under five hours. It was a smooth trip and we landed back at Ludford at 05.30 hrs. Overall Bomber Command losses for this raid were low.

29 / 30 June – Operations Fruges.

The target was a V-I 'flying bomb' launching site. This was our first daylight operation. Flying G-George LM 457, we took off at 12.05 hrs and climbed to 14,000ft. We completed this operation, bombing from 10,000 ft and returned with some flak damage.

30 June / 01 July – Operations Vierzon

Back to night flying, in G-George again, take off at 22.20 hrs, estimated flight time six hours operating at 7,000 ft and the target was the marshalling yards. This was a Group 1 'show'- just 100 or so Lancasters, and the target marking was carried out by the Group itself - no Pathfinder involvement. Due to heavy cloud the height was reduced to 5,000 ft. The bomb load was 12 x 1,000 lb bombs, many with delayed action fuses, ideal for marshalling yards. Enemy fighter aircraft were encountered immediately after crossing the coast and we were forced to take evasive action on two occasions before reaching the target area. The anti-aircraft fire was exceptionally intense, and it was cloudy so we had to circle the target area a few times before finally lining up for the bombing run. We were hit on several occasions before the bombs were finally dropped and the resounding noise on the fuselage was disconcerting to say the least. Immediately after leaving the target area we were forced to again take evasive action to avoid fighter attacks. We finally lost height to just over 2,000 ft. We crossed the coast, and then it was a quick run over the North Sea and back to Ludford. **Never was dawn so beautiful!**

Bomber Command War Diaries - state that the raid was carried out with great accuracy and was a success for 1 Group's target marking section. This would have pleased 'Butch' Harris as he had opposed the formation of PFF, in favour of each bomber group marking its own targets, but had been over ruled by the Air Ministry.

Back at de-briefing we were to discover that 101Sqn had lost three of its ten planes and each of the remaining seven had varying degrees of flak damage. The squadron loss was 30%, and the overall Group losses were fourteen aircraft missing (14%), with over half the remainder suffering severe damage. Success comes at a heavy price!

Resume and projections after the first three weeks of the Invasion.

Despite Bomber Command flying around the clock, with night and day attacks and due to determined resistance by the German army, it was to be

a further seven weeks before the invasion force could break out from the coast and start to surge inland. During these three historic weeks, 101 Squadron suffered severely.

Nine aircraft were missing with a further three crashing away from base, although the crews survived, the planes were 'written off'. A further plane had crashed at Ludford with most of the crew severely injured. In all, over a third of 101's planes had been lost and almost half of its 220 aircrew were either killed or injured. Just four of the seventy-two 'missing' personnel were taken prisoners of war – All in JUST THREE WEEKS. Only in March 1944 were the losses greater than those endured from 06 June – 30 June 1944.

CHAPTER 15   July 1944

The V-I flying bomb - Changes on squadron.

By 01 July and for the past two and a half weeks, London and the south coast had endured terrible havoc from the 'buzz bombs' - between seventy and 100 V-Is were hitting London each day. The government was so concerned, that for the next two weeks virtually the whole of Bomber Command's activities would be to locate and destroy the landing sites. In many cases the doodlebugs were aimed by mobile launching platforms which were difficult to both find and destroy.

101 Sqn only played a minor role in this period and on 04 July our crew was sent on seven day's leave. We arrived back on squadron on 12 July and observed many changes, to crews and aircraft in particular. The first thing each crew member did, was to eagerly read a copy of 'Flight', the monthly magazine which listed the latest casualties - mostly as, 'missing believed killed'.

This was not from morbid curiosity but a genuine interest in the survival (or not) of the comrades we'd encountered during training.

A large number of 'all officer' crews had been posted onto squadron during our leave. Most were instructors from Training Command, the majority having the rank of Flt/ Lt, but with not one operation between them! They were also allocated all the new planes. It was unusual for new crews to be given any definite aircraft for at least 4/6 weeks. The 'upside' to this situation was that the sergeant's mess was less congested and of far more importance, our crew was given F-Fox LM 479. The ground crew for this particular aircraft were outstanding to say the least.

The history of F-Fox LM 479.

Seven thousand, three hundred and seventy seven Lancasters were built with a further 622 to maintain the aircraft in service. Some 3,800 damaged (too severely to be repaired on squadron) Lancasters, would be taken by road to Bracebridge, and from there allocated to many contractors in Loughborough, Northampton and Derby. On average three Lancasters could be re built from every four taken in. Parts could never be guaranteed to have come from the original aircraft, thus it was said that the only genuine part of a re built aircraft would be its log book. LM 479 had already clocked up 210 flying hours in its previous history but was reconditioned when we received it. Its flying capabilities and outright performance were far in excess of anything the crew had experienced so far! The plane itself was a Lancaster Mark I. The only difference between the Mk I and Mk III was the engines. The Mk I had Rolls-Royce (Merlin 20) engines, while the Mk III used the Packard engines manufactured under licence to Rolls-Royce. I should perhaps mention that the Mk II Lancaster used the Bristol (Radial) Pegasus engines. These were not very popular with the squadrons to which they had been allocated.

Following the re conditioning of LM 479, it had been sent to 32 Maintenance Unit which would adapt each plane for its particular squadron use. In 101 Sqn's case it was the installation of the ABC jamming equipment and also bomb bay adaptations. It was 1 Group's policy to carry at least an extra 1,000 lb bomb load compared to say 3, 4, 5 and 6 Groups.

Suspension of the Archery Club.

To the delight of the remainder of the crew, the Archery Club had been temporarily suspended as apart from myself, the only other member 'available' was Flt/ Sgt Keith Austin, the navigator in Sqn/Ldr Mathews' (flight commander) crew. We two were good friends and whenever possible would tour the surrounding countryside by bicycle.

Crew Promotions.

On 14 July, Fred James was promoted from pilot officer to flying officer and myself from sergeant to flight sergeant. Apart from the additional money these up-grades were highly prestigious.

14 / 15 July – Operations Villeneuve-St-Georges, - 'Polish chaos'.

Back down to earth after news of promotions, we scrutinized the mid-day Battle Orders. They included the crew of F/O James (ours). One Flt/Sgt Gordon was listed as a temporary replacement for our mid-upper gunner. We had our flying supper at 19.00 hrs and briefing was at 20.30 hrs. Immediately after lunch, the crew carried out ground tests on the equipment they were each responsible for.

The fuel load was to be 2154 gallons, the maximum, of 100 octane. The armouries volunteered information that the bomb load was also to be the maximum the Lancaster could carry, without modifications – 12x 1,000 lbs and 4x 500lb GP (general purpose). The latter bombs were of a special delayed action type incorporating a new specification for fuses and detonators. The weather was extremely bad, heavy cloud, many showers and a bitterly strong wind. It appeared more than likely that this operation would be scrubbed (cancelled). After supper, the crews walked the three-quarters of a mile to briefing, firmly convinced that the raid would not take place. We passed the military police and entered the now familiar 'chop' (description of bad news) room.

The raised platform at the rear was already occupied by the 'top brass'. The Group Captain, Wing Commander and flight commanders - navigation, bombing, gunnery and wireless-operator leaders - duty intelligence officers and of course Isaac's Apostle, the meteorological officer. 'Isaac' was the RAF slang for the weather –Isaac Newton – gravity and in those days what went up must come down. Airforce quip: 'Yes but in how many pieces'?

Eighty airmen entered the room and received the usual greeting: 'Be seated, you may smoke'. A large blackboard and easel occupied centre stage. Once the door was securely locked the Intelligence Officer removed the cover to reveal 'The Targets for Tonight'.

One part of the force would be going to Revigny, and the other to Villeneuve, (Southern France). At this point, the navigators and bomb-aimers collected maps and charts relevant to their allotted targets. Marks would be made to indicate any heavily defended areas to be avoided. We would plot out our respective routes and mark all critical height and speed requirements. Additionally we would compute estimated wind speeds and directions. The James' crew was allocated the Villeneuve target with an estimated flight time of seven and a half hours.

The flight path incorporated two 'dog-legs', to confuse the enemy as to our correct destination.

We were advised that take off time was to be 22.05 hrs, and the operational height 8,000 ft. ETA , estimated time of arrival, would be 02.00 hrs and a bombing time of zero + 10, ten minutes after the commencement of bombing. Our actual target would be the centre of the marshalling yards. It would then be time to synchronise our watches. All bomb-aimers and navigators were issued with special chronometers for this purpose. At the completion of briefing the 'top brass', wished one and all a safe trip and the crews then dispersed. The section leaders would remain to answer any queries and give advice as required.

We were given one further warning. If for any reason the bombs were not, or could not be dropped over the target, then the four special delayed action bombs must be dropped in the North Sea, in a specially designated area. UNDER NO CIRCUMSTANCES were these 'special' bombs to be brought back to the UK. Our next stop was the crew room to collect parachutes and Mae Wests, inflatable waistcoats. Then we changed our clothing and would eventually be prepared for the night's work ahead. It was a great pleasure to board the crew bus and be taken to ones very own aircraft - at least for the present - namely F-Fox.

The rain had finally stopped, the wind became less ferocious than it had been and now it became apparent that 'ops' would be on!

At dispersal we boarded the aircraft, each crew member stowing his parachute in the appropriate housing provided. The exception to this was the pilot who used a harness and seat-type parachute, which remained attached throughout the flight. The remainder of the crew would wear just a harness and only attach the 'chute if it became necessary to leave the plane quickly, otherwise it would be too cumbersome and impracticable. This done, it was back outside for a last smoke and a quick chat to Fox's other crew, the ground staff. Then it was time to climb the ladder and enter the rear fuselage hatch.

The ladder was removed and there was a certain finality in slamming the door shut. The crew adopted their take off positions, then the signal to start engines was received from the control tower. Thus commenced operation No 7. It was sheer heaven to be in an aircraft without strong odours of cordite or oil. It was an even greater pleasure to feel the real surge of extra power as 'Fox' screamed down the runway and, despite an extra 2,000 lb bomb load (the four 'special' bombs), gracefully lifted into the air with several hundred yards of runway to spare.

Aerodynamics is a complex subject and not one to be aired here, except to say that the stalling speed of a Lancaster on take-off with low fuel and no bombs or ammunition is about ninety mph.

Fully laden however it had to be circa 130 mph to avoid a stall.

Back to the take-off – wheels up at 500 ft, flaps and power reduced at 1,000ft - perfect but from then on all planned procedures fell apart. The cumulonimbus cloud was expected between 2,000 ft and 5,000 ft. In fact the cloud base was below 1,500 ft and at 7,000 ft, the aircraft was still engulfed in what appeared to be grey cotton wool. The first problem was severe icing and ferocious turbulence. We were less than one hour into an outward flight, with an estimated duration of four hours and it was apparent that the flight plans would have to be changed, albeit risking collisions. We switched on oxygen and climbed to 10,000 ft. The icing problem was minimised but it was obvious that some cumulonimbus must be pervading the atmosphere. Turbulence was still present but some air pockets were causing the plane to drop up to 300 ft on occasions. During all this it didn't help that there was lightning dancing off the fuselage. Although Lancasters were fitted with lightning conductors, conditions such as these were still extremely hazardous. By midnight conditions had improved slightly and it was now time to change course onto the first of the two 'dog-legs' and simultaneously gradually reduce height to 8,000 ft.

After a further hour, at 01.00 hrs the course was changed to bring us, hopefully, onto the target within the next sixty minutes. The cloud had now dispersed, but a persistent haze prevented any pin-points being recognised to confirm the navigator's estimated position. The pilot was continually querying every change of direction that the navigator issued.

The wireless operator had just received scrambled messages and advised that those crews on the Revigny raid had been recalled to base. He also offered the unwelcome news that England was now covered in low cloud and that all aircraft were being diverted across the country.

It was now 02.00 hrs and there was still no sight of the target area. There followed more aggravation from the pilot, it was understandable that he was feeling the strain of this trip. Suddenly some twenty five miles to starboard, I could see the red and green TIs (target indicators) going down. This was a relief to all the crew but in particular to the navigator. His nickname was 'Vasco', as in Vasco de Gama, the Portuguese navigator. This was ironic, because of Canadian history (or the lack of it), Jim didn't know who he was!

The 'Master Bomber' was now issuing his instructions and below us the anti-aircraft fire suddenly became alive and intense. The early bombing was well starboard of the target area.

The Master Bomber issued fresh instructions, to overshoot the present markers and bomb well to the port side.

Sounds easy but this entailed major alterations to my 'run-in' and we were fifteen minutes later than the zero + 10 allotted time. In fact, we were probably one of the last aircraft to drop our bombs. Apart from destroying the target, it was essential that we had a definite 'pin-point' from which to eventually set course for home. It was a relief to turn away from the heavy flak of this area, but the feeling was short lived when once more we encountered heavy cloud.

We were some fifty minutes into the return leg when the wireless operator received another message. Many UK bases had already closed and a diversionary landing base would be advised shortly. The nearer the crew got to England the more the weather deteriorated and the turbulence and icing became real dangers. The pilot was now calling the navigator, continually querying the course corrections which were required due to frequent wind changes.

Finally the expected diversion came through, it was to be Chedburgh, an RAF training station outside Bury-St- Edmunds. We were now some twenty-five minutes behind our scheduled ETA and this diversion would add a probable increase of a further thirty minutes. In an endeavour to make up some of this lost time and to also minimise the tension of flying through the cloud and the possibility of collision with other returning aircraft, the navigator and myself suggested an increase in speed from 190 mph to 210 mph and that we commence to descend gradually. The pilot was furious – thus the crew struggled on, nerves tense and time seemed to stand still.

Now tuned into the alternative base's airwaves, the pilot called up on the TR 1196, air to ground communication, requesting permission to commence landing procedures - and also for a confirmation of our current position. The reply was startling. Having confirmed an approximate fix, the crew was to change course to 090 degrees, due east, and fly for a further fifteen minutes, away from base. At that point we were to climb to 12,000 ft and then fly for twenty minutes on a reciprocal heading of 270 degrees, due west.

At this point we were to re call base for further information. When planes were circling base prior to landing, they would normally fly the circuit with 1,000 height between each aircraft. On this assumption, at the time of the TR 1196 call, we worked out that there must be thirty plus planes attempting to land. With no other alternative the instructions were complied with, so we can 'fast forward' to when we eventually landed at almost 06.30 hrs.

It was still very cloudy and was certainly not an easy task trying to find a vacant 'parking lot' among thirty-five Lancasters from various squadrons. We were the last to land and a crew bus took us to the de-briefing room. Normally this would accommodate sixty to eighty airmen, that morning it had almost 250 of us. 'Buckets' of tea and coffee, and sandwiches were made available. Eventually crew members were dozing or just lying about in a 'switched off' way. Suddenly the O C in charge asked for confirmation that none of the special delayed action bombs had been brought back. You will remember that the Revigny raid had been cancelled and apparently some of those crews had landed here earlier. Horror of horrors, three Polish crews from 300 Squadron stood up. No, they had not jettisoned any of their bombs – the air was, as you can imagine, electric! As our crew were nearest to the exit door, a few of us offered to help re-fuel the three Lancasters, to enable the planes to hasten to the North Sea dropping zone. It was almost one and a half hours before normality returned and hopefully by then the bombs had been safely disposed of!

Seven aircraft from the Villeneuve raid were missing and there were also many collisions with subsequent loss of life. The low cloud was still persistent but at 10.45 hrs we managed to become airborne and return to Ludford, flying in formation at 500ft, in a time of fifty-five minutes. Fox received a warm welcome from the ground crew, who immediately set about with stencils to imprint a solitary gold coloured bomb on the port side of the fuselage, below the pilot's canopy. It was common practice within Bomber Command to carry out this ritual. So ended the crew's seventh trip and Fox's first. Persistently bad weather meant that only minor operations were carried out on 16 and 17 July.

18 July – Operations Manville.

Over 900 aircraft were detailed to carry out raids on German troop reinforcements, to the south-east of Caen in Operation Goodwood. There were five designated areas, all heavily fortified villages. The James crew (flying F-Fox 479) was one of 200 planes allotted Manville. Take off time was 0350 hrs and the bomb load was 11x1,000 lb H.E (high explosive), and 4x500lb G.P (general purpose) bombs. We were to bomb from a height of 6,000 ft. Flying east, it was unusual to experience dawn breaking as we were travelling on a reciprocal to our normal heading. We had little time to appreciate the magnificent colours though as this was a highly concentrated and technically difficult assignment – to bomb only a few hundred yards from the British lines . . .Wispy cloud and aircraft in all directions kept every crew member on high alert.

Although it would have been possible to bomb visually on this occasion, T.I's were dropped by marker aircraft and the bombing achieved the pin point accuracy required to avoid allied troop casualties. However, circling the target for upwards of an hour in broad daylight was not pleasant

An uneventful return flight and a landing at our home base shortly after 08:00 hrs made this operation a complete contrast to the Villeneuve trip. *The Bomber Command War Diaries* record this daytime raid as one of the most successful raids of the Invasion.

Fast forward seventy three years later, during the inauguration of the 101 Squadron memorial at the National Arboretum, a Manneville resident who endured this raid made a visit to the UK at his own expense to congratulate 101 Squadron on the accuracy of its bombing. He offered me a profusion of thanks and we exchanged many wartime stories. A very poignant and emotional twenty minutes (see also chapter 28).

18 / 19 July- Operations Revigny - 'Big Trouble' on the ground.

Sleep was rudely interrupted shortly after mid-day, by the military police switching on all the lights and screaming the now familiar, 'wakey – wakey!' All aircrew to report to their respective messes by 13.00 hrs and all personnel confined to camp, until further notice.

When we arrived at the mess it appeared that there was a complete 'flap' on. There were no definite instructions but crews were to ensure that each aircraft was in a state of readiness. Over at the flights, the ground crews were virtually working around the clock to carry out servicing on planes which had landed barely a few hours previously.

Operation Goodwood : The Bomber Raids 18ᵗʰ – 20ᵗʰ July 1944

Refueling (max 2154 gallons.) was already taking place and the armourers were working flat-out replenishing ammunition for the gun turrets and loading the many bombs required. We deduced that the target would be medium distance and probably railways, oil plants or suchlike. The maintenance crews were checking the engines, oil and magnetos, etcetera. It really was going to be a maximum effort.

Back to the messes and earlier talk of a possible 20.00 hrs take-off had receded. It was now expected to be a 23.00 hrs or even a midnight departure. Early meals were available but afterwards, still no briefing time was issued.

I decided that a shower would help the tiredness I was feeling. Although the early morning flight was of only four hours duration, we had spent almost an hour circling the target which had required considerable concentration. I told the rest of the crew that I would be back in an hour and went off to carry out my ablutions. Feeling fully revived I returned to the mess, only to find it empty. Urgent orders for an immediate briefing had arrived. In a complete panic I ran outside looking for a spare bicycle, but of course none were left. Suddenly a motorcycle appeared. I recognised the rider to be the mid-upper gunner in F/O M's crew – a blessing indeed. I shouted to the rider to get a move on, while I leaped onto the pillion of the fourteen year old Royal Enfield 500cc side valve.

With the clutch slipping, tyres screeching and the engine over revving, we set off for the briefing quarters. Ludford Magna is bisected by the main Lincoln / Louth road. The north side of the road contained domestic quarters, while the south side housed the 'sharp end' of Squadron head-quarters, hangers, dispersals and the like.

The motorcycle approached this road flat-out, probably thirty mph, the rider made no attempt to stop, didn't have any brakes – seconds later we successfully crossed the road and entered a small cinder track used by crews as a short cut. This led to a small footbridge, just and only just, wide enough to accommodate the bike and passenger. Onwards up the muddy path, the bike engine sounded as though it would expire at any moment. Luck was with us, on reaching the briefing room entrance we skidded to a standstill by dint of the rider switching off the engine and allowing the machine to fall on its side. We both rushed to the entrance to be confronted by armed special police. There were hurried consultations – after rank, name and numbers were taken, we were permitted to enter. Fortunately the briefing had only just commenced, nevertheless we could both feel the hostility of the 'Platform Brigade'.

Four raids were taking place and our crew was to be one of five to fly on the Revigny raid. Two previous attempts to bomb these important marshalling yards had failed. Revigny was a small target in southern France, almost hidden in a valley and appeared to be constantly covered in haze. We were to take off at 22.00 hrs, fly at a height of 6,000 ft and our bomb load comprised - 11 x 1,000lb bombs and 4 x 500lb GP bombs. 101 Squadron were to provide ABC cover for just 105 aircraft from 5 Group. Once outside the room I received a first-class admonishment from the pilot. No doubt this was justified but I felt that had the pilot carried out his duties as skipper of the crew and found out where I was, then the problem could have easily been avoided. I decided to remain silent and concentrate on the raid ahead. Somehow, the morning's trip had been too trouble free and now I felt a premonition of disaster.

The TOT, time over target, was to be 01.15 hrs and bombing at zero + 5. Because of two previous failures to locate and bomb this target, I had studied maps of the terrain at the intelligence section. In the time before take-off, I scrutinised flight plans and sketches of the elusive marshalling yards and tried to memorise as much of the detail and landmarks as possible. It was time to go, take-off was smooth but after 1,500 ft, cloud was encountered. While not on the scale of the Villeneuve raid, it was still a fairly bumpy trip with continual icing up of wing surfaces.

Three and a half hours into the operation we reached the rendezvous position and received the Master Bomber's instructions, for all 'Ironfist' aircraft (the night's code word) to circle the area and await further instructions. Probably about ten minutes later, the Master Bomber radioed for his deputy to take over as he (the Master Bomber) had received a direct hit from anti-aircraft fire, and was going down fast. The following is a transcript of the James' crew reaction to this message.

Flight Engineer:	'Why doesn't he just phone the Luftwaffe and tell them we are here?'
Rear Gunner:	'No need – they are already here, just look at the flamers', (Bomber Command aircraft going down).
Pilot:	'Keep off the intercom.'
Pilot to B/A (me):	'What's happening?'

B/A to Pilot: 'The target indicators are dropping all over the place – probably ten miles from the target.'

Then the deputy Master Bomber comes on the air: 'Ignore all TIs, we shall re-mark . . .' the message ends with the sound of an explosion. Finally we receive a third instruction from one of the marker aircraft (whose responsibility was to 'back-up' dying T Is). 'Bomb visually- bomb visually!'

The Main Force needed no second telling! By this time at least six planes had dived to earth – in fact twenty four Lancasters out of 110 were lost in the target area alone! During this time, I had sighted a railway line some distance to port and proceeded to give directions to the pilot to head for the area. Once I had picked up the line again it was simple to follow this to the main yards. Unfortunately the radar operated (ground) guns found us. Very soon the whole plane rattled as the flak burst underneath, followed by the now familiar rattle of shell bursts penetrating the thin fuselage. It was obvious that the gunners would shortly hit the engines or fuel tanks. I gave the pilot a twenty five degree to port, change of course and for a few minutes this gave a welcome respite from anti-aircraft fire. Eventually however it was necessary to correct the diversion. The haze for which the region was renowned suddenly returned and left me in a blind panic – I could no longer identify the area.

I gave the pilot a new thirty degree course to starboard. This brought an angry response to the effect that all the activity seemed ten miles to port. He grudgingly agreed to the new course and within minutes the predicted flak re-commenced. This indicated to me that we were fairly near to the target – a fortuitous gap in the cloud revealed signs of activity below and ahead. I called: 'Bomb doors open'. The rail lines came back into view, we made a few minor adjustments and finally I was able to shout: 'Bombs gone'! Bomb doors closed and the next two minutes flying straight and level for the photo flash, seemed an eternity. Despite the intense flak, I had already checked the inspection panel to ensure there were no 'hang ups'- unwelcome bombs still on board.

The rear gunner reported massive explosions and fires, we'd possibly hit an ammunition train or fuel tanks. It mattered not, the target had been correctly located and hit. F-Fox despite being badly damaged, was now turning west and diving at about 240 mph to clear the area. Suddenly the starboard outer engine was hit by a last burst of flak and erupted into flames.

Prompt action by the engineer using the extinguisher gradually doused the flames, he then 'feathered' the engine, allowing the propeller to 'windmill'. Shortly afterwards we were engulfed in persistent cloud, which, although ominous was preferable to fighters and flak!

On this occasion there were no diversions and after a further three and a quarter hours flying time we arrived over base, and received priority to land. Back to de-briefing and some very welcome coffee and rum (a navy tipple). Since the rear gunner didn't like the 'totty', I happily ensured that it was not wasted.

Two of the five 101 Sqn aircraft on the Revigny raid were missing (40%), whilst overall Bomber Command losses were 24 Lancasters, almost 22% of the force. M's aircraft was one of the two missing from Ludford.

As we went to de briefing in the sergeants' mess and a well- earned flying breakfast, we passed the Royal Enfield lying recumbent, just as we'd left it the previous evening. Then it was back to the billets shortly before 07.00 hrs.

A ferret 'up my trouser leg'

At 10.00 hrs I had a literally rude awakening, when the 'ferret' in charge of special police roared: 'ONE-OH-NINE-FIVE, Flt/Sgt Davies – best blues' (uniform as opposed to standard battle dress) – 'at the double! – report to the Squadron Leader'. One or two remarks came from the hut inhabitants, but most were just too tired.

Quick ablutions, dress then a long trek to HQ. I arrived at the ferret's office, saluted and was taken immediately through the labyrinth of offices. I was astounded when I discovered our destination – the Group Captain no less. Group Captain King was a remote figure always surrounded by an entourage. It was therefore a shock to be ushered into the room and observe the great man, whose desk was at the furthest end of the room. The ferret was dismissed and I was left standing to attention in front of the CO (Commanding Officer). Without preamble he removed his cap and commenced a tirade which lasted some fifteen minutes. Broken down this was to the effect that, Flt/Sgt Davies was a disgrace, not only to the Squadron but to the Air Force as a whole. He (the Group Captain) would ensure that Flt/Sgt Davies would be stripped of rank and end up cleaning latrines, for the duration of his air force career.

At this juncture, The Gp/Cpt picked up dozens of forms indicating the supposed heinous offences committed – resisting arrest by civil police, failure to stop for questioning by said police, failing to produce documents when so requested, using an unlicensed and uninsured vehicle on the highway. Then - using illegally obtained petrol in a vehicle, breaking out of camp when on standby, failing to appear for combat against the enemy – and there were more!

When I was given the opportunity to reply I admitted being late for briefing but explained that I had not broken camp, but had merely gone for a shower. I added that I had arrived for briefing on a motor bike but as a pillion passenger not the driver.

GC: 'Can you ride a motor cycle?'

Me: 'Yes Sir.'

GC: 'Who do you SAY was the rider?'

Me: 'Sgt Jones, Sir.'

GC: 'No doubt you are aware that this airman was one of sixteen aircrew failing to return this morning?'

Me: 'Yes Sir.'

Silence – then:

GC: Now holding up a target photograph – 'This was taken from your aircraft after last night's operation to Revigny and shows tremendous destruction to the target. I am informed that your aircraft was damaged by fighters after leaving the target area?'

Me: 'Not fighters Sir, predicted flak, before, during and after the bombing-run'.

Again silence. The Group Captain then selected a pipe from his rack, proceeded to pack the bowl with tobacco, picked up a box of matches, changed his mind, and then replaced these on the desk. Moving a metal waste bin to the side of his chair, he collected all the aforesaid documentation and using a lighter ensured that all were burned and the ashes deposited in the bin.

GC: 'Where is the motor cycle now?'

Me: 'To the rear of the briefing area Sir.'

The Group Captain replaced his cap – 'Dismiss'.

I then remembered the many ceremonial parades in which I had participated. Salute smartly, right arm up the longest way, shortest way down, about turn, leg movements crisp and precise until I faced the door, right arm swinging, left hand on door handle, prepare for a rapid exit . . .

Unexpectedly the booming voice of the GC: 'Just remember Flt/Sgt, for the remainder of your stay on this squadron, you will remain **under my personal observation**'.

Answering: 'Yes Sir', I opened the door and the ferret almost fell in. As we walked down the corridor towards the intelligence section, my first thoughts were: 'Silly old buffer, there are some 2,000 to 3,000 personnel on this station and with a so far unblemished record, now to have to be under continual surveillance – unbelievable!'

Over at the intelligence section there was some good news – a PRU, photographic reconnaissance unit, Spitfire had flown over the target, probably at 30,000ft and reported that fires were still burning over the whole target area.

What a stroke of luck concerning the gap in the clouds over the target, which had enabled the attack to be so successful.

Had this not been so, how would the encounter with the Group Captain have turned out, then? There was no doubt in my mind that the ferret had fabricated most of the so called allegations.

My next port of call was the link trainer unit - there was no point trying to catch up on lost sleep now. Normally it was impossible to have a lesson without prior arrangement, today however after the activity of the past few days, there was a lull. The instructor was delighted to have a surprise 'customer', so much so that he produced a very welcome cup of coffee. Forty-five minutes of 'beam and landing' practice proved to be therapeutic and I returned to the mess in a more stable frame of mind. On the way I noticed that the Royal Enfield had disappeared, never to be seen again.

There was a committee of adjusters operating on all squadrons, who would oversee the effects of missing aircrew, and in the case of vehicles, bikes etcetera, would arrange auctions for their disposal.

The monies thus raised would be sent to the next of kin. In the case of this particular motorcycle, no doubt other arrangements had been authourised by the Group Captain!

In the mess I met the navigator of Sqn/Ldr Mathew's crew and the bomb-aimer of F/O Machie's crew who were astounded as I freely recounted the day's tale of woe. Due to continued adverse weather, only a few minor operations took place. As F-Fox would be out of service for a further week we were not required.

The Tragic loss of Keith Gosling – The James' Crew Special Operator.

Our special duties officer, P/O Keith Gosling however was detailed to fly on 21 July, with F/O Meir RCAF to Homberg with another 146 Lancasters. They were one of twenty aircraft which failed to return, (well over 18% loss rate).

I would normally pen a paragraph or two here outlining Keith's short life and what was then known regarding the fate of F/O Meir's aircraft and crew but have decided to detail what is currently known, in Appendix II.

23 / 24 July – Operations Kiel – Saved by beans on toast.

We were temporarily allocated Lancaster E-Easy LM 161.

Sgt Roy Hall replaced Keith Gosling (posted as 'missing' with the Meier crew), as our special duties operator. The Squadron gunnery section leader, a flight lieutenant, flew with us as a 'one-off' mid-upper gunner.

We attended briefing at 21.00 hrs to be advised that our night's target was to be Kiel Dockyards. Our operational height was to be 22,000 ft and the bomb load some 18 x 500lb GPs, many with delayed action timers.

We took off at 23.05 hrs and had an estimated flying time of five and a half hours. We climbed through intense cloud and were glad to clear it and set course across the North Sea. The meteorology officer had predicted a wind direction from 270 degrees and speeds of 45 mph. It was established that this was a gross underestimation - and I reported heavy flak from the fortress of Sylt. The navigator now used a wind speed of 60mph – this also proved to be inadequate. Very soon the plane was being targeted by flak from the island of Texel situated off the Dutch coast, a very dangerous place and too far east of the proposed route. The navigator kept to the wind direction of 270 degrees and 60 mph speed when the actual wind speed must have been up to or even beyond 80 to 85 mph

The consequence of this decision meant that ETA over the target found us some 50 miles adrift. I reported this discrepancy but the pilot interjected to say that the fires were probably decoys. The Germans often set up fires to simulate the proposed target area and thus confuse the bombers. It was fortunate that the highly experienced gunnery leader came to my aid and confirmed that the burning area ahead was indeed Kiel.

More course adjustments and a further eighteen miles flying, brought 'E-Easy' over the target, long after the departure of the main bomber stream. As I took over for the bombing run, 'Vasco' demurred he said his calculations didn't add up and that he was positive that we were not over Kiel. The engineer advised him that if in doubt, he (the navigator) should get his butt out of his enclosed little cabin and look through the cockpit. This Vasco did and after one horrified look, he returned to his maps and protractor, uttering unprintable oaths. That was the one and only time he would visually see the target!

Meanwhile the bombing run was now in progress – there was concentrated heavy flak and search lights everywhere. Finally: 'Bombs gone'! Sweet words indeed.

It was at this time that the gunnery leader proved to be a master tactician, superior to any politician. What he said was: 'Skipper, MUG here, those beans on toast we had for supper are creating havoc with my intestines – could do with a lower altitude'.

What he meant was that we were probably the only plane thereabouts, so let's loose some height and get the hell out of here!

The pilot turned south and gradually decreased height, he requested the navigator to supply a new course at a proposed airspeed of 230 mph. Faces were thus saved all round. The tension began to relax and a two and three-quarter hour return journey, was achieved in the cover of cloud at the lower altitude. We were the last plane to land.

This completed nine operations for the James crew – but I couldn't help feeling that we had survived thus far nor because of ourselves but in spite of ourselves. This was the first visit by Bomber Command to a German city since the end of March. Consequentially the Luftwaffe were in all the wrong places, otherwise the trip could have had a very different ending.

I was up before noon (on the 24th) and went over to the photographic centre to be shown a perfect result, with E-Easy's bombs straddling the dockyards.

Walt Reif and his crew leave 101 Squadron.

It was at this time that Walt Reif and his merry men of, *The Original Four* who had also completed nine operations, volunteered for 'Pathfinder Force', No 8 Group and left Ludford Magna. They went to Warboys, PFF's HQ to undertake specific training.

24 / 25 July – Operations Stuttgart – Aborted.

The Battle Orders were posted at 14.00 hrs and indicated that the James' crew would take part. We were again flying E-Easy. During briefing at 19.30 hrs, it was revealed that 450 Lancasters and 150 Halifaxes would be going to Stuttgart, with a take- off time of 21.40 hrs and a flying time of seven hours and fifty minutes. The operational height was set at 21,500 ft. The bomb load comprised 7 x 1000 lbs GP, and 1 x 4,000 lb 'Cookie'. The Cookie was one of the largest of conventional bombs. It was also known as a 'blockbuster', and was a thin-cased high capacity bomb. It would be the first time the crew had taken a bomb of this size. The weather prediction was for heavy cloud to the coast, then clearing to the east. Bombing time was to be 01.15 hrs and our 'slot' would be zero + 5.

After the usual procedures we had a shaky take off, with a slight drift to port halfway down the runway. We then climbed rapidly to get above the cumulonimbus, followed by steady flying for two hours, at which time the engineer announced a fuel leak. After some calculations he is confident that the trip can proceed.

The skipper however has the final word and heads on a course back to base. Naturally this is highly dangerous, flying west into the main bomber stream flying east! After almost four hours, flying with a full bomb load and over half the fuel weight, we landed at about the time we were due over the target. This was an aborted operation which didn't count towards our tour total of thirty. It was a quiet and subdued crew who trooped back to the billets.

25 / 26 July – Operations Stuttgart – Aborted.

We were being sent back to Stuttgart, as the previous evening's trip had not been too successful, with 4.5% of the force being lost. Fuel and bomb loads were identical as was the course. This time the attacking force was 350 Lancasters and 100 Halifaxes.

We took off at 21.40 hrs once again flying at 22,000 ft. When we were just over two hrs into the flight the rear gunner reported problems with the turret hydraulics but added that he could manage reasonably well.

'Pilot to navigator, course for base please.'

A carbon copy of the previous evening, the usual performance in reverse and a terrifying landing. Walking back from the mess I was furious and wondered what the C O would have to say about this. The pilot hardly communicated with the crew, there were obviously problems in his mind.

Although some major attacks took place over the next few days, we were not placed on battle orders until 31 July. For this we were reunited with F-Fox, now returned and proudly displaying three bombs on the nose. The pilot had been conspicuous by his absence for this time and the crew behaved in different ways. For example 'Tich' Taylor suddenly joined a marathon card game, then very wisely de camped to his billet while he was 'up'. George Williams and I visited a few taverns and 'Vasco' became embroiled in games of 'crap'. Messrs Middlebrook and Everitt in their '. . .*War Diaries*' credit this raid, one of three to Stuttgart in five nights, as being the most successful.

Crew Issues and the V-I Flying Bomb.

The flight engineer, ice cool and efficient in the air but belligerent and undisciplined on the ground, became involved in at least two clashes with the military police and had been sentenced to 'Severe Corrective Discipline', (the glasshouse) but the sentence was to be deferred until completion of his tour of operations.

The navigator, always a heavy gambler, seemed to be continually involved in card and crap games. Even the usually steady rear gunner, had participated in a bottle fight with a couple of other Canadians.

I was now convinced that it would be impossible to survive much longer, so I took to spending most of the free time, either studying maps and statistics at the intelligence section, or taking extra lessons on the link trainer. Other times I would just go for long walks.

The newspaper headlines on 31 July contained Churchill's statement regarding the serious situation in both London and the south-east caused by V-I (doodle-bug) attacks. Some 100 per day were now being launched. In the past seven weeks 4750 people had been killed and more than 14,000 severely injured. They had also destroyed 17,000 houses and severely damaged 800,000 more. More than one million people had been driven out of London alone.

The allied armies formed a line from Avranches to Caen but the majority of launching sites were 100 miles or more to the east.

28 / 29 July – The Second Crew of, *The Original Four,* go missing.

P/O 'Pancho' (Peter) Hyland was lost with all his crew, on a trip to Stuttgart in Lancaster 'Victor Two'. One of that crew was the bomb aimer, 'our friend' Tommy Crane. This left just ourselves and Walt Reif and his crew, from *The Original Four*. *Bomber Command War Diaries* report that, during a bright moon on the outward flight, German fighters intercepted the bomber stream, shooting down thirty-nine Lancasters . . .

CHAPTER 16   August 1944

31 July / 01 August – Operations Foret de Nieppe

– Yet more foul weather.

We were on the Battle Orders with just seven other crews. When we attended briefing at 20.00 hrs it was no surprise to find the target to be V-I launching sites. We were split into two groups and would provide ABC cover for just 200 Lancasters. Our target was Foret de Nieppe. In fact this was the only target to be attacked, as the second section was recalled back to base soon after take-off. 21.50 hrs saw Fox roaring down the runway laden with 18 x 500 lb GP bombs. Our operational height was 6,000 ft and we carried just 1350 gallons of fuel, for a flight time of three hours, fifty minutes.

Only seconds after becoming airborne, the plane was engulfed in heavy cloud - would this foul weather never improve? Gradually we reached operational height but in constant turbulence. It was hard to see how the flight could continue, but continue it did. Just before midnight, the Master Bomber instructed the Main Force to orbit until the target had been correctly marked.

Eventually bombing took place and the return trip commenced with continuous Morse messages, advising of diversion details. F-Fox and crew were diverted to Gameston, Nottinghamshire. However upon our arrival, the airfield was unable to cope and it was a further seventy-five minutes before we could join the circuit. Finally landing with very little fuel left, we were more fortunate than the dozen or so aircraft which either collided, or just disappeared.

This small airfield made every effort to make the forty odd crews as comfortable as possible. Due to continuous bad weather, it was 15.45 hrs on 01 Aug before the 101Sqn crews could take off, for the forty five minute flight to Ludford Magna. The good news was that the attack had been highly successful. The next six days saw numerous raids against this pernicious weapon, however 101 took little part in this concentrated effort to eradicate the problem.

07 / 08 August – Operations Fontenay le Marmion - Aborted by B C.

We took off at 21.25 hrs to bomb troop concentrations just behind the allied front line, bombing from 7,000 ft with a bomb-load of 13,000 lbs of assorted GP bombs. Unfortunately the Pathfinders could not identify the target and after being airborne for two hours, the raid was aborted. Yet again we landed with a full bomb load and three fruitless hours of flying!

Bomber Command – New Operational Terms.

During the last few weeks of many short daylight, and some night raids, the overall losses of Bomber Command (Excluding 101 Sqn and some Pathfinder squadrons) had reduced rapidly. New operational terms were therefore announced. Rather than all operational crews requiring thirty successful operations to complete their tour, crews with ten or less would have to do forty operations.

Crews with between eleven and twenty operations completed would have to do a total of thirty-five. Crews with over twenty ops would still be screened (finished) at thirty ops.

A directive not destined to instill confidence to people such as the James' crew – the general feeling is best not recorded. With just eleven trips under our belt, this meant we would have to do another five. What joy!

10/11 August – Operations Dijon – Better weather – at last!

21.00 hrs – and F-Fox was once more sailing down the runway at over 100 mph, bound for Dijon marshalling yards.

101 Sqn was providing ABC cover for 104 Halifaxes of No 4 Group. Operational height was 11,000 ft with a projected flight time of just under seven hours. We were carrying 11,000 lbs of assorted GP and HE bombs.

The weather was a huge improvement and we had ample landmarks to confirm that we were on course. Although the target was well protected by both flak and searchlights, I was by now well versed in marshalling yard targets and we obtained a good run in to the aiming point. It was a fairly trouble free trip, six Halifaxes lost but only one Lancaster failed to return. The photographs showed we had had an aiming point success. So ended the first twelve trips but what would the THIRTEENTH be like?

12 / 13 August – Operations Russelheim – Out in F-Fox, return in C-Colander!

Not only was this our thirteenth trip but we would be bombing on the thirteenth of the month, not too good if one is superstitious! Our target was the Opel Motor Factory powerhouse. We were flying at 17,000 ft, and were carrying a 4,000 lb 'Cookie' and a mixture of 7,000 lbs of incendiaries and high explosives. We wondered if it would be third time lucky and we would finally get to drop the Cookie? There were 300 Lancasters on this raid, plus another 250 bombing at about the same time at Brunswick. Both flights were scheduled for seven and a half hours duration.

We had taken off at 22.00 hrs and were enveloped in heavy cloud immediately after becoming airborne. Once operational height had been reached the visibility improved. Unfortunately the Luftwaffe was also making the most of the better weather.

Less than two hours into the flight and our gunners were already reporting interceptions. Prompt action by the pilot, enabled Fox to continue its journey without too much difficulty. As we approached the target shortly before 02.00 hrs, roving searchlights and concentrated flak, made the selection of a good bombing run difficult. This was exacerbated when I realised that 'tracer' bullets were being fired directly at us.

Tracer fire, was when every fifth bullet in the ammunition belt was 'illuminated', to enable the gunner (normally the enemy) to judge his aim more accurately. In this case, it didn't help that the tracer fire was coming from the rear turret of another Lancaster! This must have been shear panic on the gunner's part. The effect of this interruption, was that Fox was forced to alter direction some thirty degrees to port - so I had to select another approach to the target but we now had an increased risk of collision.

By now the raid had turned into a complete shambles. Bombs appeared to be dropping indiscriminately - but well short of the target. Several flak bursts exploding just under the fuselage caused extensive damage to Fox.

To add to our problems, the rear-gunner reported a single engine aircraft within range of attack. Immediately after this warning, cannon fire was ripping through Fox's fuselage. Jinking, twisting and turning, the pilot did well to lose the fighter. I now took over and lined the bomb site graticule towards the target. We had lost two thousand feet evading the attacking Luftwaffe fighter and were now at 15,000ft. The flak bursts were above the aircraft but the bombs from other Lancasters above us, at operational height, were still hurtling down - the next ten minutes were nerve tingling to say the least!

The MUG for this trip was a youngster, flying for the first time after a serious accident in which most of his crew had been killed. He now found the situation beyond his control and lost his head. The w/op and navigator were sent aft to remove him from the turret and to give him a morphine shot. We finally dodged the intense searchlights and I was able to announce: 'Bombs gone'! We flew straight and level for two minutes (for photo flash) but just as the pilot was heading on a westerly course, the rear gunner gave warning of a twin engine aircraft on our tail and once again cannon fire hit the fuselage stem to stern. The rear gunner seemed fated to participate in these encounters on his own. As our sole gunner fired burst after burst at the attacking fighter, Fox shuddered from the recoil effect of this fire. Suddenly the attacker disappeared and gradually the target receded into the distance. The aircraft was badly holed and the oxygen supply was suspect, which meant getting below 10,000 ft PDQ.

We landed shortly after 05.30 hrs. As we taxied into dispersal we were greeted by the ground crew waving a home-made banner announcing 'HAPPY THIRTEENTH'. When they observed the state of Fox however, *they* were not too happy.

Over at de-briefing, the full extent of the losses slowly became apparent. 101 Sqn had three planes missing and two more had crashed in England, with serious injuries to both crews. Losses were over 30 % for the squadron. Bomber Command as a whole lost over sixty-five planes missing or crashed – almost 15 %. Worse was to follow, both raids had been virtual disasters, on the Brunswick trip little or no damage had been inflicted and many bombs fell up to thirty miles from the target. At Russelheim most bombs fell well short of the Opel works, so it was all the more pleasing to discover that Fox's bombs (including the Cookie), had virtually wrecked the power station.

A Further tragedy resulting from one of the losses of 12 / 13 August 1944.

One of the three missing crews from the Russelheim raid, was that of Flt/ Ltn Marham-Tucker, the deputy leader of 'B' flight. He was also the senior fighter affiliation instructor. His flight engineer was Sgt G H Eaton, a popular NCO. Eaton was also the proud owner of a Triumph Tiger 100 Speed Twin, at that time the top of the range of British motorcycles.

A couple of days after the Marham-Tucker crew had been reported 'missing', Sgt Eaton's brother, a petty officer in the Royal Navy, arrived at Ludford to collect this precious possession. He was entertained well in the sergeant's mess and so decided not to return to his base at Chatham, until the following day.

We received the unwelcome news shortly afterwards, that as he crossed London on his way south, he had been killed by the blast from a V-I flying bomb. We all prayed that this was a case of mistaken identity. For a mother to lose one son is tragic enough, to lose both sons within a week – unthinkable!

The 'Top Brass' visit Ludford Magna.

In the late afternoon of the day we returned from Russelheim, and just as crews were sauntering into the mess, there was an interruption as the SWO, the station warrant officer, called all aircrews to stand up .Who should walk in but Air Commodore Bluck. A/C Bluck had been an ex-operational Blenheim and Wellington pilot and was now AOC, Air Officer Commanding, Faldingworth, Kelston and Ludford, all 1 Group bases. He led a very informal meeting and was interested to know what the crews who had taken part in last night's operation, believed had caused the chaos and subsequent heavy losses.

Almost to a man, the consensus of opinion was the lack of experience of many of the crew's participating. It was commonly believed, that many of the crews who had been operating on the easier and shorter daylight raids, had become less alert than say 101 and the one or two other squadrons flying on night attacks and used to heavy opposition. At this point a spokesman brought up the unfairness of the recent decision to increase, for most crews, the standard thirty operations which constituted a 'tour'. The AOC agreed wholeheartedly and assured all 101 squadron aircrew that although no special treatment could be offered, he and the 101

squadron Group Captain would ensure that all crews who had flown consistently over the last two and a half to three months, would not have their tours extended.

15 August – Operations Volkel Fighter Base.

09.50 hrs saw us airborne and climbing to an operational height of 15,000 ft. We were eager to pick up our fighter escort for this daylight raid. As Fox was indisposed following the Russelheim operation, we were flying in M-Mother PB 239 with a 13,000 lbs assorted bomb load. Wisps of light cirrus cloud hindered but didn't hamper the trip, so we were over the target area at 11.00 hrs. The Master Bomber and his deputy were broadcasting continuous warnings regarding the need for accurate bombing - and the raid was halted periodically to ensure the target was being accurately attacked.

It was after 11.30 before we finally released our bombs and headed back for base. Just the previous day there had been seven raids carried out in support of the Normandy landing troops. Something went irreparably wrong however and many Canadian troops, vehicles and equipment were hit. This is believed to be the only occasion when Bomber Command had killed and injured allied troops. To be fair however there could have been mitigating circumstances. It was claimed that the Canadian ground forces were using yellow ID flares while PFF used yellow T Is . . .

After landing back at base, we received confirmation that the front fuselage section of F-Fox had been peppered with .303 bullet holes, from the Russelheim raid of 12/13 August. The Germans considered this calibre as useless so it could only have come from 'one of ours'. It certainly justified my instruction to the pilot to take evasive action.

16 / 17 August – Operations Kiel Dockyards.

At 21.45 hrs on 16 August M-Mother was once again airborne, with F/O James driving and his 'merry' band of men on the alert. During a dark and cloudy take-off, we had another unpleasant swing to port half way along the runway. This didn't exactly fill me with confidence, as I already believed that we were living on 'borrowed time'. The bomb load was 'only' 12,000 lbs and was of the cluster variety. Since Kiel was once again the target, the idea was to create maximum damage in a concentrated area.

Mother was one of 350 Lancasters flying at 17,000 ft. On this occasion the weather and conditions were considerably better than on 23/24 July. The flight time was to be just under five hours and the searchlights and flak, as we were running in to the target were intense. To quote the rear gunner: 'Jeez, just look at those flak bursts, you could get out and walk on it'.

There was however little activity from the Luftwaffe, possibly due to the heavy attacks the previous day to both Belgian and Dutch airfields. M-Mother landed shortly after 03.30 hrs, thankfully undamaged.

Later in the day I visited the photographic section to discover that we had achieved accurate bombing on the aiming point and that much of the port and dock area were destroyed. Unfortunately many bombs fell to the north-east and thus the main impact was minimal. We were now exactly half way through our first tour of, hopefully no more than, thirty operations.

The V-I and V-2 'Flying Bombs' - My Ear Problems.

Being minus both a plane and MUG, the James' crew spent the next few days doing minor air tests and being on 'stand-by'.

Until 22 August, there were only sporadic raids on Germany and the raids on V-I sites were petering out. Some 450 aircraft had been lost and over 2,900 aircrew killed while engaged on V-I raids. This had certainly been a heavy price to pay but on the credit side, it was calculated that without those raids, the London and south-east death toll would have been five times higher. Had the original German plan of commencing the V-I attacks in January 1944 taken place, it could have influenced the outcome of the War.

The fresh menace was the V-2 rocket. Known in Germany as, 'Vergeltungswaffe 2', or Retribution Weapon 2. This in fact was a supersonic ballistic missile. The V-2 was some forty six foot long and five foot six inches in diameter. It would soar fifty to sixty miles into the stratosphere and would approach its target at a speed of 2,500 ft per sec.

It could be launched from orchards and suburban parks, using mobile launchers. Already a few of these rockets had exploded in London but the population was advised that the explosions were due to gas leaks! It was only in November that the Prime Minister divulged a little of the threat from these 'Terror' weapons. Naturally from then on, they were referred to as 'flying gas pipes'.

Meanwhile, Bomber Command explored the feasibility of carrying out concentrated raids on the launching sites (when known). From 21 – 25 August, I flew with different 'drivers', experimenting with practice bombs at the local bombing ranges, but of course not knowing the real reason.

It was during this period that my ear problems developed.

101 Sqn Take Heavy Losses during August 1944.

Eight aircraft went missing during August with the names of sixty-three airmen being added to the Roll of Honour as 'killed in action'.

Additionally P/O Jack West flying in P-Peter (another war weary kite), encountered very heavy flak on a daylight trip to Bec-d'-Ambis oil storage sites. Despite the loss of an engine and being severely injured, P/O West continued to the target and dropped their bombs. They returned to England at just above stalling speed, finally crashing at Ford (Southampton area) where the pilot was rushed to hospital. For his bravery P/O West was awarded an immediate Distinguished Service Order (DSO), the only one to be awarded to a 101 Sqn member in 1944. Two other crew were also injured. The crew however received no awards and after returning to Ludford Magna by train, found themselves split up and posted separately to other squadrons. In the same month, two aircraft landed back at base with dead gunners. A further aircraft returned with a decapitated bomb-aimer (Sgt Smart from Northern Ireland), who was flying on his fifth operation.

The raids to Germany recommenced with a vengeance. From the 26th to 29th August, raids took place on Russelheim, Kiel, Stettin and Konigsberg. Heavy losses resulted with Ludford losing five aircraft in two nights, one of these was 'our' F-Fox, LM 479, just back from its extensive repair! It was flown by F/O Foster and was shot down over Stettin with the loss of all the crew.

31 August – Operations V-2 Rocket Sites – Aborted by B C.

We took off at 05:00 hrs on one of nine raids to V-2 rocket storage sites.

The aircraft was C-Charlie NF 924, our bomb load was 4,000 lbs of assorted HE bombs and the operational height was to be 16,000 ft. By now my ear infection had become extremely painful and it was partly a relief when after one and a half hours in the air, the wireless operator received the instruction to return to base for yet another abortive trip.

After having landed with a full bomb load on board, we reported to de-briefing to discover that six Lancasters had been lost out of just 125 dispatched. There was no information regarding why the operation had been cancelled or indeed why such a high percentage of planes had been lost.

CHAPTER 17   September 1944

3 September – Operations Gilze Rijen – Aborted.

15.50 hrs saw C-Charlie again airborne and, with the James' crew aboard, climbing to 15,000 ft with an assorted bomb load. Together with 675 other Lancasters, we were heading for five airfields in southern Holland, our target being Gilze Rijen. With only twenty minutes flying time to ETA, a sudden burst of flak hit the starboard inner engine. It was quickly feathered by an 'on the ball' engineer and by his speedy use of the fire extinguisher, an all-out fire was prevented.

Despite being in severe pain from my ear problem, I expected that we would continue with the operation. I was amazed to hear the pilot requesting a course back to base. Normally I would just have been irate, but would have at least waited until back at Ludford, before giving vent to frustration. Maybe it was a combination of the ear problem, previous aborts and now another wasted trip, that led to my sudden outburst of temper. Whatever the cause the pilot resented my interference and threatened (rightly so) to have me placed under arrest for insubordination and conduct not conducive to the safety of both the plane and the rest of the crew.

Frustration was so great that I told him to do whatever the hell he liked on return to base but that I felt strongly that the trip should have continued and that I intended to make my feelings known once we had landed. This was foolish of me. In the air the captain's word is final and in any well-disciplined crew, should never be questioned. It was a silent and miserable flight of almost three hours wasted time. The crew bus arrived and duly delivered us all to de-briefing.

The duty intelligence officer accepted the pilot's reason for aborting the trip. No mention was made by any crew member of the altercation that had preceded the return journey. As the crew left the room, the pilot muttered that on this occasion he would not take the insubordination charge any further but asked for an assurance that it would not happen again.

I was now almost frantic with pain from my ears and replied that there would be no re-occurrence of any criticism but that I would not retract any of my opinions. In this delicate situation, I regretted my frustration and appreciated that the pilot was responsible for the safety of both his crew and the aircraft.

The Dreaded 'Twitch'

In 1944 the words 'stress' and 'pressure' were unheard of.

There was however a much more ominous and terrifying expression, called 'the twitch' – involuntary movement of the muscles, usually facial but which could in fact migrate to any part of the body, depending on the seriousness of the condition. This problem was also associated with LMF, Lack of Moral Fibre – it was a term commonly used by Bomber Command during WW II and was the greatest fear of all fliers. Today of course the term would be, Combat Stress Reactions.

There had been an epidemic of this syndrome since the beginning of the year and consequently many airmen who were genuinely ill, became afraid of reporting sick to the medical officer, in case they became LMF suspects. The matter was further complicated because, like back problems today, the line between sufferers and malingerers was a very fine one, especially in cases like mine regarding ear infections. The consequence of all this was that I had flown the last two operations in great pain suffering stupidly. In later life I paid the penalty of chronic deafness. I could now no longer carry on so with great trepidation I reported to sick quarters. I was therefore extremely surprised, when upon an examination of my ears, the medical officer immediately grounded me for a minimum of two days. He reprimanded me for leaving it so long and instructed me to report to sick quarters each day, for medication and medical attention. I was now determined to reflect on my operational experiences to date and to reject any superfluous problems.

Corn and contemplation.

By the middle of the following morning, 04 September 1944, I had reached a point some eight miles from base at Ludford, in the Faldingworth area –

after a frantic 'pedal' taking an hour and a half on a borrowed service bicycle. I came to a corn field where the farmer was harvesting the crop and asked for permission to go into an adjacent field, which had had the crop already cut, to rest. The farmer wasn't pleased and suggested that a fit and able fellow would be better employed helping him to stook (stacking in sixes or eights), the sheaves of corn being thrown to the ground by the binder – a primitive form of today's combine harvester.

The binder, drawn by a pair of horses, had a cutting action adjacent to the front and took a five foot swathe of corn. This would land onto a sheet of canvas, which was operated by a windmill in order to rotate. In turn the sheaves were forced onto two more canvas sheets rising at an angle of 75% from the first canvas and were handled by a series of levers at the very top of the contraption, to finally be tied with bailer twine.

These sheaves would then topple down to the ground. The binder operator was perched well above the ground at the rear, to enable him to both control the two horses and to ensure the smooth and continuous operation of the machine.

On practically any other day I would have been more than willing to help. Today however I was very aware of my limitations, being both mentally and physically weary and additionally had a tormented mind to contend with.

Declining the farmer's 'kind' invitation, I walked back to my bicycle. Suddenly I heard him apologise and give me permission to use his fields anytime. After finding a good spot to rest near the gateway, I removed my tunic and began to enjoy the sun which, due to the appalling spring and summer of 1944, had been in very limited supply. Due to Double British Summer Time being in force, noon was really only eleven o'clock but the sun's rays were already very powerful, and it was probably one of the best days of the year. Apart from one or two Lancasters flying on air-tests, at about 10,000 ft, the only sound was the whirring of the binder in the next field. This together with the porcelain blue sky and the penetrating warmth of the sun combined to give a soporific effect. I began to feel my spirits rising and now felt strong enough to analyse my state of mind and start to divest myself of unnecessary problems. Later that same day, I did help with the harvesting and also took part in the traditional rabbit 'shoot'. As the corn was harvested, the many rabbits were deprived of their cover and attempted to return to their warrens . . .

The second half of the James' crew tour of operations - 101 Squadron.

By 08 September we had still not received a replacement F-Fox, which had

not flown since our return from the Russelheim raid on 13 August. So we took E-Easy LM 161 on a bomb-sight and camera test flight. 'Easy' was normally flown by F/O Machie whose crew shared the billet next to ours, the crew was on leave at this time.

12 September – Operations Stuttgart.

We took off in our first brand new Lancaster! – F-Fox NF 936.

The camera and intercom connections were faulty but our 12,000 lb bomb load was accurately delivered from a height of 16,500 ft.

Twenty-five Lancasters failed to return but the operation was generally regarded as being successful.

More importantly our crew integration had become vastly improved and it felt good to be part of a successful team. The flight duration had been seven and a half hours.

Tragedy over Loch Lomond.

15 September saw us carrying out another air test in another new aircraft - this time D Dog NF 983. Simultaneously another 101 Sqn crew were air testing Lancaster PB 456. This aircraft was last seen diving into Loch Lomond with at least one engine on fire. The crew of seven perished.

22 / 23 September – Operations Neuss.

On this sortie we were tasked to bomb marshalling yards at Neuss. Although a success for us, this operation saw the loss of twenty-two Lancasters. One of the lost crews was flying in M-Mother PB 237 piloted by F/O Machie, you may remember that they were billeted in the next Nissen hut to ours. The crew had joined 'A' flight at the end of June and were sadly missed. All eight crew member's names are listed on the Roll of Honour situated in Ludford Chapel.

We completed two more raids in F-Fox NF 936 before the end of September. We attempted a trip to bomb the German defence positions in Calais on 25th of the month. Due to inclement weather we were unable to bomb and the Master Bomber ordered our return to base.

It was not until mid-September, that we eventually received a permanent MUG replacement for Sgt AN Other. He was F/O Ken Gibb DFC, already a survivor of seventy-five trips –three tours of operations. Amazingly he had joined 101 Squadron to extend his number of trips to – yes – 101! This meant that after we had finished our tour (God willing!) Ken intended to carry on flying . . .

An attack, on 26 September on Cap Griz Nez was more successful. We bombed visually from 3,000 ft (low), and helped to destroy the shore batteries. A short, three and a quarter hour trip.

101 SQUADRON
Lancaster Pilot F/Lt F.G James DFC & Crew
Taken at Ludford Magna, Lincs

CHAPTER 18   October 1944

The Flooding of Walcheren Island.

Antwerp and its port were captured by Allied Forces in early September 1944. The Germans however had mined the approaches via the Scheldt Estuary. They had also built massive concrete gun emplacements along Walcheren Island. These effectively prevented Allied access to 'minesweep' the adjacent estuary, the approach to Antwerp itself. It was Eisenhower's intention to use Antwerp as a supply 'staging post' to facilitate the taking of the Ruhr.

At this time Germany was also robustly holding the ports of Boulogne, Calais, and Dunkirk - thus severely restricting the supply line to allied troops. On or around 07 September, Hitler himself issued orders that the Allies had to be prevented from using the port facilities of Antwerp by means of the Walcheren Island gun emplacements.

On the following day he backed up these instructions adding the words, 'at all cost'. [Paul M Crucq – *'We never blamed the crews'.*]

Shortly after mid-September, the 2nd Canadian Corps felt that the flooding of Walcheren Island was desirable in order to support allied forces spearheaded by the Canadians themselves. It is salient when considering the probable loss of life of the Dutch population of Walcheren after flooding, to confirm that Bomber Command had had two attempts to bomb the gun emplacements directly. Although there were several near misses, it became clear that this tactic was not going to silence the guns.

On 02 October, warning messages were sent to the Walcheren residents, without revealing exactly what was going to happen or where. The BBC broadcasts gave specific details concerning the immediate evacuation of their homes and indeed the island itself. The radio broadcast was backed up by the dropping of warning leaflets by the Americans using B-17's.

03 October – 1 and 3 Groups go 'dyke busting' - Operations Westkapelle.

Bomber Command despatched 240 Lancasters from 1 Gp and 3 Gp to carry out a daylight raid. The intention was to breach the sea wall at Westkapelle, the most easterly point of Walcheren Island.

Four Lancasters and four Mosquitos from 8 Gp Pathfinder Force, were detailed to mark the target. PFF also controlled the pace of the operation, by the use of a Master Bomber. As it was a daylight raid, forty-six Spitfires of 11 Gp Fighter Command were detailed to protect the Main Force. PFF supplied a further three Mosquitos for photo reconnaissance and meteorology reconnaissance.

'The Dambusters' – 617 Sqn (5 Gp) had aircraft on 'standby' in case the Main Force did not achieve their objective - we shall return to them later.

The operation comprised eight 'waves', with the 120 Lancasters of 3 Gp, bombing during the first four waves and the 120 aircraft of 1 Gp, attacking during the last four waves. We were due to bomb at 14.55 hrs, towards the end of the last four waves.

On the way out we experienced heavy cumulus cloud at low altitude. We decided to climb to try to clear the cloud. Just before we reached 10,000 ft there was an ice build-up on the aircraft and the controls became sluggish. The pilot reported that he had lost control and in Fred's words: 'Fox began to "flutter" towards the sea'.

This disconcerting situation continued until we cleared the cloud at about 3,000 ft. Slowly, the ice build-up broke away and control of the aircraft was regained. On reaching the target we saw that the dyke had been breached and we bombed in order to widen the gap. The bombing took place from a height of 4,000 feet.

1 Gp and 3 Gp success save The 'Dambusters', valuable Tallboys.

Had the dyke not been breached by the Main Bomber Force, 617 Sqn had eight Lancasters and two Mosquitos (617 Sqn generally did their own target marking) ready to form a ninth wave of attack. The Lancasters were carrying 12,000 'Tallboy' bombs designed by Barnes Wallace.

Unknown to us at the time, the 617 Sqn Commander, W/C 'Willie' Tait DSO and three bars, DFC and bar and his deputy Sq/Ldr Gerry Fawke DFC, were circling around in the Mosquitos as we made our bombing run. The Tallboys which 617 Sqn were carrying were extremely expensive and also in short supply - they were only to be used as a last resort. Tait and Fawke observed 'very accurate bombing right from the early stages', which had clearly breached the dyke.

Tait conferred with his deputy leader and they agreed that Main Force had succeeded in creating a breach and furthermore, were continually enlarging it. He saw no reason to waste their precious bomb load. Tait therefore turned back his eight Lancasters before they commenced their bombing run. All landed with their precious (non-human) cargos intact.

The Tallboy was designed as an earthquake bomb, at twenty-one feet long and thirty-eight inches in diameter it required that standard Lancasters receive considerable bomb bay modifications to carry it. The bomb was of thick skin construction and largely hand made. This process was very labour intensive, so the tallboys were both extremely expensive to produce and in short supply.

Just four days later, 617 Sqn used Tallboys in a successful (special) attack on the lock gates of the Krebs dam, using – Tallboys. In all probability they were still warm!

The remainder of October proved to be a hectic month when the James' crew clocked up eleven operations to an assortment of targets.

5 October 1944 – Operations Saarbruken – Marshalling yards.

Raid requested by American ground forces advancing this way to halt

German rail communications and troop reinforcement movements. Bombed from 16,000 ft in F-Fox, with a return trip of five hours and forty minutes. Accurate bombing causing severe damage was reported.

6 October 1944 – Operations Bremen.

We took off at 17.45 hrs flying H-How DV 302 at a height of 17,000 ft. We had been the 'stand by' crew that night. This often meant waiting until all aircraft detailed for that raid had taken off - and then returning to our barracks. On this occasion one of the detailed force lost an engine on take-off – at least we got to cross another op. off the 'thirty'. *Bomber Command War Diaries* report the raid to have been an outstanding success helped no doubt by accurate target marking and clear moonlit skies. [Our own target was the marshalling yards.]

The transport network was seriously disrupted and a shipyard, aircraft factories, a major electrical works and other vital war industries suffered severe damage. Bomber Command's ability to find the target, mark the target and bomb the target, had now advanced to the extent that, the 1942 One Thousand Bomber Raid to Bremen, produced far less damage to war industries than this raid, which used only one quarter of the force, (246 Lancasters).

7 October – Operations Emmerich – Front line support.

A daylight raid, we took off at 12:15 hrs and bombed from 14,000 ft. This was a successful attack with a flying time of four and a half hours. The German threat to the allied flank, through this 'gap' had now been largely removed.

9 October – Operations Bochum.

Took off at 17.30 hrs in F Fox NF 936 to bomb at 20,000 ft.

Due to bad weather and visibility the Pathfinder Force had marked the target using 'Wanganui' - illuminated target markers hanging on parachutes above the cloud. Main Force aircraft therefore, bombed without seeing the target. It was a five and a half hour return trip and a rough one due to the weather. For whatever reason the results of this raid were disappointing.

Thirty two aircraft were lost this night mostly to German fighters, but much industrial damage was caused, especially to steelworks. This was Bomber Command's last trip to Bochum.

11 October – Operations Fort Fredrich Hendrich – Gun batteries.

Another daylight trip and yet more bad weather. We took off at 15.20 hrs in our faithful 'Fox'. Due to heavy cloud we lost height from 4,000 ft to just 2,000 ft (uncomfortably low!) for the bombing run and encountered heavy ack-ack fire. Flying time was a total of four hours.

It was on the Fort Fredrich Hendrich sortie that we were flying just to the starboard of Y-Yorker LL 771, piloted by Sqn/Ldr Mathews, the 'C' Flight Commander and his crew, when they received a direct hit from an ack-ack battery. As we were flying at just 4,000 ft at that time, the crew had no chance of survival. Sqn/LdrMathews and his crew had served on the squadron for almost six months, so would have been close to the end of their tour.

The James' crew takes seven days leave.

23 October – Operations Essen (Ruhr).

A 'rough', five and a half hour return trip to the Ruhr, (referred to by Bomber Command as 'Happy Valley') industrial centre to bomb Essen. Due once more to bad weather, we bombed on Wanganui markers above the cloud level. Even in reasonable weather the Ruhr area had always been covered by industrial haze, making precise target identification at night, problematic.

25 October – Operations Essen – German gunners punish 'Fox'.

Back to Essen again after only 48 hrs but this time in daylight. Take-off time 13.50 hrs to bomb from 18,000ft. For once the target was cloud free and we bombed visually. Accurate flak caused severe damage to the bomb aimer's compartment (my office), and the fuselage. Following this attack 'Fox' was out of service for a few days. It had been a five hour trip.

The Krupps steelworks in particular were heavily hit by these two raids and sustained perhaps more significant damage, than on any other WW II raid. This raid probably marked the beginning of the end for Essen as one of Germany's major industrial centres of production, although further Bomber Command raids did take place.

On 5 October we lost P/O Mason and his seven crew members, in A Apple LL 758 during the Saarbruchen trip. On 15 October P/O Hunt and his NCO crew were posted missing in LL 774.

28 October – Operations Cologne.

Back to the Ruhr again in a repaired 'Fox', tasked to bomb an aircraft factory. Bombed from 18,000 ft, visually – incurred slight flak damage – another five hour trip completed. *Bomber Command War Diaries,* state - local reports confirm that much damage was caused to power-stations, railways and harbour installations on the Rhine.

29 October - Return to Walcheren Island – Extremely low level bombing by later 'waves' of the Main Force.

On this occasion we were detailed to bomb battery/strong point W 18. This was situated near Domberg, just a few miles N E of the Westkapelle dyke, which as you may recall was successfully breached by Bomber Command on 3 October 1944. This raid was different from most of the others we had been engaged on during our tour.

It was one of the few daylight raids and we eventually bombed from the lowest height ever. We had been due to bomb from a height of 1,500 ft, which would have been very low. In the event, because of maelstrom and haze from the efforts of previous aircraft, we actually dropped our bomb load from just 800 ft! On this occasion we carried a 13 x 1,000 lb armour piercing bombs. This type of bomb required a safety height of at least 1,000 ft.

On night raids we would generally bomb from considerably higher altitudes. The target always appeared to be a lifetime away and reaches the bombsight graticule with agonizing slowness. A bomber is at its most vulnerable to flak and fighters, when it is flying straight and level and at a constant speed, on the 'bombing run'. This raid was completely different. Just as we were about to bomb, the Master Bomber instructed the Main Force to ignore the green TI s, which had fallen in the sea and to bomb on the 'reds'. Because of the low altitude, everything happened rapidly and it required all my powers of concentration to line the Lancaster up with the bombing run. Just as suddenly the target was in the bombsight and the bombs were released (at 13.32.30 hrs). We remained flying straight and level for the mandatory two minutes for the camera to record our efforts. The whole world seemed to rock and the Lancaster shuddered as if it was due to disintegrate.

This of course was the up blast from our own bombs - then it was all over. On our return, I was credited with an 'aiming point photo' for the raid.

Other crews bombing from a similar altitude to ourselves reported flying *through* red Pathfinder TI s! One even reported fragments of bomb casing falling out of one of their engines, on landing!

German occupation crumbles on Walcheren.

The 'ground' attack of the Island commenced just two days later. The troops detailed were mainly Canadian and Scottish. British Commandos did however make a seaward approach – sailing through the breech in the dyke made by the 03 October, 1 and 3 group raid! The Island fell to the Allies after a further week of intense fighting. By late October the estuary had been cleared of German mines and the first convoy reached Antwerp on 28 November 1944.

31 October – Operations Cologne.

Took off at 18.20 hrs in 'Fox', once again due to inclement weather we bombed on Wanganui sky markers. This was another rough five hour trip.

CHAPTER 19   November 1944

We make the magic 'thirty'!

A five and a half hour duration flight to Dusseldorf, on the night of 02 November saw the James' crew become 'tour expired' - with one exception. It was Bill (Paddy) Orr who needed one more trip to reach the magic 'Thirty' operations. The Dusseldorf trip was flown at 17,500 ft and was the last trip the James' crew made in F Fox NF 936. We expected that the whole crew would fly one more trip but two crew members refused. I decided to accompany Bill on one more operation. Incidentally this operation was the last major Bomber Command raid on Dusseldorf of the war.

Paddy's last trip.

On the night of 04 November we took off at 17.00 hrs for Bochum. We were in aircraft J- Jig LL 829 and our pilot was F/O Barber RCAF. The trip went comparatively smoothly for us – so now the whole James' crew was 'tour expired'.

It was pleasant to subsequently hear that my very last trip had been particularly successful and that we had been 'spared' the attentions of the many German fighters in the target area that night.

On this attack, 32 aircraft were lost.

A clandestine motor cycle journey – I lose more friends.

Our beloved F- Fox NF 936 was also airborne on this trip. Its new skipper F/O Edwards and his crew had, since mid-September shared our Nissan hut. They were aware of the high regard in which we held this aircraft and were 'allowed' to take it over.

The navigator for this crew was one Chris Terriere, who hailed from Mauritius. Chris had an uncle in the UK. This relative had sometime in October, kindly sent to Louth Railway Station, a 1934 250cc BSA motorcycle for Chris' use while on the airfield. On an afternoon 'stand-down', Chris and I travelled to Louth to collect the machine.

Needless to say there were many problems – not least a supply of petrol and also the machine had a flat accumulator battery. It took some time to sort out our difficulties and also to acquire two torches . . . Eventually, with the engine revving and Chris perched on the back holding one torch in front of him and one behind, we set off. I quietly prayed that Gp/Cpt. King's threat, that I would be under continual observation regarding any further misdeeds, would be hindered by the darkness, as the torch didn't exactly 'light up the heavens'. My prayer was answered and eventually, after narrowly avoiding excursions into the ubiquitous Lincolnshire ditches which flanked the road, we arrived back safely at Ludford. Chris then learned to ride the BSA, which became very useful to both crews.

Now back to the Bochum trip of 4 November. The aircraft which failed to return, included two Lancasters from 101 Sqn. These were F/O Twiss in X X-Ray ME 865, and Chris Terriere and all his crew in, 'our' F Fox NF 936.

We had booked an extension at the Sgts. Mess bar to celebrate the end of our tour. This was cancelled – in the event it didn't seem appropriate. By the time Paddy and I had returned to our billet, Chris' motorcycle had disappeared. The special police and Committee of Adjustments had already removed the missing crew's effects . . .

Two days later I ensured that the ground crew of 'Fox' were taken to the White Hart and entertained as well as was possible in wartime.

The Story of the Lancaster, accurately records NF 936 as having gone missing on 4 November 1944, having achieved 144 hrs flying time. All of these hours had been logged by the James' crew.

The following day, I set off on the long journey across the country for seven day's leave. I arrived home to find a telegram addressed to 'Pilot Officer' Davies', advising me of an immediate commission. The first shock was that this promotion was totally unexpected. The second, was that it had been proposed by none other than my 'old friend' G/Capt King (Revigny raid 18/19 July). The promotion had been seconded by Air Commodore, soon to be AVM, Bluck. A further telegram interrupted my leave a few days later and instructed an immediate recall to Ludford Magna.

Promoted :
Pilot Officer Davies

My Thoughts at the end of a successful tour of operations.

After seventy odd years my precise thoughts are rather sketchy. More recently however at the end of a talk I had given to The Wirral Aeronautical Society, I was asked the question: 'Which was your most difficult operation.' It took only a few seconds of reflection before I responded: 'All of them.' I further explained that by 'all' I meant the thirty one operations which I had completed but also the seven which for various reasons were aborted.

Even comparatively uneventful trips involved:

Hours of waiting after the 'Battle Orders' had been issued.
Extensive Operational briefing.
Changing into flying - clothing / collecting parachutes, life jackets etcetera.
Ground testing and finally climbing into the fully fuelled and bombed - up Lancaster.

As senior NCO it was my responsibility to close the rear door, (after the removal of the access ladder by the ground crew.) The resounding clang resonated as if a coffin lid was being shut on all eight crew members!
From that point and until our return WE WERE ALONE.

That is what sticks in my mind now.

PART SIX

VITAL 'RESEARCH AND DEVELOPMENT' FLYING – SOUTH WALES AND HAMPSHIRE.

CHAPTER 20 – CCDU Angle – South Wales.

In mid-November 1944, the James' crew was seconded to 'Coastal Command Development Unit' at Angle in South Wales, a remote and desolate base situated on the very south west tip of Pembrokeshire, some eight miles west of Pembroke itself. As we were not using ABC equipment at this unit, Sgt Roy Hall joined a RCAF crew at 101 Sqn, in order to complete his tour of operations at Ludford.

On completion of a first tour of operations, crews were frequently 'rested' by being seconded to training stations, as instructors in their particular field of expertise. This task sounded as if it could be a lot more exciting. Due to inclement weather, the James' crew, in a brand new Lancaster (V Victor) were diverted to Boras in N Wales, where we spent two days before we were able to continue our journey.

Paddy faces the music.

As we taxied to our allocated dispersal area at Angle, the crew (especially Fred), were startled to find the rear exit of the Lancaster blocked by a special police (RAF) vehicle! Three men, two of whom were armed, arrested Bill Orr for an alleged fracas aboard a Belfast ferry the previous week. Despite strenuous denials, Bill was taken away, charged and sentenced to eight week's detention, at Sheffield Air Crew Corrective Centre (the Glass House).

Our replacement flight engineer.

Paddy's replacement was a Coastal Command 'spare bod' called Rob. In July 1943 Rob had been the flight engineer on a Coastal Command Halifax which had attacked, and sunk, a U-boat off the south west coast of Ireland. The Halifax was however fatally damaged and ditched in the sea.

Three crew members were killed in the crash. The six remaining crew survived without rations, in a single-man dingy for **twelve days** before being rescued.

The pilot, Flying Officer Hartley had been awarded the DFC for sinking the U-boat. This amazing episode is described in Charles Bowyer's - *Men of Coastal Command*. There was no doubt that Rob was far from fit enough to be deployed on such demanding flying.

For his part in the crew survival over this period, Rob (then a Flt Sgt) was 'Mentioned in Dispatches' and promoted to Pilot Officer. Thus he and I were the new boys in the officer's mess! Consequently we had many deep conversations about life as we knew it.

It was here that Fred (a martinet to the rest of the crew), went into overdrive and, recognising his own difficulties following a traumatic experience, extended the help and patience that Rob required to regain his self-confidence. Ten weeks later on the return of Bill Orr, Rob left the crew, a much more relaxed and self-sufficient airman.

What price patriotism?

On March 18th 2016 a leading national newspaper published a photograph taken by one of the crew of the rescue destroyer, with all the graphic details. The paper reported that the now deceased pilot's family were placing the DFC (Distinguished Flying Cross), log book and diary of F/O Eric Hartley into auction and were hoping to raise £3,000. Compare this with the nearly £200 million transfer fee recently paid for a football player.

The other crews.

When we settled in at Angle, we were advised that we were to carry out R & D work, with five other 'tour expired' crews. Two of the crews were from 1 Group, ourselves from 101 Sqn and that of F/O Shorney, formerly of 12 Squadron based at Wickenby. The other four crews were ex 617 Squadron ('The Dam Busters') from 5 Gp, and consisted of:

Flt/Lt John Williams DFC - John was the Flight Commander of our detachment.

Flt/Lt Arthur Fearn,DFC.

Flt/Lt M L ('Mac') Hamilton, whose DFC was gazetted in January 1945.

Last but certainly not least:

F/O Nicky Ross, DSO DFC.

The task in hand.

The objective of this detachment was to develop specific techniques to enable *moving* targets to be accurately bombed. Up and until this time, very little progress had been achieved in this direction.

At the Quebec conference in September 1944, Winston Churchill proposed that a large part of Bomber Command, (250 to 400 heavy bombers) be transferred to the Pacific theatre, once Germany had been

defeated. This was to be a British / Commonwealth bombing effort, called 'Tiger Force'. Tiger Force planned to use Lancaster, Lincoln and Consolodated Liberator bombers, to attack the Japanese fleet based at that time in the vicinity of Okinawa.

That this research was both serious and urgent, was brought fully home to us, by the fact that each of the six crews was allocated a brand new Lancaster. Ours was V Victor PD 417, if only this had been available six months earlier! All the main bomber groups (1, 3 and 5) used the mark XIV bombsight. 617 Sqn (and 9 Sqn) however, used the Stabilized Automatic Bombsight (SABS). SABS was a much more technically advanced bombsight than the MK XIV.

SABS had only been used operationally for the first time, by 617 Sqn on 11/12 November 1943, on the Antheor Viaduct raid. They were all hand-made, cost a king's ransom and were in very short supply. We two 1 Gp bomb aimers were very excited and privileged to get our hands on them.

Before I say more concerning the bombing of moving targets, it may be helpful to briefly highlight the difficulties encountered when bombing a *static* target. To enable the bomb aimer to know when to release the bomb load, the bombsight must take into account, at least, the following factors:

    Aircraft speed and height.

    Wind speed and direction.

    Bomb aerodynamics and weight.

    Changes in air density (when bombing from high altitude).

Using the above data, the bombsight has to estimate the path which the bomb will take on release from the aircraft (roughly parabolic).

For example a 500 lb general purpose bomb dropped from 20,000 ft, will travel forward approximately 6,500 ft or well over one mile, before impact. It is not too difficult therefore, to imagine how much more complex the task will be when the target is also moving!

John Williams firstly divided the unit into two sections, 'A' and 'B'. Each section comprised two 617 crews and one 1 Gp crew. We found ourselves in 'B' section together with the crews of Arthur Fearn and Nicky Ross.

I hear about the Petwood Hotel for the first time.

As previously mentioned, Angle was remote and lacking in many refinements. Of our contingent of forty-two aircrew, there were fourteen or fifteen officers. As I had received my commission at the completion of my tour with 101 Sqn, I was allocated, together with the other officers, a cold and spartan Nissen hut and we were also supplied with one batwoman.

This differed little from my former life as a senior NCO at Ludford Magna. It was however, a far cry from the accommodation and facilities, to which the 617 Sqn officers had been previously accustomed.

From early January 1944 when 617 Sqn moved to Woodhall Spa, they had their officer's mess located in the Petwood Hotel, situated about a mile from Woodhall village centre. The Petwood is a broad and pleasantly rambling, stone and (black and white) timbered building, which has many of its internal walls clad in oak paneling. These would of course have been boarded up during wartime occupation by the RAF. The hotel is situated in magnificent wooded surroundings and is set in twenty-six acres of gardens. Being billeted in The Petwood and having your morning cup of tea brought by a batman, or woman, must have made for a pleasant existence – except of course for the war. The 617 boys' description of this stunning hotel intrigued me, but it was to be sixty-three years before circumstances conspired to allow me to see it for myself.

However back to Angle and as autumn turned to winter, bringing shorter days, we found ourselves settled into a routine of flying all available hours.

We used what little leisure time remained, by taking advantage of the somewhat limited facilities available, such as cards and billiards, within the officer's mess - yet another converted Nissen hut but with very little added to ensure a comfortable lifestyle.

A bolt from the blue.

At the beginning of December, one of the Lancasters was scheduled to return to Lincolnshire to collect additional spare parts for the detachment's aircraft. As I had been re called early from my last leave, I had been unable to collect my officer's uniform from the tailor in Chester. Until now I had made do with my old battledress with the NCO insignia removed and replaced with a single blue band, which signified the rank of pilot officer. To enable me to collect my uniform, I was granted a forty-eight hour pass to travel as far as Cosford , Shropshire, in the Lincoln-bound Lancaster. From Cosford I could complete the journey to Chester by bus / train.

At 15.25 hrs on 08 December 1944, I travelled as a 'passenger' on Lancaster U Uncle PD 810, a new aircraft only recently delivered from the factory. Our scheduled flying time was to be fifty minutes, in daylight and all over friendly territory! Nicky Ross DSO DFC was the pilot for the trip. He was all for flying at the minimum required height of 4,000 ft, the navigator however insisted that this be changed to 6,000 ft, due to the proximity of high ground. Due to the passage of time, I cannot recall the navigator's name.

For me it was a luxury to be flying this route as I would otherwise have had a full day's journey by road and rail.

Approximately half way into the flight, I was standing in the fuselage behind the pilot's canopy, contentedly looking through the perspex astrodome when, without any warning whatsoever, the Lancaster nose-dived earthwards. Within seconds I was plunged to the floor of the aircraft, to be immediately bombarded by .303 ammunition belts from the mid-upper turret.

The G forces were so great that it was impossible for me to move. It was surprising therefore that under these conditions, the pilot and engineer were able to arrest the downward spiral – albeit only a few hundred feet above mother earth! Shortly after control of the aircraft had been regained, the pilot said with some feeling: 'I could certainly do with a drink after that'! Immortal words indeed. We soon returned to the planned route and only suffered a twenty minute delay, landing at Cosford at 16.35 hrs.

Having collected my uniform from Chester, I returned to Angle by train. Our routine was flying every day, weather permitting and often twice a day. By now a trajectory and ballistics scientist had joined the team and was present at all flight briefings and de briefings. The scientist was one Sqn/Ldr Richardson, who was nicknamed the 'talking bomb' if my memory serves me.

He would later, also fly with each crew to monitor co-ordination between the pilot, bomb-aimer and navigator. These briefings were a busy time for all crew members but especially for the pilots, navigators and bomb-aimers.

Extract from my logbook for Nov / Dec 1944.

Flew in Lancasters V Victor PD 417, U Uncle PB 810, T Tare PB 803 and S Sugar PB 809 with, (variously) pilots F/O James – F/O Shorney – Flt/Ltn Hamilton DFC and F/O Nicky Ross DSO DFC. Static bombing practice using Mk XIV and SABS bombsights at bombing ranges situated at – St David's Head, Honeybourne and Bristol.

Normally used 12 lb PB's (practice bombs) and executed six runs, using two bombs per run. Bombing height set at 3,000-5,000 ft but after experimentation was changed to, from between 500 ft (or lower) to 10,000 ft. These tests were to enable the 'Talking Bomb', our ex 617 Sqn 'egghead' to produce various ranges of calculations, before we attempted to attack simulated moving targets. These would usually be High Speed Launches (HSL's) or Motor Torpedo Boats (MTB's).

1945 beckons.

Despite the primitive conditions, both Christmas 1944 and New Year 1945

passed pleasantly enough and I particularly enjoyed the stories relating to the adventures of the famous 617 Squadron - but especially those of Nicky Ross. Nicky didn't discuss his exploits very much but everything he related was pertinent. One quickly understood what made him stand out head and shoulders above most people.

The U Uncle 'incident' of 8 December 1944.

The results of the investigation into the incident aboard U Uncle, were announced at the end of that month. It appeared that a connecting-rod linking parts of the automatic pilot mechanism, known as 'George', had failed. There were sighs of relief at this news, as the problem had *not* been judged as pilot or aircrew error.

Nevertheless, a major catastrophe had been averted due to, a) the diligence of the navigator by insisting that an additional 2,000 ft be added to the height of the original flight plan - and b) the remarkable ability of the pilot, Nicky Ross.

Bad News from Ludford Magna.

News filtered through from 101 Sqn base at Ludford, regarding three separate incidents which occurred within just six days of each other. The crews involved were much less fortunate than those of us aboard U Uncle. The first occurred on 22 December 1943, when by co incidence a 617 Sqn Lancaster was attempting to land at Ludford in the fog. Ludford Magna was one of the few airfields equipped with a fog dispersal system called FIDO. The port wing touched the ground and the aircraft began to break up and caught fire. The bomb-aimer and one of the gunners were killed but the pilot and remaining four aircrew survived albeit with injuries.

You may remember that Flt/Lt Walt Reif and his crew trained with us during 1943/44 and initially also flew on operations with 101 Sqn. Later they their transferred to 582 Sqn of the 'Pathfinder Force' (PFF).

We now heard that on 23 December 1944, Walt and four of his crew had been killed on a raid over Cologne. That was to have been their final trip before being screened. This now left the James' crew, as the last remaining of *The Original Four*.

The third piece of bad news came on 27 December 1944. F/O Ken Gibb DFC who, you may remember, had joined our crew as the third replacement mid-upper gunner in September, had been killed flying with

Flt/Lt Parke. All eight crew members had perished. Ken joined our crew with many operations under his belt and the stated intention of completing one hundred and one operations with 101 Sqn. He was killed on his ninety-sixth trip.

Extracts from my log book for January 1945.

Flew in Lancasters Y Yorker PB 418, T Tare PB803 and V Victor PD 417, with (variously) pilots F/O Shorney – Flt/Lt Williams DFC and F/O James. Bad weather restricted flying and the HSL's rarely appeared.

CHAPTER 21   The unit relocates to ASWDU, Hampshire.

In mid-January 1945, Coastal Command Development Unit (CCDU) at Angle closed down and our small unit of Lancasters was transferred to Air Sea Warfare Development Unit (ASWDU), at Thorney Island in Hampshire.

We took off from Angle just before lunch time on 15 January and, led by Nicky Ross, our six aircraft circled the airfield to give one of the finest impromptu displays of close formation low level flying ever seen at Angle. It therefore seemed somewhat churlish that the Angle station commander was not (definitely not!) duly appreciative.

On arrival at Thorney Island there were reprimands in abundance. Relations between Coastal Command and Bomber Command had always been strained and our parting display at Angle did little to heal that rift.

During the one and a half hour trip from Angle to Thorney Island, George Williams, our rear gunner reported that there was an aircraft *without a propeller.* flying just behind us. We all remonstrated with George for imbibing too much the previous evening. As it turned out of course, it was the new Meteor jet fighter . . .

High Jinx at Thorney Island.

During our stay at Thorney, two incidents occurred which demonstrated that not only Bomber Command crews could behave in an unruly manner, to 'let off steam'. These incidents also highlight the fact that Thorney Island was a multi services base.

A Coastal Command Sq/Ldr's wife had just given birth to a son. He and one of his pals decided to celebrate the event.

He rode his motor cycle into the officer's mess creating mayhem for the incumbents. Rumour had it that he paid £125 for damage to fixtures and fittings, a small fortune then, even on a Sq/Ldr's pay. Prompt settlement of this sum probably avoided a court-martial.

The second incident was much more serious. One Saturday evening, the Station Commander's Hillman Minx was removed from outside the officer's mess. The miscreants responsible, drove the car onto the main runway and attempted to 'take off'. The empty wrecked car was discovered at daybreak. All officers were immediately ordered to visit the mess, with an account of their whereabouts at that time.

Eventually an ultimatum was issued to the effect that unless the culprits confessed to the crime, all officers would be medically examined for injuries. Fortunately the culprits, four members of The Royal Naval Air School realized that the 'game was up', and admitted the offences. This saved the rest of us the indignity of an inspection.

There was one further incident, but to whom the responsibility could be attributed, was never discovered . . . Towards the end of 1944 I had acquired a bicycle. Since the officer's mess was adjacent to the flight headquarters I had little need for the machine. George Williams however was billeted some distance away and borrowed the bike to save a long walk. After just a few days however he reported that it had: 'just disappeared'.

A full church service and parade was laid on to celebrate the Easter holiday and it was mandatory for the whole station to attend. As we marched towards the parade ground and saluting area, and in full view of all, we saw the missing bicycle attached to the top of the flag pole. I decided that it was better to lose a bike than get involved with explanations. Such is life.

Extracts from my logbook for February to May 1945.

February / March.

Flying with F/O James, (now DFC) in V Victor PD 417. Combined bombing and photography – also experimented with Wind Finding Apparatus – results eventually discounted due to grossly inaccurate results.

Now using data sheets compiled from our experiments to improve bombing results on moving targets (usually three HSL's towing targets).

Exercises now stepped up to include moving targets taking evasive action. Also trips to Bristol simulating attacks on static targets - for example, ports and shipping areas, practicing attacks on - maybe Okinawa? Also two trips at 15,000 ft and a return to target at low level – complicated but some good results reported.

April / May.

Formation flying at 500 ft with Liberator – photography and bombing. More experiments with 'wind finding' and many simulated attacks on moving targets, interspersed with trips to Lowestoft and Ely – for mock attacks on ports and shipping.

More experiments with newly developed 'instruments', recorded as being successful. There were still more successful simulated attacks on moving targets while they were taking evasive action. The majority of these exercises were carried out in PD 417 flown by F/O FG James DFC.

The work was hard but fulfilling and long flying hours, combined with continual assessment meetings, continued to be the order of the day. Unlike CCDU Angle however, there were compensations in the form of the many facilities located at the nearby towns of Havant, Chichester and Bognor Regis, of which we took full advantage!

Conclusion. The results of the experimental work which we were carrying out were good and improving all the time.

Atom bombs were deployed against Hiroshima, (Little Boy, a Uranium device) and Nagasaki (Fat Man, a plutonium weapon) – within three days of each other in early August 1945 by the Americans. I have little doubt that if these nuclear bombs had not been utilized, that our efforts would have almost certainly resulted in the decimation of the Japanese Fleet. Such was the aim of most of our research and development work at both Angle and Thorney Island.

I have to say that I thoroughly enjoyed those six months of flying, hazardous and tiring though it was. When six Lancasters are flying wingtip to wingtip, often at very low level, in pursuit of MTB's which suddenly take evasive action, even the most experienced pilots find the concentration exacting.

It was no picnic for the rest of the crew either – our rear gunner George Williams (an ex rancher from Alberta) mooted: 'Hey Skip, if I'd wanted to get my feet wet I'd have joined the navy'!

We served at Thorney Island until just before VE day in May 1945.

We then returned to 101 Sqn at Ludford Magna.

CHAPTER 22   Our return to Ludford Magna.

Still officially on the strength of 101 Sqn, **we now returned** to hand over our trusted Lancaster, V Victor, together with many valuable spares.

Way back in September 1944, 'A' Flight was commanded by Sqn/ Ldr Gordon-Black. The previous month's heavy casualties had for some obscure reason, prompted him to introduce compulsory physical training, for all crew members not actually flying that day. This created resentment and tension among us all. To compound matters further, Sqn/Ldr Black on one of his early night trips, flying A Apple, inadvertently landed at the nearby Killingholme, instead of at Ludford.

This caused chaos and confusion to the remaining aircraft still circling Ludford and awaiting permission to land! At the next PT session, the Squadron Leader heard the chanting of a group of dissidents:

'Who moved Ludford Magna – Squadron Leader "Killingholme" Black'!

The PT lessons were suspended but Sq/Ldr Black did not forget those crew members he suspected of being the perpetrators of the rebellion . . .

On our return to Ludford many months later, we found that 101 Sqn was commanded by, now, Wing Commander Gordon-Black. Among the airman Black believed responsible for the chanting, he had not forgotten that at least one of the suspects was a James' crew member. We were dispatched post-haste to a transit camp. The Canadian members of the crew were repatriated and demobbed. Fred and the remaining members of the crew (with one exception) were posted to Transport Command to fly Dakotas.

The exception. as noted above, was myself. I was allocated, ironically, to Tiger Force and posted to South East Asia Command. During my time there I served at Mauripur (Karachi), India and later at Dum Dum, Calcutta, joining the second wave of troops to relieve Singapore and finally to Kuala Lumpur, (Malaya). It was to be fifteen months before I returned to England and with constant movement in Asia, I lost all contact with my former crew members.

PART SEVEN

SOUTH EAST ASIA COMMAND

CHAPTER 23   The Far East Beckons

When one is married, few 'single' overseas postings in wartime are ever convenient. This one was doubly inconvenient. My wife had informed me of her pregnancy (child due December 1945). We had been sharing a home with my wife's mother near Wrexham, N. Wales.

Now that the European war had ended, two of my wife's brothers, ex-prisoners of war from Dunkirk, had been repatriated and were living at the same house. I will not go into detail regarding my lack of success at 'house hunting' in the Wrexham area but after ten days searching, I became more and more despondent. Just before I was due to report to Bourne, some friends from Llangollen, later to become famous for its annual music festival, pointed us towards a flat to let in that town. The landlord had more than forty applicants, whether it was my uniform that swung the decision in our favour I never found out. The flat was very small, up two flights of steps and deemed as 'not suitable for children'. We however had run out of options.

One bright spot at that time was notice of my promotion to Flying Officer. This entitled my wife to an adequate allowance. She had had to give up her job in a Wrexham factory due to the move to Llangollen.

At Bourne and out of thirty odd officers I would share the flight to India with, I became particularly friendly with one Bob Clarke. Bob immediately set out to cultivate my interest in bridge, something I would be more than grateful for over the coming years.

A general election was held on 5 July 1945. It would be a further three weeks before the results were declared. When our flight departed from Oakington in Cambridgeshire to Castle Benito in Libya, on the first of four 'legs' of our journey, we were unaware of the sort of government we would return to. That is *if* we returned, as the prospect of fighting the Japanese was an awesome one.

For the seven and three-quarter hour flight to Castle Benito, approximately thirty of us and our kit, were confined to the bomb-bay of a converted Liberator bomber - which looked and sounded clapped out! It was a very bleak journey indeed.

We were allocated tented accommodation for the stopover and served a very unpretentious meal. The following morning we arose early to prepare for the next leg of the journey. For the first time I began to appreciate how much the temperature dropped after sun set in Africa. Our flight to Cairo West in Egypt took just under six hours. At this point the Liberator developed engine problems and we were given a forty-eight hour 'stand down'. To break the tedium, a party of us took a trip to the desert where we viewed The Sphinx and also one of the lower tombs of the Pyramids. Afterwards we called at that well known watering hole – Shepherds. Sadly, I think it was later a casualty of an explosion.

On the third day, we travelled in a replacement Liberator and made a four and a half hour flight to Shaiber in Iraq - an RAF trading post. After refuelling and a light meal, we took off once more, in mid-afternoon for our last leg of the journey, bound for Karachi.

At that time Karachi was in India, today of course it's in Pakistan. The flight duration was six and a half hours of which four and a half were night-flying. Flying in the dark doesn't make much difference when you are ensconced in the bomb bay of a Liberator!

Tiger Force becomes a damp squid.

The transit camp and trading station were based at Mauripur. In common with the many transit camps I had been stationed at over the last four years, this one was both grim and forbidding. Tiger Force was the formation of Lancaster, Lincoln and Liberator bombers, planned, with support from American Air Force fighters, to attack the Japanese. It was expected that the island of Okinawa would be one of the targets. Air and ground crews had been hurriedly assembled with little or no thought or organisation. The accommodation was again in tents, with marquees provided for dining and recreation. Morale was at a low ebb and the administration did little to enliven the situation.

As yet there appeared to be no sign of the promised Lancasters. There was hardly any news from England, so it was little wonder that resentment and disenchantment set in rapidly. As if this wasn't enough, a plague of dysentery broke out, and visits to the primitive latrines – never pleasant – became a nightmare.

Eventually the results of the General Election filtered through. The Labour Party for the first time in history had achieved a working majority with a landslide victory to the political left. The new government came to power with over 140 seats more than the opposition.

Despite the general consensus of opinion for 'change', I can't recall much euphoria at that camp.

Hiroshima and Nagasaki – Recollections of an RI class at school.

In the late evening of 06 August 1945, the shock news emerged that not only had an Atom Bomb been produced, but that the Americans had dropped one on Hiroshima. We heard no further news at this time, except that Hiroshima was a base for the Japanese army. The general response was that: 'This must be the end of the war out East'. Another week later, a further nuclear devise was dropped on Nagasaki. Suddenly I remembered an incident at Wirral Grammar School, back in the early 1930s. A religious instruction class had, on that occasion been taken by the wood and metalwork master, a Mr Jones. One pupil asked him to explain the function of, The Christion Scientist Organisation.

His reply was indeed passionate: 'Don't talk to me about scientists - they will end up blowing the world to pieces'! He then added as an afterthought: 'By the time this class reaches my age, you will have breakfast in England, climb aboard an aeroplane, fly to America and land just in time for another breakfast'.

At the time the class was amused – now just a decade and a half later the first part of his remarkable prediction proved correct. As we now know Concord commenced its transatlantic flights in May 1976, thus confirming Mr Jones amazing second prophesy!

Tiger Force is disbanded – yet more travelling.

Back to India, Tiger Force was disbanded and its members were dispersed to various stations across the Far East. If I thought I was a long way from home, I had another thought coming. My first posting was to Dum-Dum, seven hours flying time away via Dehli. Shortly afterwards I received a posting to Kuala Lumpur, Malaya, (now Malaysia) and moved to the transit area at Park Lane, Chowringee, Calcutta.

While awaiting transport for onward transition, we reported daily to the RTO (Rail Transport Officer) for news. At the same time I succumbed to another bout of dysentery, added to which was 'prickly heat', where the whole body erupts into rashes.

There was some delay therefore before I departed on yet another leg of this interminable journey. By way of a change it was to be by Liberty ship (built for speed not comfort) which was manned by the American Merchant Service.

The Liberty ship lacked any really adequate amenities. They were so basic that one was even built in under five days! We sailed from Calcutta to Singapore, a journey taking eight nights and seven days. Due to a shortage of space, myself and thirty other junior officers were billeted in the hold, with hammocks and bed rolls provided - it was not quite as unpleasant as it sounds.

Sixty-five years ago there was a services' saying to the effect that: 'You haven't been east until you've sailed the Bhramaputre'. I was to discover just how true this was - it was a fascinating journey and after the turmoil of the last few months, it was also very therapeutic.

I 'settle' in Singapore.

A week later we arrived in Singapore. It is impossible to describe the utter chaos and confusion resulting from the collapse of Japan. All Japanese service personnel were taken into custody as 'prisoners-of-war'. Simultaneously, allied forces' personnel were released. In most cases they had been Japanese POWs for almost three and a half years. These men were suffering from malnutrition and exhaustion. Many had been the subjects of torture and bestial treatment by their captors. Their average weight would have dropped from say, ten to twelve stones, to maybe six stone - or even less! Few were fit enough to travel 12,000 miles home, and rehabilitation camps were established to help with these problems. These were just a few of the issues facing the new arrivals tasked with the repatriation of allied forces personnel.

I suffered from yet another bout of intestinal illness but felt guilty about reporting 'sick', having witnessed the indescribable condition of the allied POWs. The situation was partly resolved for me, as there was no transport available for Kuala Lumpur. This being the case, the RTO changed my posting, temporarily, to Kallang Airport. This was a civil airport on the island, allocated for the relocation and onward transportation of many of the ex POWs. Some had been released from Changi Jail, others had worked in 'camps' further afield. I am quite sure that there can have been very few people who witnessed these terrible sights and conditions, who were not in some way traumatised by the experience.

Life was frantic for some two months or so, while repatriation of the POWs was taking place. Many of them would require weeks of nursing and/or rehabilitation before they could be moved. Concurrently, the liberating forces were attempting to re-establish law, order and of course food for the incumbents.

The upper echelon of the new regime, quickly commandeered all the accommodation in the coastal and high quality suburban areas for themselves. Meanwhile the remainder of us were either under canvas or in primitive barrack type huts.

By contrast, many first wave relief forces discovered a world beyond their wildest dreams. Due to the rapid removal of the Japanese and in some cases local collaborators, expensive motor cars were abandoned, with keys left in the ignition, in roads and driveways. These cars constituted the finest quality vehicles of their time. Motors such as open tourer Lagondas, Alvis and Armstrong Siddeleys.

Cars which, the few examples remaining today, command a high premium - if the owners would sell them. Sixty-five years ago they were available in Singapore ready to be driven away, which is exactly what happened. Not only that, but it was a common sight to see army privates and RAF 'other ranks', driving these vehicles around the island. Quite where the petrol came from I never discovered, nor what eventually happened to the vehicles themselves

We were being moved so fast that we were, 'leaving mail behind' and it took some time to catch up with us. Due to the restriction of space on the Airgraphs (a microfilmed brief letter), the news was stilted but emphasised the continuing rationing at home. It actually now seemed to be worse than during wartime.

A six week dock strike exacerbated the situation and already the new government was proving much less popular than had been expected. They seemed more concerned with nationalising industry and issuing restrictions in all aspects of civilian life. A war-weary nation wanted acceptable accommodation and relief from queues and rationing. Unfortunately both would be a feature of post-war Britain for some time to come.

The Atom Bombs.

More details concerning the recent bombing of Japan also became available. We heard that each bomb contained as much explosive power as 2,000 of our massive ten ton conventional bombs.

For those of us who had taken part in the war in Europe, it was a timely reminder that Hitler had also been not that far from producing nuclear weapons, and would almost certainly have done so, had the war gone on for much longer.

CHAPTER 24 Life in Kallang – Winning the Peace in Asia

By now the colonial civil administrators had returned to power. One of the first orders given, was for the RAF to move from Kallang Airport to the base at Changi and arrangements were put in hand for a rapid withdrawal from the airfield. At this point I had fully expected to finally be on my way to Kuala Lumpur. To my amazement I found that as a junior officer (aka dogsbody), I had been placed in charge of some thirty or so 'other ranks' and one sergeant (at Kallang). Our task was to have the buildings and their surroundings put into apple-pie order. We had a period of four weeks to achieve this before the ceremonial handover to the authorities.

I had had no previous experience in these matters and looked to the sergeant (a strong character fortunately) to deploy his immense experience. The control tower and administration area was allocated as our headquarters, complete with sleeping / cooking / recreational areas for the sergeant and the 'other ranks'.

At the same time I met the only other RAF personnel left on the station, one Flying Officer George Power, the acting signals officer for the area. George had been a pre-war RAF regular and had been a navigator on Fairy Battles during 1939 – 1940. At that time they had been stationed in France. Later George flew in Blenheims and Bostons. Now however, due to an accident, he was ground based and in the process of applying for a permanent commission. George had already requisitioned a large house in the prestigious area by the coast. This house was close to the Lido and more importantly, adjacent to the messing quarters of air-crew members of the Australian airline, QUANTAS. George invited me to join him and I gratefully accepted. I was however slightly concerned regarding the lack of transport, as the house was some distance from our HQ. George was completely un-fazed and produced from the signals stores, a BSA 500cc side valve motorcycle. The machine was no youngster, had a twisted frame and displayed evidence of many knocks and scrapes but was reliable and immediately became my constant companion for the next few months. Additionally, George could always produce a can of petrol when required. A firm friendship developed between us despite the decade or so of age difference.

In those days the relationship between the Aussies and the Poms (English) appeared friendlier than seems to be the case in the twenty-first century. Although the food was in short supply we were always welcome to share their rations. My memory of this period seem to revolve around pineapples - natural for breakfast, sauted for lunch and fried in the evenings. There would be additional treats when relief crews flew in from Australia.

Our clear up operation was reaching the end of the first week, when suddenly there was a complete panic. The runways at Changi Airport had been pronounced 'Unsafe', for four engine aircraft to either land or to take off. With immediate effect, Kallang had to accommodate all the four engine planes which formally used Changi. Our small detachment was to be responsible for all the aircraft re fuelling, AND for all aircraft spare parts and replacements, by an AOG agreement.

The petrol bowser and crew arrived within hours. We discovered that petrol was not delivered straight to the storage tanks but in ten gallon drums. It required daily teams of five groups of five men each, to transfer petrol from the ten gallon drums to the storage tanks. Twenty five Japanese prisoners arrived each day to carry out this heavy manual task. After a few days of trial and error, we eventually produced an efficient method of solving this problematic task.

Japanese POWs try our patience.

It has to be said that, despite our loathing for the Japanese POWs, they were hard working. Each day they would arrive by truck and remove their immaculate white shirts (how did they get their dhobiing done?) and fold them carefully away. Taking only water bottles with them, they faced the intense heat and headed off for their daily tasks. Our sergeant insisted that he be saluted both on their arrival and before they left in the evening.

Inevitably the day arrived when one Japanese refused to salute: 'No officer - no salute'. Quick as a flash the sergeant commanded: 'Put your shirt on NOW'! After a few moments hesitation the prisoner's arm was going up and down like a Clapham Junction signal: 'Sorry Sir – sorry Sir', he wailed. I decided that the sergeant had this situation fully under control, so I made my exit . . .

The second problem occurred just a few weeks later. Twenty-four Japanese prisoners and an officer arrived one morning. The officer refused to work: 'Geneva Convention, officers no work', was all he said.

At that time I was struggling to hold a telephone conversation. The system was antiquated and even local calls could be endless, so when the sergeant entered the office I was not best pleased. When he asked me if I had read the Geneva Convention I almost blew my top. While he waited for me to calm down, the Sgt explained that we would be one team of five short because of the problem. He then produced a large piece of wood with long nails protruding from one end. His next question was even more bizarre

'Mr Davies, does it say in this Convention that I', (the Sgt), 'can't chase this officer around the quadrangle with this stick and prod him whenever he falters?'

Visualising court martials, cashierment and similar, I could only weakly reply that it was not possible. The sergeant then suggested that I moved my chair so I could not overlook the quadrangle. I silently complied with this helpful suggestion. After about fifteen minutes, curiosity got the better of me. I looked out of the window to see the sergeant going like a bat out of hell right behind the Japanese officer with the nailed stick firmly implanted in the prisoner's rear.

About half an hour later the sergeant re-entered my room with a broad grin on his face. 'Trouble resolved SIR', he said and departed. At this point I must confess I began to shake with hysterical laughter. I thought of the incredible five and a half years which had passed since I had wandered the quiet lanes of Poulton cum Spital in England with nothing more difficult than a team of horses to command.

Fatherhood and the daily round

In Early December 1945, I finally received the news that I was now the father of a seven and a half pound baby boy. Normally this would have involved 'wetting the head' celebrations, but in fact there was little time or energy for partying.

Our day began at 06.00 hrs or even earlier. I would shower, have a quick game of deck quoits on the lawn then saunter over to the QUANTAS mess for breakfast. Then it was back to the house for another shower (due to the humidity). Start work by seven and put in five solid hours until midday. Back on the motor bike to the Lido for a swim, then a siesta until 16.00 hrs or so. Back to the office for a further two to three hours, or longer if problems arose. I would return to the house to freshen up before dinner.

We then walked for about forty minutes, to the 'Happy World', an entertainment area on the Island much frequented by the Royal Navy. George and I would have one or occasionally two halves of beer before we walked back. By this time we were physically exhausted and virtually collapsed onto our beds. This went on for seven days a week.

It was always uppermost in my mind just how incredible life must have been for those allied prisoners of war – their existence must have been almost unbearable.

I think that there may have been one or perhaps two visits to Raffles, that well known 'watering hole' for the services. Apart from the logistical problem of using the motor cycles off the station limits. Raffles was extremely expensive and was visited mostly by the 'higher echelon'.

Demobilisation looms.

As the new year of 1946 progressed, the first stage of my demobilisation was announced. I was advised that I would be released towards the end of May, or in early June – a target date to look forward to. However what little news we heard from Britain was by no means inspiring. With both wars now over, the Lend-Lease arrangement we had with America which had supported our country since the autumn of 1940, was now suspended. A much tighter and tougher arrangement was enforced by the Americans. Our cousins from across 'the Pond' had never approved of the British Commonwealth or Empire. Additionally the new Labour government was now contemplating nationalisation on a grand scale. They were also proposing social security and national health schemes. There was therefore no alternative but to accept the stringent terms attached to the new $3.75 m loan. For myself with neither a job, nor even the prospects of one in the offing, the future looked 'pretty damned bleak'. 'Ah well' I thought, 'nose to the grindstone and just carry on.' One small aside while on this subject was that QUANTAS did make me a job offer.

The job itself interested me and appeared to have prospects. The down side however was that the position would be in Australia. I would have been required to pay my own outward fare and – the real killer – I would not have been able to bring my family over for three years! The offer was regretfully a non-starter. In years to come there have been occasions when I have regretted this decision but as we all know, hindsight is an invaluable possession.

The Commander in Chief of SEAC, Lord Louis Mountbatten, had taken up residence three-quarters of a mile from the house which I occupied with George Power. Mountbatten had no such pressing personal problems but his responsibilities must have been enormous. We occasionally caught glimpses of his entourage, perhaps cavalcade would be a more apt description. The security would have easily done justice to the King and Queen. George Power commented from time to time: 'Best keep the motorbike out of sight when the patrol's about'.

British Overseas Airways Corporation, today known as British Airways, started a new route from west to east with their four engine flying boats.

This was a twice a week service and having landed they would regally taxi up the estuary and anchor almost adjacent to our headquarters. A launch was then sent out from the small landing stage to collect the passengers, of whom there would usually be about a dozen - and the crew also. They would be taken to waiting limousines, to be whisked effortlessly to the world famous Raffles Hotel. It made an interesting break for us when that plane landed and even more so on its departure. We really felt at the heart of civilisation!

For our part, we were gradually making life more acceptable for the small but loyal and hardworking contingent of 'other ranks'. We engaged the services of a No 1 Boy – a local Chinese worker aged fifty-something. For a small remuneration plus my cigarette ration – an advantage of being a non-smoker – he would ensure that a bucket of tea was available throughout the daylight hours and would supply practically everything that we required. Additionally 'No 1' organised the dhobi women, who were 'washer ladies'. Despite soap being unavailable, they would produce the most prestigious laundry service I have experienced anywhere in the world.

Word got around the island concerning our tea service and we would receive a constant flow of visitors throughout the day, just to enjoy 'a cuppa'. It's a strange thing about tea, it is just as enjoyable in temperatures of 100 plus degrees in the shade, as it is welcomed in the depths of a bitter winter in England.

A welcome diversion.

There was one occasion when our tea proved to be the Sustenance of Survival, for the ten or twelve passengers and crew of an old Halifax bomber which had landed at Kallang.

The aircraft was en route from Britain to Australia and suffered a catastrophic breakdown while landing. We organised the vital replacement part from Yorkshire, England, under our AOG (spare parts) agreement. It would be seven to ten days however before the part could be delivered to Kallang. The passengers and crew were virtually penniless and we quickly heard their tales of woe. We mustered what hospitality we could while we listened to their story.

The pilot was an ex Bomber Command type who had managed to get himself de mobbed early on in the year. He had then purchased 'for a song' the obsolete Halifax bomber. In one of the leading daily papers back in Britain, he had advertised for: 'Paying guests to work their way to the 'Promised Land'.

His advert remarkably, or perhaps not considering the inhospitable attitude in Britain at that time, received numerous replies. These included a navigator, a Spitfire pilot and a handful of flight engineers.

Last but by no means least, was a female well into her 'eighties'. This lady wished to join her son in Sydney, Australia and acquired the wherewithal by selling her flat.

Eventually we found items such as mosquito nets, bed sheets and other essentials, to enable the males to sleep either in the aircraft or under its wings, depending on the climate.

The elderly lady was taken to our HQ during the evening and allotted the few little luxuries we had available. Early the following morning she would be escorted back to the aircraft. Sustenance was provided for all. I have to say that our thirty or so ORs were magnificent in their assistance and generosity towards the 'stranded' Brits. Fortunately the required part arrived on time. The pilot had credit facilities in place with one of the major fuel suppliers, for the purchase of oil and aviation spirit. This enabled us to supply the Halifax with a full tank for the next section of their 3,000 mile journey to a QUANTAS outpost in Australia.

I have related this story for two reasons. Firstly to highlight just how difficult conditions were, back in Britain, for people to contemplate and scrape the money for such a doubtful venture, in order to emigrate. Secondly the ORs under our command were poorly paid, their living conditions basic, food miniscule and yet for no reward they willingly shared what little they had. I found it then, and even more so today – inspirational.

Unwelcome diversions!

Unfortunately however, the other side of the coin was disturbing to say the least. Scarcity of all the essentials of daily existence invariably creates a breakdown of the scruples of a few individuals. Singapore was at that time no exception. Black marketeering became rife and thieving, from petty incidents to major robberies, quickly became prevalent. Few of the average service personnel failed to become victims of pilfering, including myself and George Power. While we were asleep in our house we 'lost' cash and all removable personal property.

On a larger scale, the weekly deliveries of cigarettes, alcohol etceteras were often hi jacked. Many items of equipment such as clothing and utensils just disappeared. This created a general feeling of despair among the many people affected. These feelings of apprehension, together with new threats of personal attack, gave rise to unrest and feelings of frustration at the lack of control and security of the community.

An even greater worry was the information coming from visiting aircrews with regard to the unrest in India and especially Calcutta. There were reports of hostility from the native population, both Hindus and Muslims, towards British personnel. Occurrences such as service vehicles being hi jacked and the occupants stoned to death were now not just isolated incidents.

The Crisis in India.

A very complex relationship existed between the British, led by Lord Wavell - Jawaharial ('Pandit') Nehru, who represented the Hindus - and Mohammad Ali Jinnah, the representative of the Muslims. After I had (fortunately) arrived back on UK soil, a general strike or Direct Action Day, aka The Great Calcutta Killings, was held on 16 August 1946. This was intended to be a protest in favour of the creation of a separate Muslim state in Pakistan. It is unclear who started the riots but within a short space of time 3,000 Hindus and 7,000 Muslims lay dead, with many more injured.

In March 1947 Lord Louis Mountbatten was appointed viceroy of India, his function was to plan and coordinate the British withdrawal. On 15 August 1947, almost exactly a year after the Calcutta riots, the Partitioning of India took place.

I prepare to depart.

The runways at Changi Airport were still not operational for heavy aircraft in June 1946, by which time my de mobilisation number had arrived. I was however unable to leave Kallang until a replacement had arrived, which delayed my departure until the end of June.

I bade a sad farewell to George Power and the thirty plus staff at HQ - once more it was 'packing time' - this was probably about the twenty-fifth occasion in six years! I journeyed to the transit camp at the main Singapore docks, to await transport for the 12,000 mile journey home.

There was an ENSA variety show at the local theatre, Tommy Trinder was the star of the show so I decided to attend for the evening.

By what seemed then quite a co incidence, his leading lady was Gwen Lancelyn Green. Gwen was the elder daughter of Major Lancelyn Green, the land owner and landlord of our farm back home. I had lived within a few hundred yards of 'The Hall' for almost a decade but had never really

seen the lady before. It was likely that she had spent most of her time at boarding school. There were at that time, rumours of a liaison between her and Tommy Trinder. Several years later they were married.

'Blighty' bound.

With the arrival of the *Empress of Australia,* my stay in the Far East was finally over. The ship was a superior type trooper which had recently had a major refit. In 1918 the Kaiser proposed that it become his royal yacht and as such the vessel became a 'prize' for the victors during reparations.

As the liner departed the dockside, with many of the passengers lined up facing the shore and waving farewells, the steering seemed unbalanced. A collision with another ship berthed nearby was only narrowly averted. In consequence instructions from the 'Bridge' issued the following warning. For the remainder of the journey and while entering or leaving ports en route, 'other ranks' were to remain below deck. All officers and first class passengers would be confined to either the lounges or cabins. Our route was to be via Columbo, now Sri Lanka, then to Bombay, now Mumbai and across to Aden. We would then take the Suez Canal to the port of Suez and cross the Mediterranean to Gibraltar. From there we would head for the Port of Liverpool – a total journey of approximately thirty-three days.

There were probably around 5,000 passengers on board, with constant arrivals and departures at each port. I shared a cabin with five other junior officers and we slept in three tier bunks. We had the services of a shared steward and the privilege of the use of the first class lounges. This was my fourth troop ship journey since joining the services and it was certainly the most luxurious. We cruised steadily at fifteen or sixteen knots in mostly good weather. For the first time for some years I had the pleasure of reflection and meditation. Thinking back to school days, I remembered being taught the 'history' of the great British Empire on which 'the Sun never Sets'. I was grateful for the opportunity I had had to visit many of these places, as it was obvious that the days of a British Empire were numbered.

Deck walking for exercise never became boring, because of the spectacle of the sun glinting off the flying fish which escorted the liner on its journey.

The time passed pleasantly and finally we approached the Suez Canal. Cruising down the Canal was quite an experience and the many British troops stationed in Egypt would stop and wave to us. That was until one service 'wag' on the ship yelled, 'What's it like to be stationed near home'? Their replies were unprintable. We refueled and took on food and provisions at the Port of Suez. We then crossed the Mediterranean with a rather long stop at Gibraltar, then set off for the last leg of the journey home. We arrived at Liverpool in mid-afternoon on a Saturday in early July. It was wet and miserable - welcome home! The Port itself still showed signs of the intense damage inflicted by the Luftwaffe, over the period from August 1940 to 26 May 1941. Next to London, Liverpool had been the most heavily bombed city in the country.

Disembarkation took place over a period of some four hours and we witnessed many acts of vandalism and theft. Hold luggage had been deliberately damaged and no doubt valuables pilfered. Each person was hoping that it wouldn't be their property which had been targeted.

On entering the port of Liverpool, a squaddie ignored all instructions to remain in his quarters. He was observed running along the deck hotly pursued by two military policemen. The soldier was yelling at the top of his voice: 'It's me own bleedin' country - I can look at it if I want'!

We were entrained to the demob. centre outside Stafford. Service revolvers were handed in, clearance chits made out and cheques written by ourselves to cover any deficiencies.

Wearing my new demob suits and trilby, and tightly grasping my ration vouchers and travel warrants, I made my way to the nearest train station bound for Llangollen, my wife and young son.

Thus ended my six year service career and I disappeared into the ranks of the three million newly unemployed .With my constant movement in Asia, all contact with my fellow members of the James' crew was lost.

PART EIGHT

POST WAR BRITAIN AND DISCOVERY OF THE 101 SQUADRON ASSOCIATION – Late 1990s.

CHAPTER 25   Post War Britain.

It took quite a few days to acclimatise myself to a post war Britain and to envisage the efforts which would be required, to make a new life for myself and my family. I fully expected to have to climb a few hills but was overwhelmed by the scale of the problems confronting us. Rationing of food, clothing, fuel etcetera was in fact worse than it had been during wartime, as bread had now been added to the list – it had never been rationed during the war.

The American Marshall Plan distributed grant money to re build Europe (and resist communism) but was not available until three years after the war in Europe had finished.

The housing situation was absolutely shambolic. There were tens of thousands of, mainly ex-servicemen and their families, 'adopting' empty service barracks and even 'squatting' in unoccupied houses.

Despite the 'coffers being dry' the new government was preparing a ten year nationalisation plan. It proposed Social Security Benefits and (in 1948) established the NHS service, all of which were highly expensive. Most of our manufactured goods had to be exported, to build up sterling and due to supply and demand, those goods which were available in the UK were horrendously expensive. The country lacked cohesion with regard to the immediate problems and the work force was exhausted. Even pre-war levels of prosperity didn't return until well into the 1950s

We had known that the Llangollen flat was unsuitable for a family with a young child. Until now however, I had been in Asia and so had been unavailable to look for alternative accommodation. An additional problem was that the flat rent was double what a three bed council house rent would cost - not that there was a hope in hell of getting one. Before we could resolve our housing difficulties, there was the somewhat pressing problem of my obtaining gainful employment. A return to the family farm was not possible. Since my call up, my younger brother was now into his third year as a farmer. The introduction of tractors and other machinery, had rendered redundant the skills with horses which I had acquired.

I enquired regarding an Emergency Teacher's Training Scheme - this had placements for no more than 1,000 trainees and a waiting time of over one year! I had even been rejected as a fireman as I was deemed too short by one inch! So it went on. It felt as if we had won the war only to lose the peace.

After months of traipsing the length and breadth of England and Wales and after some three months of applying for virtually anything available, an offer was made and accepted. I was to train for thirteen weeks at the Wrexham store of my prospective employer and then to transfer, on a permanent basis to their Crewe depot. This entailed a return journey of eighty miles each day. The salary was not brilliant but the need for an income was paramount.

For transport I purchased a brand new AJS 350cc motorcycle, thinking that it would be more reliable than a 'war weary' ex services machine.

Wrong again. It was highly unreliable and outrageously expensive to repair and service, as the guarantee was very limited. When I confidently applied for additional fuel coupons, I was in fact turned down flat as: 'Not being a deserving case'. This was despite a letter of confirmation from my prospective employer that my request was legitimate. Fortunately my employer allowed me fuel from their company bulk fuel ration.

At around the time that I started work at the Crewe depot, I began a house search in the local area. After some time I put an offer in on the only property within my budget. This was a three bed semi-detached house in Davenport Avenue, for which I offered £775. I was only in the position to afford to pay this amount, due to having served for fifteen months abroad without home leave. I had also accrued the payments of 'hard living allowance' (no mess facilities) and sixty nine cents per day Japanese War Subsidy, through limiting my spending while in Asia.

I received the response that an offer of £800 had already been received. A farce, worthy of any Whitehall theatre now commenced, with me trying to out-bid the vendor's 'supposed' offers, which rose in small increments until they stopped at £1125. My offer of £1150 was only then accepted. I had no means of knowing whether the many increases of offer to the vendor were legitimate. The vendor had recently purchased the house for £550 and therefore turned in a profit of 109%, in under a year. Nice work if you can get it! The vendor of this property had allegedly been a Rolls Royce employee based in Derby. In 1939 he was transferred to their Crewe factory and rented the said property until 1946, at which time he went back to Derby. He 'proved' to a gullible jury that, had the war not intervened, he would have purchased the property at pre-war prices!? Puzzled – so was I.

The following decades progressed conventionally, virtually all my energies went into putting bread on the table for my family which expanded in 1954 to include a daughter, Susan. By rights the story should end here – I have never ceased to be amazed that it didn't.

CHAPTER 26   Fast Forward Fifty-Two Years!

A letter in the paper re kindles my wartime memories.

As I read the Daily Mail on 19 February 1998, my attention was drawn to a letter entitled – 'Burning Injustice'. Some nine years previously, a British Midland 737 had taken off from Heathrow, bound for Belfast. Due to a malfunctioning engine, the captain decided to make an emergency landing, at East-Midlands Airport (co incidentally the former RAF Castle Donington).

The pilot was unable to maintain height and the aircraft crashed onto the M1 motorway at Kegworth. Prior to the arrival of emergency vehicles, several passing vehicles stopped to render assistance. One of these drivers had successfully sued the airline for 'stress and shock' and had recently been awarded the sum of £35,000, by way of compensation.

The letter writer was appalled and related the details of an accident which happened when he was piloting a Wellington Bomber on 09 December 1942. They had crashed on high ground in the UK on the way home, in bad weather. His crew members were either killed or were severely injured. A local doctor visited the scene to offer his assistance. He later wrote to the Air Ministry, not to ask for money but for clothing (ration) coupons, to replace his clothes damaged by exploding ammunition. The reply was both brief and brutal. Since the good doctor had not been asked for his assistance, he must be considered an intruder on air ministry property!

The letter writer signed himself off as – 'F G James – Bakewell, Derbyshire.'

I wrote to Fred via the newspaper and remain indebted to them for passing the letter on. He advised me regarding which crew members were still alive and their state of health. They had kept in touch with each other and the squadron (101) since the end of the war. Unknown to me, 101 Sqn were one of the few not disbanded after the cessation of hostilities in Europe. In 1979, 101 Sqn Association was formed and Fred had rarely missed an annual reunion since that time.

101 Squadron - still operational!

I soon discovered where 101 Sqn had been based and what aircraft they had operated since I had left, in 1945:

June 1946 - Re equipped with Avro Lincolns, (based at Binbrook).

May 1950 – 1st squadron to receive Canberra jet bombers, (Binbrook).

October 1957 – Joined the V-force equipped with Vulcans, (Finningly / Waddington)

1963 – Three 101 Sqn Vulcans, using air to air refuelling, establish new record of 17 hrs 50 mins to fly to Australia.

1982 – 101 Squadron was involved in Op. Blackbuck – bombing Falklands Isles runway.

May 1984 – Equipped with VC 10s to carry out air to air refuelling, (Brize Norton)

Very active in all theatres, including the Gulf Wars, Bosnia and Afghanistan - refuelling many UN airforces.

I joined the Squadron Association and attended many annual reunions - these are two day affairs, normally held on the first weekend in September. On Saturday, lunch and the AGM were followed by dinner and speeches in Lincoln Assembly Rooms. Sunday saw most members trek the eighteen miles east to Ludford, for a magnificent church service, parade and wreath laying ceremony. This would be followed by afternoon tea at the Ludford WI.

Weather permitting, the BBMF Lancaster would make four low level passes of the village, which most members viewed from the field behind the WI building. Local residents also proudly came out to watch their very own private air show! On the mighty bomber's banked turns they were easily low enough for the crew to wave back to the crowd and be clearly seen themselves.

The James' Crew.

As of February 1998 the status of the crew was as follows:

Pilot – Fred was in robust health and with his wife Myfanwy, regularly attended the Sunday gathering at Ludford.

Navigator – Jim Coleman. Jim had died in his seventies.

Flight Engineer – Bill 'Paddy' Orr. Paddy was immobile and had been left speechless after a stroke.

Wireless Operator – George 'Titch' Taylor. 'Tich' was house bound with 'internal' problems.

Special Operator – Roy Hall. Roy was living in Spain and in robust health. We met when he came over (with his two sons) for one of the Squadron Association reunions.

Rear Gunner – George Williams. George was still resident in Alberta, Canada.

CHAPTER 27 Into the New Millennium - 101 Sqn Reunions and Lincolnshire Lancaster Association Open Days

The George Owen saga.

During the early years of the Millennium, I came into contact with an ex radio operator who had served in the merchant navy. His name was Les Owen and we met regularly at the September reunion. Les had joined 101 Squadron Association, as an associate member, in order to hopefully meet any veteran who had known his brother George. George had been killed in action and had flown with 101 Squadron during 1944. Les had been searching for a couple of decades, for any scrap of news he could glean, but without success.

Les had approached me on several occasions. As George Owen had served on a different flight from the James' crew ('B'), I had had to sadly tell Les that I couldn't help him.

It was in about 2002, that I entered the Church of St Mary and St Peter in Ludford for the annual 101 Sqn memorial service. I entered a pew with just one other occupant. I sat down and slipped onto one knee for a moment or two of, 'holy thought'.

As I focused through the dark interior of the small church, I saw that the other occupant of the pew was - Les Owen. Once again Les requested that I think deeply, in case I could recollect even the tiniest snippet of information regarding his brother George. This time however Les threw me the key to unlock this longstanding conundrum. He told me, for the first time, that his brother George had NOT been killed with 101 Sqn - but had been transferred *from* 101 Sqn to The Pathfinder Force, in mid-1944. My mind raced! – the only crew to transfer to PFF in mid-1944 was, of course that of Walt Reif. One of *The Original Four.*

I told Les that not only had I known George, but had known him over a period of eight to nine months. Les was ecstatic as I recounted the name of the pilot and also the names of the remainder of his crew members. I felt as if I had reunited Man Friday with Robinson Crusoe!

Over the years Les and I have remained firm friends. In retirement Les is a keen artist and I have him to thank for a large painting of a Lancaster Bomber, which takes pride of place on my dining room wall.

This painting is very special, as it's both an original and it has the correct 'SR' 101 Sqn markings on the side of the aircraft fuselage. I also have a sizeable collection of hand painted Christmas cards of Lancasters, from Les to add to my treasures.

The Hon. Michael Benn affair.

On 08 November 2004, the Daily Mail serialised part of a book written by former Labour minister and MP, Tony Benn - *To Be a Daniel – Then and Now*. Mr Benn describes the events leading up to the death of his elder brother, Michael Wedgewood Benn, in a flying accident on 23 June 1944. This subsequently led to Mr Benn inheriting his father's hereditary title. In his description of his brother's accident, the story tells how Michael's RAF Mosquito 'lost' its air speed indicator. Another Mosquito was used to guide the stricken aircraft in for the landing. In the serialisation, this scenario occurred at Tangmere, the famous Battle of Britain airfield, from where Michael was taken to St Richard's Hospital in Chichester. He died there the same day.

   Checking the time and date - 03.15 hrs on 23 June 1944 – this incident just had to be the one which occurred simultaneously with our crash landing at Thorney Island, following the 'Rheims Raid'.

   I wrote a letter to Mr Benn (via the Daily Mail) giving him the details which I have related in the description of the Rheims raid in this book and persuaded him that the accident could *not* have happened at Tangmere, an

 inland fighter station, as he had previously believed. I also pointed out that Chichester was situated adjacent to Thorney Island. Mr Benn subsequently telephoned me and we exchanged further correspondence. He was extremely grateful for my correcting an important fact relating to his brother's death in 1944. He suggested I might like to tell 'my story' to the Daily Mail. I thanked him but declined due to the fragile health of my wife and my 'great age', (well into my eighties).

Cyril Roebottom comes out fighting
[CR : 1922 – 2013. Ex 101 Sqn Navigator]

I only met Cyril the once, out of all the Squadron Association reunions I have attended over two decades. It was however an occasion I shall never forget. Early in the twentieth century we were seated together side by side, on a bench seat at the Squadron Association's hot – pot lunch at Lincoln's Assembly rooms.

There were about 100 other Association members dining and it was totally pot luck who sat where at the long refectory tables. As I asked Cyril to pass the red cabbage, my first impression was of an avuncular type who would gently brush a fly from his seat to avoid crushing it.

I struck up a conversation; the first question being, when did you serve on 101 Sqn and, what plane did you fly? I was delighted when it appeared that we were both on Squadron in early June 1944, but perplexed when we learned that we had both flown in F – Fox! Cyril clarified the apparent conundrum by explaining that his last flight in Fox was on 7th June. After this date he and his crew were transferred to 300 Polish Squadron @ Faldingworth. The official reason given for this most unusual transfer was that it would bolster moral! Cyril however disclosed that the real reason was, 'An altercation between myself and that b------ Flt Ltn XYZ.' A fellow sitting on the opposite side of the table must have still been in possession of excellent hearing because he leant across and asked, 'Who did you say that b------ was?' Thinking that here was another airman who had been unfairly treated, Cyril repeated XYZ's name.

By now I was an interested party and listened carefully. We were flabbergasted when the chap opposite stood up and exclaimed loudly, 'I am XYZ – why am I a b------?'

Firstly it must be understood that 101 Squadron flew for the duration of WW II and the chances of meeting even one person who had been on Sqn at the same time as myself was remote – now I had two!!
Not to be out witted Cyril also stood up. His florid face mirrored the pent up resentment of sixty years of injustice It was obvious that he was going to have his say. It wasn't just I who was paying attention. Due to jutting jaws and raised voices, half the table turned their heads and re tuned their hearing aids!

Cyril advised XYZ that he had endorsed Cyril's Logbook with red ink (a severe reprimand), following Cyril's return from an operation to St-Lo in Normandy on 7th June. Cyril's pilot, P.O. Arnold had ignored the set flight plan for their return to Ludford Magna and XYZ had blamed Cyril (the navigator). In 1944 a pilot was captain and no crew member could question his decisions. Cyril was rightfully indignant, especially with regard to the subsequent transfer to a mainly non-English speaking operational unit, such as Faldingworth. So strongly did Cyril put his case forward that XYZ, by now aware that many eyes were watching, and many ears listening, offered that he would remove the said endorsement should Cyril present his log book to XYZ.

At this point Cyril almost exploded, claiming that nothing XYZ could do could make amends for effectively having his service life wrecked. It was about ten minutes before he calmed down (by which time all our lunches were ruined). It's doubtful whether an acceptable solution was ever reached, but eventually both parties calmed down.

As I have mentioned that was the only time I ever met Cyril, I would however encounter XYZ on many other reunions but there was never any sign of recognition.

Cyril passed away in 2013. Despite being ill for four years his widow Maureen generously donated on Cyril's behalf the sum of some £5,125 to the 101 Sqn Centenary Memorial. This demonstrates that it is possible to dislike someone intensely without losing one's loyalty to the institution he also belonged to. Even so, a very sad epistle.

The Petwood Hotel – Lincolnshire Aviation Heritage Centre.

Over a period of about ten years I attended the Squadron reunions fairly regularly with my son. We stayed in a hotel facing the Brayford Pool and its charismatic marina. It was convenient for the sequence of events held over the two day week end. I had thought of basing ourselves at the Petwood Hotel in lovely Woodhall Spa, but the circa thirty mile round trip from Lincoln was a downside.

East Kirkby lies approximately eight miles east of Coningsby, the base of the Battle of Britain Memorial Flight. RAF East Kirkby was a bomber

station, the wartime home to Nos 57 and 630 squadrons, of 5 Group.

Most of the original airfield had, long ago, been turned back to agricultural usage, but some aprons, part runways and a control tower remain. It is on this site that the Panton brothers, Fred and Harold, have established a memorial to their elder brother Christopher. Christopher was killed in a Halifax HX 272 on 30/31 March 1944, during a raid on Nuremberg. This was Bomber Command's 'Black Friday', when they sustained the greatest losses of the war. The Lincolnshire Aviation Heritage Centre is home to Lancaster 'Just Jane', privately owned by the Panton family. Jane is not airworthy, but is licensed to carry passengers for a short taxi ride and was only the third Lancaster in the world to be able to move under its own power.

In 2006 I renewed my acquaintance with the inside of a Lancaster, (a 'fear' provoking experience!) for the first time since 1945, by taking the taxi ride in 'Jane'. It was too far from The Wirral, to contemplate the outward and return journey home the same day. Being situated just eleven or twelve miles away, there was now no excuse not to stay at the Petwood Hotel – but more about this unique hotel later . . .

A High-Flying Birthday Party.

The Squadron (101) had been formed on 12 July 1917, at South-Farnborough as a night bomber squadron.

In order to celebrate the ninetieth anniversary of its 'birth', the Squadron, based at Brize Norton and the 'Association' committee members got their heads together. What they proposed was this – that one of the Squadron's (then) current VC 10s would carry 'one hundred and one' passengers, comprised of Squadron veterans and family members, on a tour of all the UK bases that the Squadron had operated from since its inception. Lunch was to be served on board the tanker.

I was fortunate enough to receive an invitation and on Thursday 12 July, accompanied by my son, made an early morning dash by car to Brize Norton. Our 'Master Bomber' for the trip was non other than Flt Lt Gary Weightman, 101 Sqn VC 10 air-to-air refueling Captain and long-time 'Association' magazine editor.

We had all gathered together for a pre-flight briefing, when Gary announced with a suitably glum face, that a problem had arisen and instead of the planned 'jolly' the designated crew and aircraft was going to have

to go to 'work' - in their air to air refueling role. He paused theatrically, just long enough to let a sense of disappointment set in, and then with a smiley face told us that we were going along too! When we got to the designated aircraft we were delighted to see that on the engine covers had been painted the words, '90TH ANNIVERSARY' - and that 'tail-art', in the form of the Squadron number and a lion issuant from battlements (part of Sqn badge) had been applied, with lion and Sqn number picked out in yellow against a dark background. Magnificent, and unique as XV 105 was the only 101 Sqn aircraft to have been decorated in this fashion.

Once on board we took off, with Gary at the controls, bound for a designated AAR rendezvous over the North Sea and adjacent to Berwick-on-Tweed. The VC 10 refuels from the rear, so it is almost impossible to get a clear view from inside the aircraft, except from monitors in the cockpit.

Normally the fast jets would take on fuel and continue with their tasking for that day. Today however and by special arrangement, immediately after refuelling, the jets came alongside the VC 10, flying so close that one could identify the features of the crew!

We had refueled both Tornado GR 4s and Typhoon Eurofighters. By looking through the tanker's windows, I could see between one and three fast jets mere metres away. This was one of the most spectacular peacetime feats of flying I had ever seen. We could also, in small groups access the flight deck to witness the refuelling process via the monitors! By mere coincidence I had a window seat just at the front of the VC 10 wing so didn't even have to move to get the best view! A day to file in the memory banks as one of the very best!

Now – Back to the Petwood Hotel

The Petwood was built as a private home by the heiress to the Maple Furniture fortunes, Baroness Grace van Eckhardstein, later Lady Weighall, in the early 1900s. It was built in a 'Tudor to Jacobean' style as a low level, almost rambling building and slips into the magnificent grounds in a most unobtrusive fashion.

It also has official approval to fly the RAF ensign from its chimney tops.

Since 1998, most of the visits to my old stamping grounds of Lincolnshire, had had to take into account the health of my wife and so were never for more than a two day duration. My wife died in late October 2007. I felt the need to alleviate the stresses of the previous weeks and months. A stay, for more than one night this time, at the Petwood Hotel was duly booked for 13 November.

The thought of staying in the lovely Woodhall Spa for four or five days, both wound me down and perked me up, to absorb all the memories and fresh experiences, I had planned.

For all too obvious reasons, not so many people holiday in the UK in November! Walking through the unmade road which splits the golf course in two, revealed trees and shrubs in the most magnificent autumnal colours, I had ever seen in Britain.

During another walk, we strolled into the village to scrutinize the 617 Squadron memorial. This is huge and has been fashioned in the shape of a breached dam.

**VC 10 AAR Tanker in Anniversary Livery
12th July 2007**

There are details of all 617 aircrew lost during WW II. The names of those lost on the night of 16/17 May 1943, The Dams Raid, would have been familiar, via books and the eponymous film, to many people. John ('Hoppy') Hopgood brought down over the Mohne dam. Henry Maudsley having limped away from the Eder, 'Dingy' Young crossing the coast on his way home, Barlow and Byers crashing even before reaching designated targets. All spine tingling stuff.

Then it was back to the hotel lounge and a comforting fire, glowing within the 'baronial' stone chimney piece. I found myself staring into the flames and imagining what it would have been like sixty five years ago, when Nicky Ross, Arthur Fearn and the others had enjoyed these same surroundings.

The rooms are even grander now that the wooden wall paneling had been restored to pre wartime condition – after the RAF occupancy. My son suggested: 'Who knows? Perhaps you will "meet" some of them here'. I thought he was getting carried away by the well-known 'transporting' effects of the fire.

We had an early start the following morning and made our way the twelve miles or so, to the East Kirkby Aviation Heritage Centre. Our previous visit had concentrated on the briefing for and the actual, Lancaster taxi ride, leaving no time to explore the centre's many features. Apart from housing 'Just Jane', the hanger has been turned into a museum of, mainly Bomber Command artifacts. The original concrete control tower has been refurbished and contains models acting out the landing scenario, including taped speech/sound effects, of aircraft returning after a wartime raid on Berlin. Very convincing and certainly not a place you'd want to visit at midnight!

One of the last of the original 'Dambusters' keeps a low profile.

As it was the end of the season and a Thursday, we were surprised to find 'Just Jane' outside on the apron, basking in the frosty sunshine. The reason soon became apparent. A compact film crew was setting up photographic and recording equipment around the venerable warhorse. Sitting in one of the film crew's vehicles was an elderly chap, of about my age. He was keenly observing the film maker's endeavours …A question to the film director solicited the reply: 'We're making a film about an ex 97 Squadron chap'.

A Fast Jet Salutes Us : 12th July 2007

We had a long but interesting day. I remembered that Arthur Fearn and his bomb aimer, Flt/Lt Chadwick DFC, had flown about twenty trips from this station with 57 Sqn. Nine or ten of these had been to Berlin (the Big City). Berlin was a long journey from UK and its defences were formidable. That was quite an achievement for any crew in 1943 – but even more so in Arthur's case. At that time he was pushing thirty, almost ten years older than the average pilot, so was commonly referred to as 'dad'.

Arthur and Nicky Ross were two of the greatest advocates of 'The Law of Twos' - today referred to as synchronicity. I became a willing student and since then my whole life seems to have revolved around this 'law'.

In the main hanger there were display boards, for most if not all WW II Bomber Command squadrons. Each board displayed two, maybe three crew photographs. These were taken from the many hundreds of photos of crews who would have passed through each squadron, throughout the duration of the war. Imagine my amazement, when on the 101 Squadron board was, staring back at me, a photo of the James' crew, taken at the end of our tour! At that time I had no idea whatsoever who put it there.

We arrived back at the hotel and were disgruntled to find a large party of golfers occupying our favourite fireside seats - and indeed most of the others in the commodious lounge also. We squeezed ourselves into the last two unoccupied chairs at the far end of the long lounge. I sat down and straightened my tie. It was my RAF tie and it was only on rare and mostly formal occasions, that I wore it. I was not even sure why I chose today? Maybe it was in remembrance of the 617 boys I had flown with and who had regaled me with unique stories of this place.

Whatever the reason, the tie immediately attracted the attention of another non golfing party, one of whom pointed to it and asked, 'Bomber Command'? I recognised this chap as one of the film-making crew we had spotted at East Kirkby earlier. His colleagues strolled over to us and I became bombarded with the usual questions – squadron – group – when had I been on operations and the like. My proud response of, '101 Squadron, 1 Group and...' was cut short by the elderly man, who appeared to be the subject of the film. He pontificated that it was only 5 Group which really counted!

One of the film makers explained that he was George 'Johnny' Johnson, who had first served with 97 Sqn and then volunteered for 617 Sqn, at its formation. 'Johnnie' went on to describe how he had been the bomb aimer in Joe Mc Carthy's crew on the night of 16/17 May 1943, when they had been tasked to attack the Sorpe Dam. In 2007, only a handful of the airmen who had taken off for the Dams Raid, were still alive.

Nicky Ross 'joins the party'!

Slightly taken aback by this attack on my flying credentials, I explained that I had flown with four ex 617 tour expired crews, on research and development work.

This seemed to raise some interest and 'Johnnie' asked for the names of those involved. I told him they were, Ross, Fearn, Williams and Hamilton. I was now warming to the discussions and related the tale of a Lancaster diving out of the sky over England with a sweating Nicky Ross attempting to regain control of the recalcitrant bomber.

To give the story some spice I repeated Nicky's heartfelt words: 'Gee, I could certainly use a drink' . . .

I couldn't have guessed the reaction these words would produce, especially as there was no way of knowing whether Ross was even alive.

The film crew director cut in and advised: 'Well, he hasn't changed much. We were at his home in Scotland last Tuesday - and he had the whiskey bottle open before mid-morning'!

I was both astonished and delighted, to have yet another gem to add to my lengthening list of examples of 'The Law of Twos'. Now the ice had been broken, 'Johnnie' explained the details of the bombing run for the Sorpe dam. Unlike the Mohne and Eder Dams, the run in took place parallel with the dam, not at right angles to it.

The 'Upkeep' depth charge was not to be spun - they were to drop the weapon as close to the dam as was feasible and from a height of only thirty feet above the water level. And don't forget, all this took place in the dark. It was little wonder that it took nine dummy runs before the weapon could be released!

Subsequent conversation revealed another co incidence. After the war George Johnson remained in the RAF. He was posted to Binbrook as bombing leader and instructor, during which time he introduced the

Stabilised Automatic Bomb Sight (SABS) to 101 Sqn, who had moved from Ludford Magna in 1946. The film crew now dragged the venerable 'Dams Veteran' away for further taped conversations. As he headed off he turned around and shouted to me: 'We were the only ones who could give instructions to the pilots'!

Shortly after our return, a serious accident incapacitated me for some time, with the result that I missed the showing of the documentary which had been made by the team based at the Petwood.

Dams Raid anniversary – a day to remember.

By 16 May 2008, I had recovered sufficiently to be able to attend the sixty-fifth anniversary of the Dams Raid. With the help of the Lincolnshire Lancaster Association (LLA), we were fortunate to obtain tickets for a flypast over the Derwent Dam, situated deep in rural Derbyshire. The significance of this venue was that, not only was the dam used as practice for the actual raid but that the squadron C/O, Guy Gibson himself, had used it to test the feasibility of low level flying over water at night. There were significant similarities with the Mohne and Eider Dams, as the Derwent Dam also had a tower on either side. These towers were used to establish the aircraft's distance from the dam and at what point in time to release the revolving depth charge. Some of the flying sequences for the 1955 film were also filmed over the Derwent reservoir and dam.

Present at the display were direct relations of Wing Commander Guy Gibson, who led the operation and of Barnes Wallace, the inventor of the weapon, almost always referred to as the 'bouncing bomb'. Additionally there were three guests of honour.

Richard Todd who memorably played Guy Gibson in the 1955 film, 'The Dam Busters'.

Les Munro came over from his native New Zealand and was the last pilot then alive to have taken off for the Dams Raid.

The third was George Johnson. I didn't get to meet him this time as he was with the other dignitaries and relatives viewing the proceedings from the 'road' over the dam. It gave me a good feeling to be there and I felt privileged to have met him.

The BBMF Lancaster is one of only two in the world that are airworthy and which fly on a regular basis. After a short service of remembrance, the vintage machine flew just 100 ft above the water of the reservoir but - merely forty or so feet above the parapet of the dam itself. That is, below the tops of the two towers! The Lancaster was closely followed by a Spitfire and a Hurricane, also from BBMF at Coningsby. Only a few minutes later, this fantastic display was backed up by two 617 Sqn Tornado GR4s from the squadron's operational base at Lossimouth. These modern day jets were flying only a touch higher than the WW II aircraft - but of course at twice the speed!

We had been indeed fortunate to obtain tickets and take up our 'ringside seats', as we were only about fifty metres or so from the action. On the other side of the Derwent reservoir, on the steep hillside about half a mile away, hundreds of people appeared who had trekked two or three miles over the moors, to also witness this magnificent event. Just before the first aircraft arrived, there must have certainly been in excess of 2,000 spectators in total, some sources say 10,000, all of whom had a day to remember, with pride.

A Warrior departs for Valhalla.

Shortly after returning home from the Derwent flypast, I was given a number of copies of newspapers containing the obituary of Flt/Lt Nicky Ross. Ross DSO DFC, had died on 18 April 2008, aged ninety. I read that Ross had completed seventy seven sorties, the last twenty eight with 617 squadron and was forcibly removed from operations. Among descriptions of 617 Sqn's significant sorties was that carried out on the Gnome-Rhone aero engine works at Limoges, on the night of 8 February 1944. The factories were surrounded by French workers' houses.

Up and until this time, absolute pin point accuracy of target marking of sensitive targets was not being achieved. Leonard Cheshire the 617 Sqn C/O at that time, was convinced that only by dive bombing the target before dropping target markers, could absolute accuracy be achieved.

Needless to say he struggled to gain Bomber Command approval for his proposed new method, especially as it had to be carried out at very low level! On this occasion he used his Lancaster to drop the markers, *from under 100 ft*, which were bang on target. Nicky Ross was one of four 617 crews who scored direct hits on the target each with a 8,000 lb bomb. After the results, and as there were no French casualties, Cheshire's method was officially sanctioned by Bomber Command and he was supplied with the Mosquitoes he had requested.

Shortly after being withdrawn from operational flying, at the same time as the great Leonard Cheshire VC, Nicky Ross was awarded an immediate DSO (an award second only to the Victoria Cross). The citation stated that:

'This officer has completed a very large number of sorties and the successes obtained are testimony to his great skill, courage and resolution. He is a model captain whose strong sense of duty, gallantry and resource have set an example of the highest order'.

I couldn't suppress a smile when I read that Ross enjoyed: 'fiddling with old Jaguars and . . . *had a passion for Scotch'.*

2009 - 101 Squadron reunion and LLA member's day.

On the night of 29/30 August 1944, F/O Foster and his crew were killed during the Stettin raid. They were flying 'our' F Fox LM 479. Fox, you may remember, had been extensively damaged during our thirteenth raid to Russelheim, on 12/13 August, 1944. Stettin was the first return to operations that Fox was to make after repairs had been carried out ...

During dinner at the 2009 Squadron reunion (sixty five years later!), we met the nephew of Flt/Sgt Chalmers (RCAF), the navigator in the Foster crew - and the niece of P/O Cousins, the special operator. All had travelled from Canada to attend the reunion.

In late September we attended the Lincolnshire Lancaster Association (LLA) Member's Day held at RAF Coningsby. Coningsby is the home of the BBMF fleet, in addition to being a strategically vital current RAF station, from where two frontline Eurofighter Typhoon F2 squadrons operated.

The weather was set fair for flying priceless vintage aircraft. On the day, the Lancaster, three Spitfires, two Hurricanes and a Dakota flew in various combinations, including an unforgettable V formation of all of the aforementioned aircraft, led of course by the Lancaster.

We felt massively privileged to be there. Also present that day was the military historian, Jim Shortland, with whom I struck up a conversation. I was amazed to learn that Arthur Fearn had been close friends with Jim, before his death some ten years previously. As Jim was the first contact I had had with Arthur in sixty four years I was delighted to listen to his stories of this enigmatic airman. You will not be surprised to learn that I notched this up as yet another example of the 'Law of Twos'.

2011 – Spirits of the past.

Back to Lincolnshire in an early October heatwave, for the LLA member's day and the now 'obligatory' stay at the Petwood Hotel. During one particular stroll through the enchanting gardens, the thought occurred to me as to whether 'Mac' Hamilton was still alive. The reason for this was that I knew that Nicky Ross and Arthur Fearn were deceased - that only left John Williams and 'Mac' Hamilton out of the 617 Sqn men I had flown with.

Back in 2007, information in the hotel's 617 Squadron bar advised that the president of the association was one 'Mac' Hamilton. He would almost certainly have visited the Petwood in 2007 to officiate at the May Dam's raid anniversary. Only minutes had passed since the thought entered my mind, when I stopped to read a small weathered brass plaque fixed at the foot of a young tree. I had to re read the plaque several times before the words sunk in. It said quite simply:

Sqn Ldr M L Hamilton DFC

PILOT – 617 Squadron

Passed away 20 April 2008

Probably a heartfelt token from his family, I thought, rather than something the squadron initiated. There was only one other dedication in the garden and that also was to a 617 Squadron airman.

George Williams : our rear gunner; died December 5th 2009

'George was born and raised on a farm in Viking, Alberta. Rodeo was a consuming pastime after high school. This pastime was cut short by the outbreak of World War 2. The war soon took him to England and Europe where he was a tail gunner aboard Lancaster bombers.

When the war ended in 1945, George left the Air Force and returned to civilian life. He then worked in construction for a number of Canadian companies including Peggott Construction, Poole Engineering and Federal Electric Corporation as a heavy Equipment Operator and Diesel Electric Mechanic. George also spent three years in the Arctic working on a site of the Distant early warning (D.E.W. Line).

After retirement, George spent much of his time on his acreage overhauling diesel equipment and a cable control bulldozer. George is survived by his friend, Maxine Pedersen, brothers; Reg and Bernard (Evelyn), sisters; Dorothy and June. He was predeceased by sister-in-laws Anona and May Lou and brothers-in-law, Milton Schalin and Ernest Saunders.'

Other 'Recent' Events

Two other tragic events from my operational period with 101 Sqn, have recently made news once more...and an unexpected surprise.

The crew of Peter 'Pancho' Hyland, were the second out of *The Original Four* to go missing. They did not return from the Stuttgart raid on the night of 28/29 July 1944. Recently, remains of their Lancaster, Victor Two, were found in south west France. Tommy Crane had been one of the crew members. 101 Sqn Association arranged for family members of the crew, to attend the unveiling of a commemorative plaque, erected by 'locals' in their memory. I believe that Tommy Crane's sister attended the ceremony.

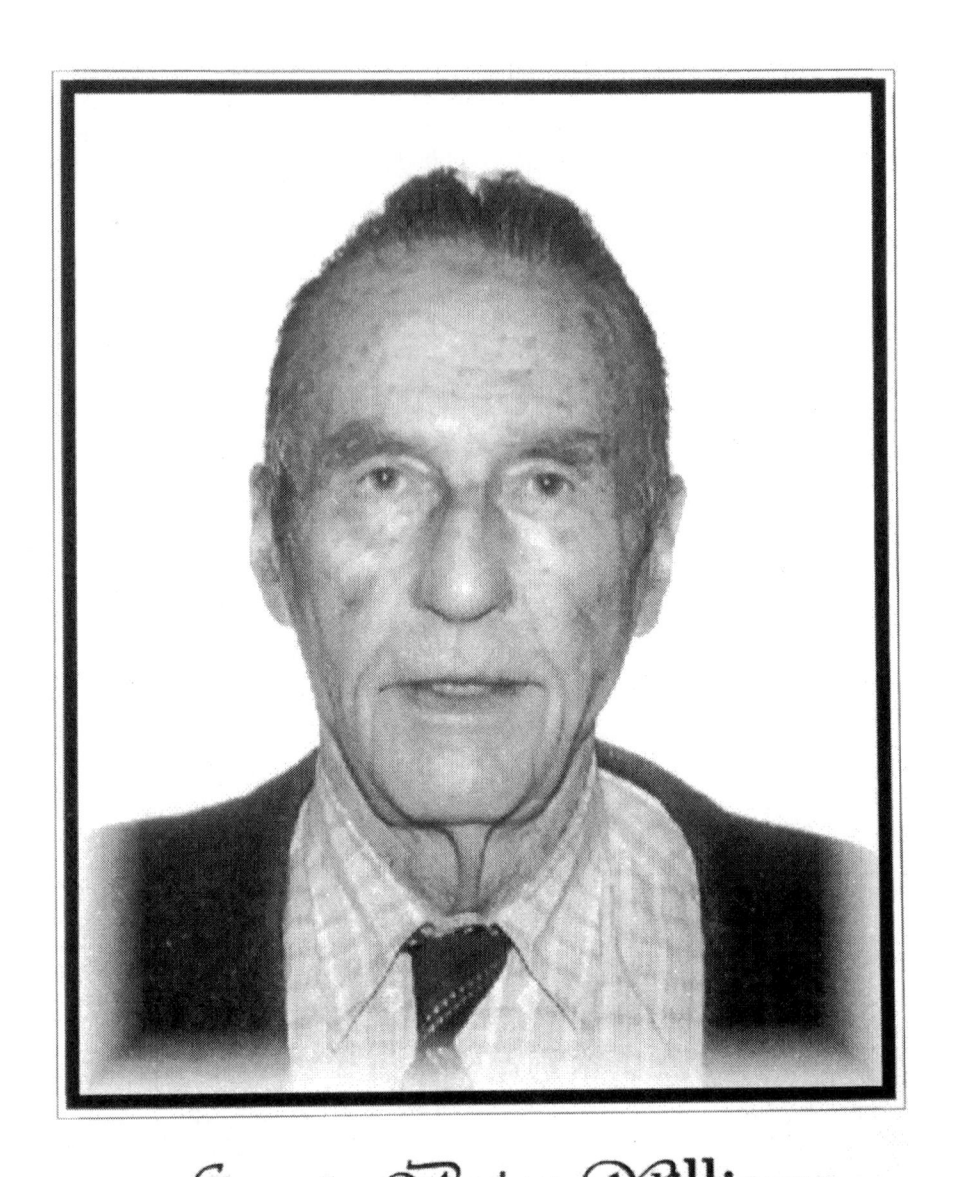

George Bates Williams

James Crew Rear Gunner
Died December 2009

On 15 September 1944, a 101 Sqn Lancaster PB 456 on an air test flight, plunged into the ground at the south-east end of Loch Lomond. The crew of seven (probably no need for a SO on this air test), all perished. Over a period of some years in the 2000s, significant parts of the aircraft were excavated and a documentary film based on these findings was shown on TV. I believe that one of the Merlin engines now resides in a local museum.

CHAPTER 28   More Adventures Beckon

The Legion d' honneur Award

Just under four years ago (August 2014) the French President, Francois Hollande, in a moment of belated largesse, announced the award of the Legion d'honneur to all (living) service members who had taken part in the liberation of his country seventy years before. Bomber Command (including 101 Squadron) was deeply involved before, during and after The Battle of Normandy, (5 /6 June 1944 to 16 August 1944). My nomination was forwarded to the French authorities in September 2014 and I duly received my medal on 15 February 2016. The rank of the award is 'Chevalier' meaning Knight: a horse borne warrior. I was born to a father who worked with and was passionate about horses (and indeed I have worked with these intelligent animals myself); my life has travelled almost full circle, so I feel it most appropriate that I now have an official title associated with horses.

I feel very proud, both for myself, but especially for those brave soldiers, sailors and airmen who, for whatever reasons, did not live long enough to receive their much deserved award.

Editor & Publisher note : The ceremony, appropriately, took place in the Churchill Suite at Chester University Campus in the presence of the eleven recipients, their families and friends. Ron was joined by son Peter, niece Ann, step-daughter Lindy and publisher Dave Gregg. The 'do' showed the usual British restraint by limiting the after award 'dinner' to coffee and biscuits. To make up for this Ron and the others had the full attention of TWO French consuls and numerous photographers. Overall it was a grand day out. Ron had made sure the car boot was full of books for sale just in case.

'Selling the Book' : Hooton Airfield and Beyond When we produced the first edition of 'From Landsman to Lancasters', Ron informed his editor, and son, Peter that his target was to sell a thousand copies. Peter informed the publisher, myself, Dave Gregg, and we wondered once more at Ron's unbounded enthusiasm…but surely a 1,000 books target was out of reach? This was to foolishly underestimate Ron's determination. From the inception Ron's purpose was to support charities from the book sales. The main initial recipient became St. John's Hospice on the Wirral who cared for Ron's daughter Sue in her final days in 2015. It is a worthy, respected organization deserving support. The Hospice is just yards from Rising Sun Farm where our story began. Other charity recipients include The Salvation Army and the Royal Star & Garter Homes.

Help Wirral Hospice keep serving our community

Mr Peter Davies
29 Greenfields Avenue
BROMBOROUGH
Wirral
CH62 6DB

05 December 2017

Dear Mr Davies

I am writing to thank you and your father for raising an incredible £680.00 from the sales of your book 'From Landsman to Lancasters'. Please find enclosed certificate for your father in recognition of his achievement.

We very much appreciate your support as voluntary donations such as this make a major contribution to our fundraising income and enable us to continue with the very special care we provide for our patients and their families.

The aim of Wirral Hospice St John's is to warmly welcome people with progressive illness which has failed to respond to curative treatment, into the quiet calm of a highly professional, caring atmosphere which 'comforts always' both them and those who are important to them. We aim to enable patients living with advanced disease to achieve the best quality of life.

Thank you again for your support. Please do not hesitate to contact me should you require any further information or alternatively you may like to visit our website at www.wirralhospice.org.

With kind regards

Yours sincerely

Jacinta Warwick
Fundraising Officer

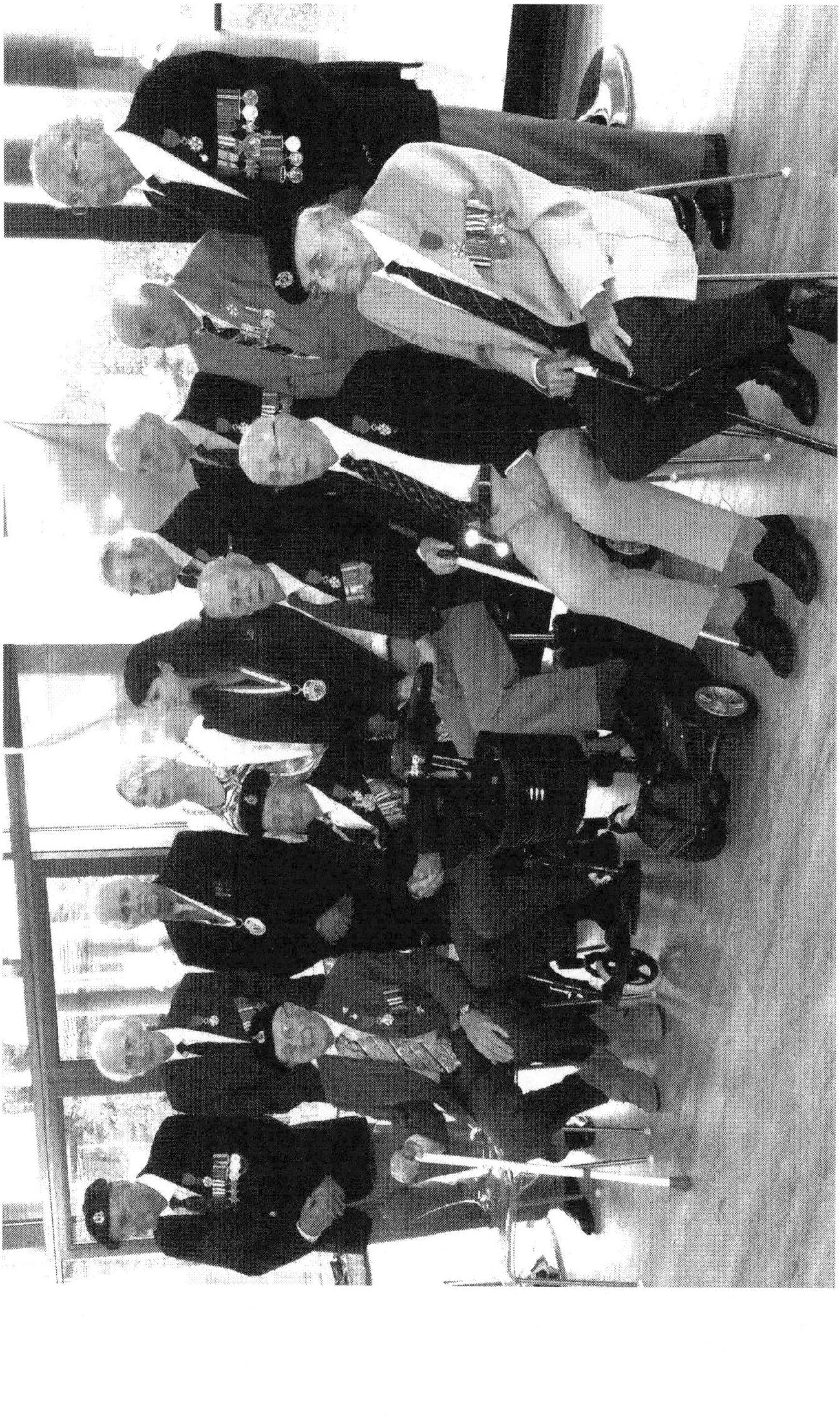

Ron Davies Receives His Legion d' honneur

University of Chester, Churchill Suite, 2016

Ron and his comrades received their medals from not one, but two, French Consuls. The recipients and their guests then dined sumptuously on coffee and biscuits, no doubt due to Le Austerity.

A 1,000 book sales target was as nothing to a man who had taken part in a 1,000 bomber raid. On that basis a plan of campaign was quickly evolved beginning with a reconnaissance mission to establish the landscape of the 'Historic Militaria Enthusiasts Community'. Peter discovered that an annual militaria event was to take place at the site of the old Hooton airfield not far from Ron's home in Bromborough on the Wirral. Hooton was a pre-war aerodrome which later became a wartime RAF airfield defending Merseyside.

The exhibition space was in one of the old hangers noted for its original, magnificent wooden roof. Here Ron and Peter set up a display table featuring 'From Landsman to Lancasters' and other military history books for sale. Ron also proudly displayed his commendation from the Charles Holland Awards group for their annual Brave Britons Award.

He was one of five military veterans nominated. He had attended the awards ceremony at a grand dinner in London with his granddaughter Briony…another adventure.

There were of course many other display tables at Hooton selling books, photographs, uniform items and a fierce array of Allied and Nazi weaponry up to and including Wehrmacht anti-tank bazookas.

Many of the enthusiasts were in period dress including village policemen, NAFFI 'girls' and army platoons. The soldiers tended to be both overweight and grey haired so the effect was more Dads Army than Eighth Army but the genuine enthusiasm could not be faulted. This was just as well since the hanger was unheated and the temperature remained below zero all morning. To show family solidarity Ron's niece Ann and stepdaughter Lindy turned up to brave the cold while the frozen publisher took photos.

Ron spoke to many enthusiasts and made valuable contacts in the community. This lead directly to invitations to give talks to local societies which Ron enthusiastically accepted.

Ron had brought with him and displayed his uniform tunic which soon attracted attention from the collectors. In the end he parted with it knowing that it would be looked after and preserved as a 'valuable' historic item in the militaria community…along with his story in the copy of the book which went with it. It is to be hoped that all such stories will be preserved and remembered. British military history and bravery did not end at Agincourt nor at Balaclava.

Dedication of the 101 Squadron Memorial, National Arboretum

Due to a serious malfunction in my port inner eye I was sadly forced to abort an invitation to visit Brize Norton. Time over target was to have been 12:30 hrs on 12/07/17 and the master bomber was to have been the Princess Royal! All joking apart, the occasion, of course was the 100th anniversary of 101 squadron.

This made me think about the next trip (which I was now especially determined not to miss), the dedication of the 101 Squadron memorial, to be held at the National Arboretum on 23 September 2017. I have no particular expectations of receiving a 'telegram from the Queen' (she would have to be ninety-five herself!) but being in the final quinquennial certainly focuses the mind. Two things dominated my thoughts: how to turn a trip into a mini adventure, and to relish the two month planning, time as the event itself would be over in the blink of an eye, and opportunities for days out at my age are limited.

Due to a combination of Anno Domini and accidents, my joints no longer respond to a quick squirt of WD 40! Mobility is something the young take for granted – the elderly have to be more creative. Just when I was despairing at the thought of spending five hours (two and a half each way) cramped in a car, a thought occurred to me; Andrew Mills a good neighbour who had demonstrated a particular interest in Bomber Command was the owner of a 'something' UV - let's just call it a people carrier. The advantages of this kind of transport were that I could sit in comfort without impeding my circulation (or anything else for that matter!). After several coffee-and-a-dram sessions masquerading as planning meetings, we had the bones of an idea and Andy went off to 'make it happen'.

One of the problems was that the time we would have to set off from home meant it would be far too long to go without a substantial meal until the availability of a buffet meal after the ceremony. Andy did stirling work locating an inn a) within thirty minutes of the Arboretum and b) prepared to open for us half an hour early and pre order our meals from their extensive menu. It took a couple of weeks by the industrious Andrew to finalize the arrangements which provided continuous interest for myself.

'Came the day', we set off promptly at 09:30 in Andrew's gleaming chariot. The 'we' included Professor David Gregg (rtd), the publisher of this book, another good friend.

The hostelry chosen for lunch was the Dog and Partridge in Marchington a winner of the best kept village in East Staffordshire, where we had arranged to meet six-foot five Adam James from Northamptonshire. Adam is a keen and successful distributor for *From Landsman to Lancasters*.

Mine host, Margaret (who had agreed to open the Inn half an hour early) was especially helpful and expressed an interest in the display of medals adorning my blazer, (the first occasion that I had worn them together). The repast was both fabulous and economical and an occasion I shall certainly NEVER FORGET. I suspect that Dave, Andy and Adam felt likewise. All too soon we were reluctantly forced to make a move towards our main appointment of the day, still some thirty minutes' drive away. My parting gift to Margaret was a signed copy of this book. She received it with the rejoinder, 'Thanks so much, you have made MY day.' I almost felt tearful myself.

After such a mid-day indulgence it will not surprise the reader to hear that we were only just in time for the ceremony, the main party being seated and ready. Far from being relegated to the back row we found that seats had been saved for us on the front row AND we were not put on a charge for absenteeism!

The ceremony commenced on time and after a short introduction the Venerable Ray Pentland CB QHC, stepped up to commence his ecumenical duties. Ray obviously saw this dedication as a serious effort because five years previously he decided to get some practice in – Ray oversaw the Bomber Command memorial dedication in Green Park London (in his pre-retirement role of Chaplain in Chief, the Royal Air Force).

The service which followed was very poignant (especially I would say for all the veterans attending). Finally the wraps covering the memorial were removed by 'Rusty' Waughman DFC, AFC, nominally the oldest ex 101 Squadron member and SAC Paige Wardle, the youngest. Meanwhile the (then) incumbant Officer Commanding the squadron, Al Tano read from the Bible – John 15, 9 – 14. After the prayer of Dedication, 'Rusty' Waughman carried out the reading 'They shall not grow old...'. This was followed by The Last Post, and finally:

THE SILENCE
THE REVIELLE
THE BLESSING.

There were few dry eyes among the Attendees by the end of some forty minutes of an extremely moving ceremony.

The Aftermath

Freed from convention the guests started to mingle and many contacts were made before the mandatory buggies arrived to take us to the last part of the proceedings. As we made our way to the tented area two thoughts struck me: firstly I realised just what an enormous area the Arboretum covered. The atmosphere really was restful, each site projecting its purpose and the thoughtfulness behind the individual designs. Official statistics confirm that over 300 memorials are contained within 150 acres of ground having 30,000 maturing trees, many chosen to compliment the adjacent memorial. For example the area surrounding the Police Tribute memorial (The Beat) is covered by London Plane trees and Horse Chestnuts. (The latter was the wood from which the first police truncheons were made). With similar intent the British Korean Veterans memorial is cloaked by the indigenous (to the Far East), Dawn Dogwoods. I noticed that the visitors' car park was jam packed, an indication of just how many people were paying their respects to, in all probability very distant relatives, with a quiet air of dignity.

Secondly I remembered that the main purpose of my own visit was to remember some 1,150 personnel from 101 Squadron who lost their lives between 1939 and 1945 and the 730 of this number who sacrificed their

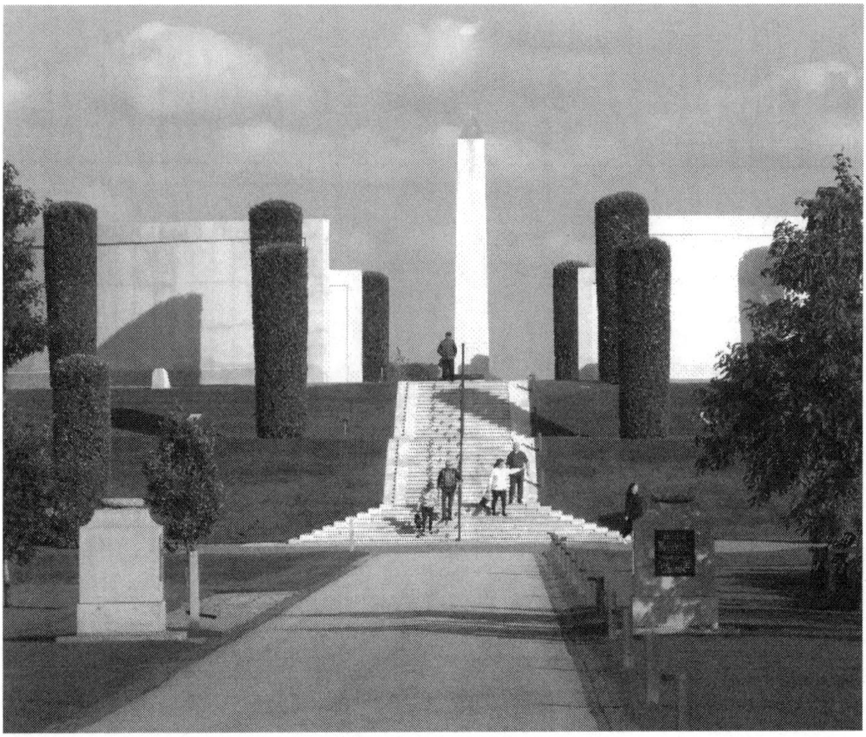

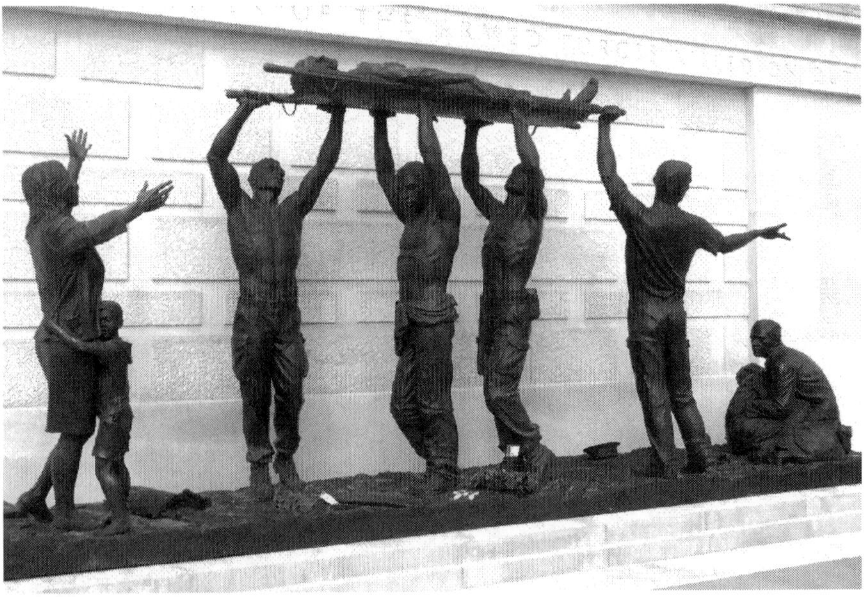

future while flying from Ludford Magna. In particular and foremost in my thoughts were the 230 plus who died during my own time on the Squadron. This last number of course included personal friends and room- mates. Naturally my thoughts hovered over recollections of two members of my own crew. P/o Keith Gosling aged just nineteen years was (you may remember) killed in action on his seventh operation, (refer to Appendix II). F/O Ken Gibbs DFC, our replacement mid - upper gunner killed in action on his ninety-sixth trip.

Now back to the reception, we were ushered into a lavish tented area which was luxuriously furnished and created an air of pomp and ceremony in harmony with the occasion. Our ample lunch seemed eons away and we were looking forward to an outstanding buffet to complete an outstanding day. Myself, Adam, Andy and Dave were joined on our table by The Venerable Ray Pentland and his wife and also ex – Air Vice Marshall Eric Macey, a 101 Squadron C/O of the Vulcan Bomber era, whom I had met at 101 Sqn reunions. The last two seats were taken by a lady and gentleman who seemed rather remote from the general conversations.

After some attention by the press I was approached by a Frenchman suitably decorated with the medals of his country. During July 1944 101 Sqn had bombed his village but he recognised that it was to drive out the common enemy so HE DID NOT BLAME THE CREWS (see the P.S.).

The next person to approach me did so in a very direct manner: 'Were you in the crew of F/O James?' he asked. After I answered in the affirmative he began to discuss the War - time activities of 101 at Ludford Magna. So deep was his knowledge (far beyond the reach of my own memories) that I deduced that he was some sort of historian. When I put this to him his response astounded me. He explained that he was in fact one of the two farmers whose acreage covered the wartime extent of RAF Ludford Magna during 101's occupancy. As this book contains much information about that period he immediately purchased a copy!

Suddenly the last two occupants of the table began to enter into the conversation. The man's father had been a 101 Squadron 'special operator' and had only recently died and his son became yet another customer for this book.

As we prepared to depart I was again approached by another person apparently seeking me out. A lady tapped me on the shoulder and said

'You won't remember me?'

Looking up I immediately recognised Myfanwy James, the widow of my late pilot, Fred, who had died on 6/4/2011, and I was pleased that we had met once again.

A walk back to the vehicle, a pleasant two hour trip home and so ended an exhausting but pleasurable day.

Publisher's Post Script : Memories of the Mannville Raid

At the dedication of the 101 Squadron memorial in 2017 Ron encountered many memories. The French military visitor in the glasses was a native of Mannville near Caen in Normandy and recalled as a child stories of the great RAF raid in which Ron took part. It seemed that the local Wehrmacht commander expected his massed troop and panzer concentrations to be attacked by air and warned the villagers of Mannville to flee the area... just in time. When they returned nothing remained except bomb craters and the shattered wreckage of overturned, 54 ton Tiger tanks (see page 122).

In 2016 Peter, Ron's son (and editor), and Dave Gregg, the Green Man Books publisher, made a pilgrimage to Normandy to retrace Ron's

RAF sorties. By one of those strange coincidences, while Ron was 'bringing the whirlwind' to the Nazi hordes that July, Dave's father, Bombardier Philip Gregg, (92 Reg. RA) was at Escoville, three miles to the north of Mannville, shooting down Messerschmitt bf 109s with his 40 mm Bofors AA gun.

By the kind of serial coincidence Ron Davies enjoys (his 'Law of Twos') Dave's second cousin is now the curator of the Pegasus Bridge Museum east of Caen and a few miles from Mannville. By accident, due to a logistical SNAFU (Situation Normal All Fucked Up) in the invasion schedule, for some days after D Day + 5, Philip Gregg's misplaced marching party had been 'volunteered' to reinforce the famous F Troop / 92nd Regiment AA guns defending the strategically critical, and now famous, Pegasus Bridge which had been taken on D Day by glider troops.

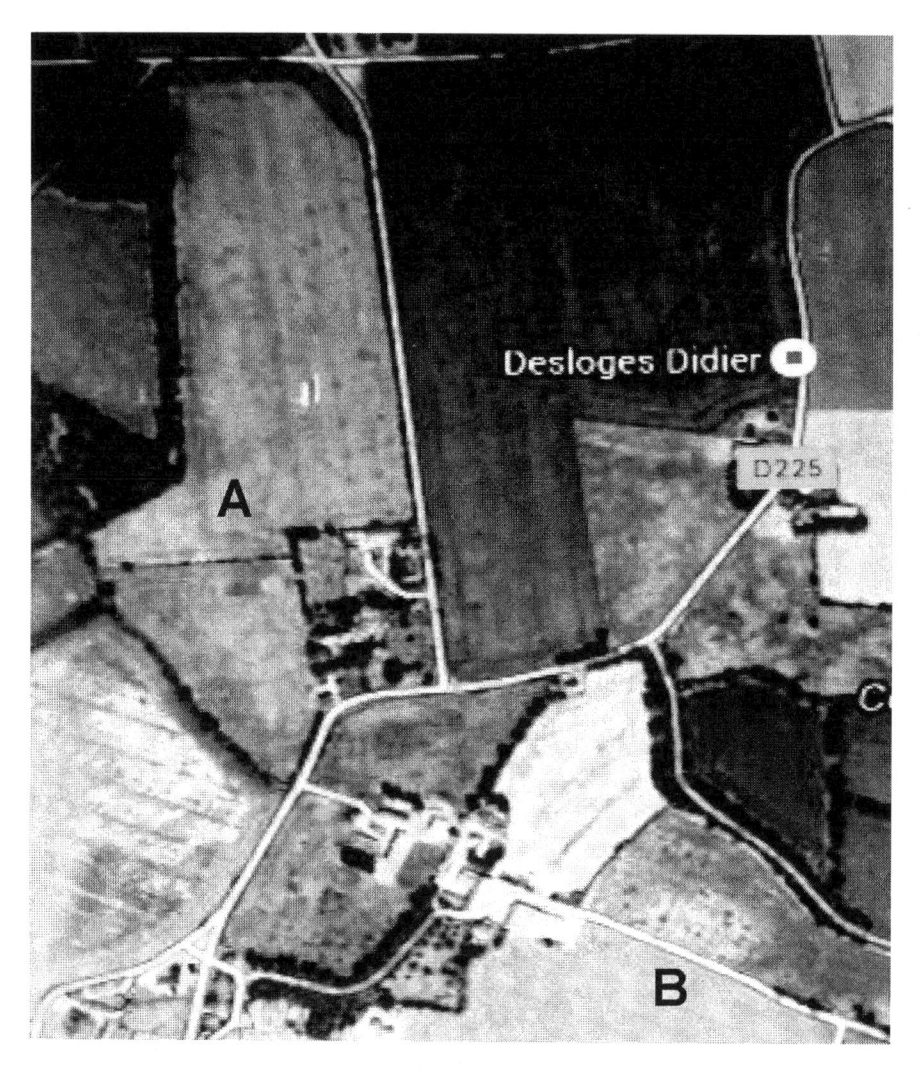

Peter and Dave visited the now peaceful Mannville fields but nothing could be seen on the surface after seventy two years. However satellite images show the fields all around to be peppered still with huge, bomb crater crop marks. Here are two such fields labeled A and B and a close up.

At the excellent 101 Squadron Memorial tea, while Ron concentrated on pushing 'the book' at his table, Dave went in search of our Mannville Frenchman to sell him one. Alas, despite reading Ron's personal record of the Mannville Raid and several others over Normandy, he declined to purchase a copy! No doubt Le Brexit was to blame.

The Bomber Command Memorial Visit to Lincoln

Ron's next adventure in April 2018 took him back to Lincolnshire and the finally completed International Bomber Command Centre and memorial. Ron and crew had decided to miss the busy opening, which Ron could have attended as a Bomber Command veteran, and visit a week later under quieter conditions. This strategy worked out well.

Every adventure requires a good lunch and this time it took place at the Inn on the Green at Ingham which Ron and Peter had visited before on their Lincoln trips. Ron, Andy, Adam and the publisher were warmly welcomed at the pub and the food and beer were as good as promised. A short drive south then brought us to the memorial site set on a high promontory to the south of Lincoln with magnificent views of the cathedral and city across the valley. Since the main memorial is a very tall steel spire it can be seen from miles around which seems fitting given the history of the area. Here are recorded, on concentric rings of vertical, perforated steel sheets, the names of all those who died in WW II in Bomber Command and in associated forces.

Because of the long distances involved in exploring the site Ron used a light weight wheel chair and donned his green jacket and medals for the visit. This arrangement had the advantage of attracting many convivial conversations with the centre staff and visitors. Ron's chief objective in the visit was to identify a long list of names of fallen crew mates and others on the memorial's steel walls and to mark them with poppies. The centre staff kindly supplied a box of poppies for this purpose free of charge.

We set off along the long paved stone path which leads to the memorial itself but did not get far before conversations broke out. Ron was approached by a uniformed lady, with a certain aura of authority about her, and a middle aged man. This lady, I believe, was the centre manager who was delighted to talk to Ron and the man was a local journalist and history enthusiast who listened avidly to Ron's story. This was a good start!

We eventually reached the rings of rusted steel sheets bearing the crew names. It would be fair to say that the logic used to allocate blocks of names to particular sheets and the sequencing of the sheets around the central spire, was arcane. Apparently this occurred because the sheets had been erected in several phases. The publisher, who was once a mathematician, could not follow the explanation offered. Fortunately Adam had a list and ground plan and by sending out search parties the key names on Ron's list were found and marked with poppies, including that of the young Keith Gosling which was important to Ron (see Appendix II).

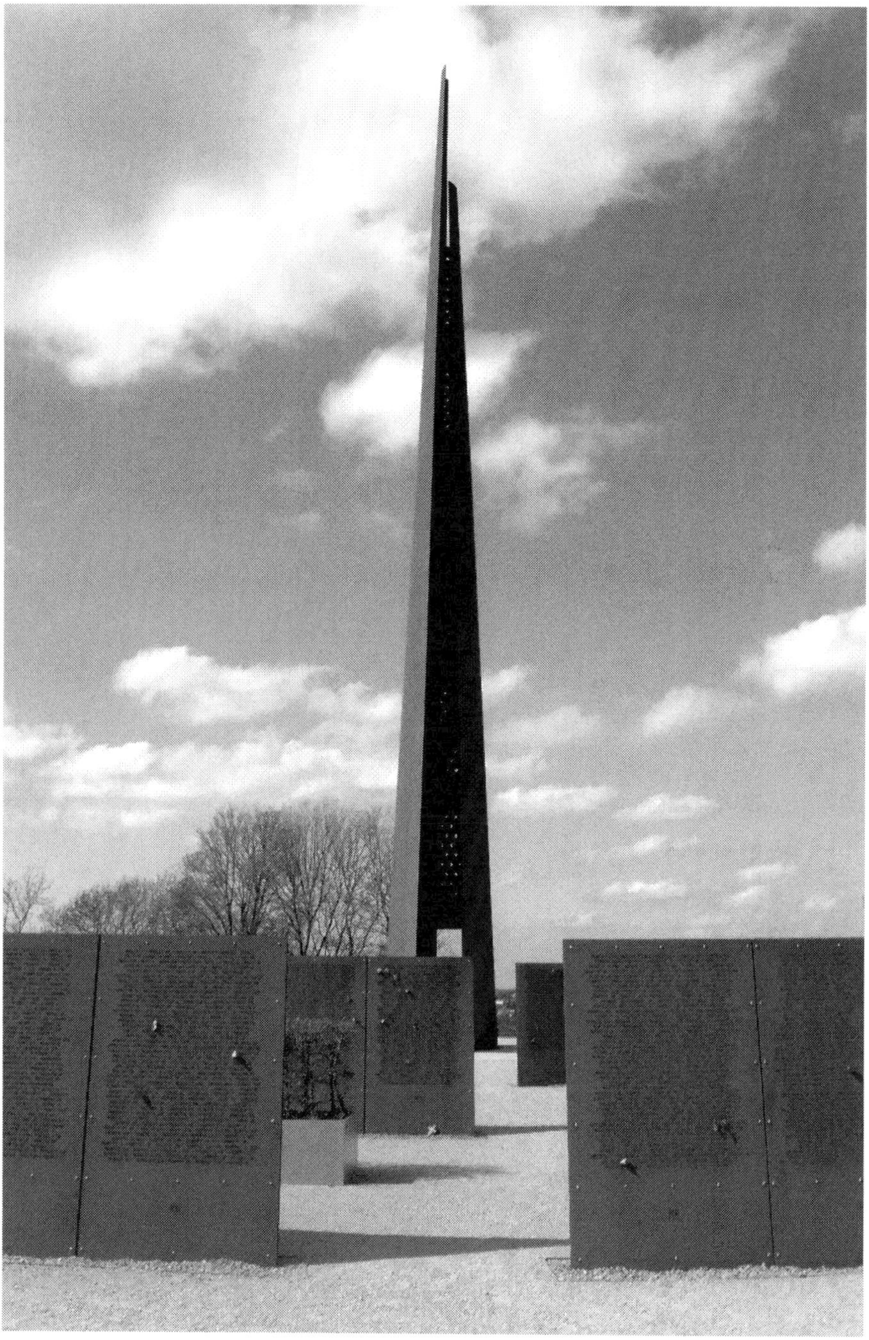

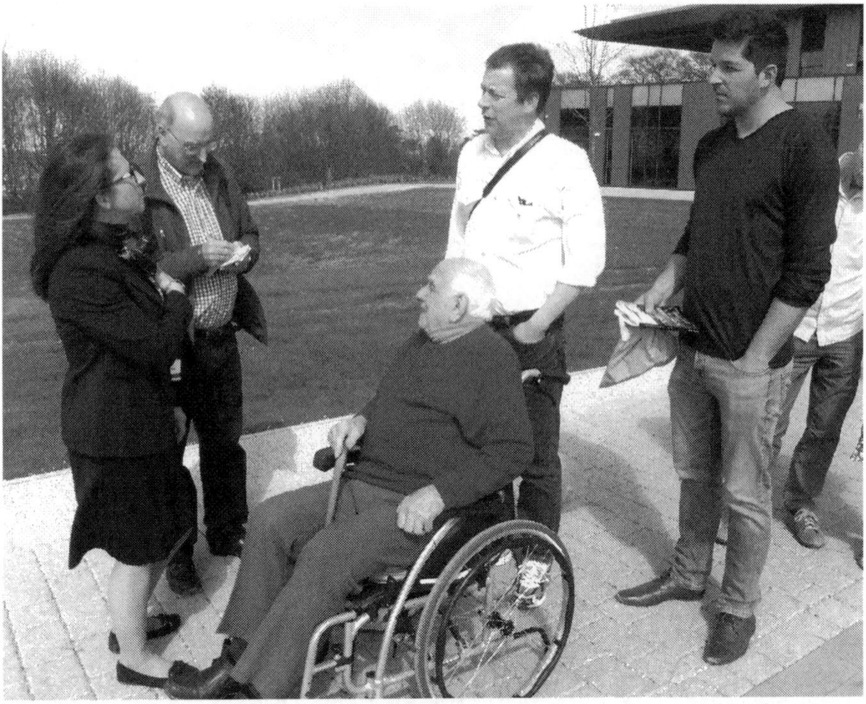

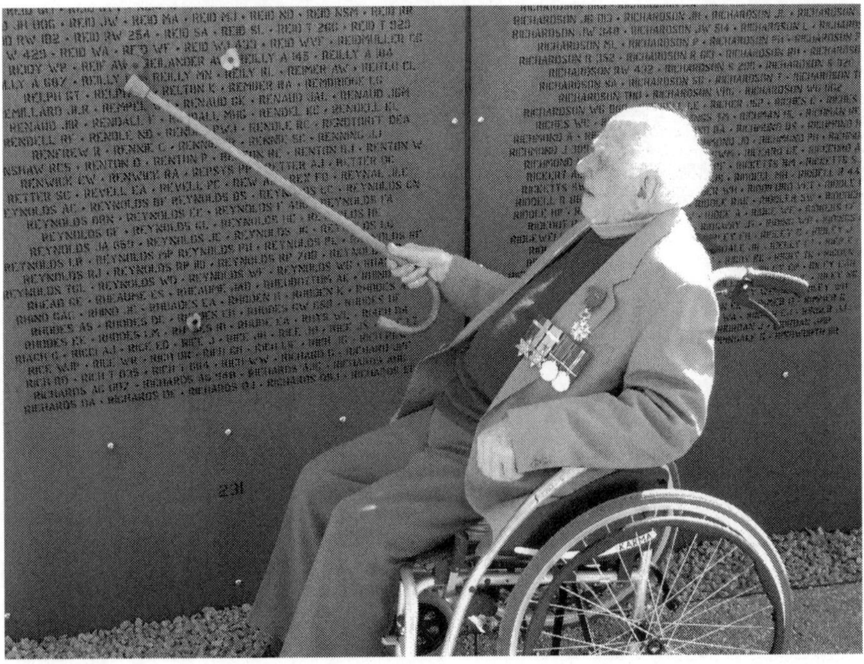
231

GORNALL
GORWOOD JE
GOSLING K
GOSSIP AB
GOUGH

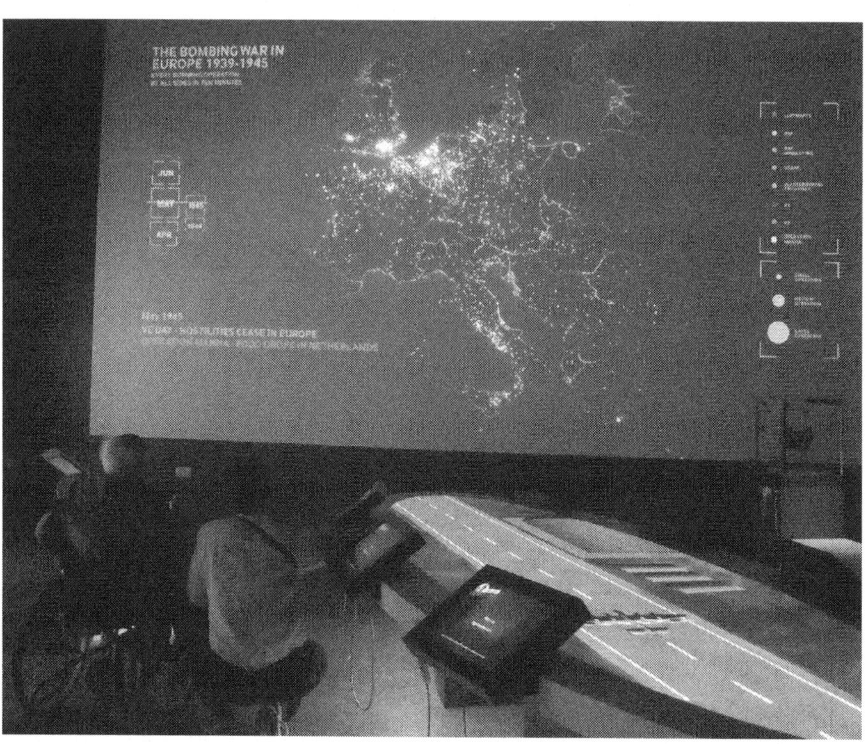
THE BOMBING WAR IN
EUROPE 1939-1945

After an exhausting effort, from Adam in particular, the task was done and over twenty names had been found and marked. We retired to the centre for tea and coffee and a rest. The centre had a museum shop but this one had a particularly good range of biographies and autobiographies by Bomber Command air crew. Out came a copy of the book which was passed to centre staff and contact details were exchanged for later follow up. Just before closing Ron went into the War Room which had a giant computer display screen showing the pattern of bombing raids by the Allies and Axis, day by day, all through WW II. Ron and the rest of us were very impressed with this display. He watched the whole twenty minute sequence.

As we departed the site Adam had a surprise for us. He knew that the Battle of Britain Memorial Flight Lancaster was due for a test flight that afternoon and, although it was too late to drive down to Coningsby, he showed us the take off, live, on his phone. But alas the Lancaster did not come our way. We did watch a giant AWACS aircraft doing circuits around us: a reminder that the price of freedom is eternal vigilance, a sobering end to a poignant and thought provoking day. The drive back home took us across the high, wild Pennines via the Woodhead Pass in beautiful evening light …another reminder of what it was that our forces fought so hard to defend in WW II.

            The Publisher

The Author with 'The City of Lincoln' on an earlier visit

APPENDIX I

Uncle Ned and the Ice Cream Factory

Did the RAF target German civilians deliberately?

The above question was the title of a debate section inviting reader's letters, which appeared in a daily newspaper in 2009, the like of which crop up with metronomic regularity. They serve to perpetuate the on-going controversy which this subject has created, over many years. It did however make me feel that it was time to relate the story of the life of my late Uncle Ned (c1888 – 1940). For those of you who may wonder what on earth Uncle Ned's life had got to do with the RAF targeting German civilians – read on.

Edward Davies was born circa 1888, the eldest child of William and Mary Davies, at The White Cottage, Raby Road, Raby, Wirral. Ned eventually had eight siblings, five brothers and three sisters. White cottage was a small farm worker's abode having just two small bedrooms. Raby was, and still is, a tiny hamlet having a schoolroom and an inn – The Wheatsheaf, aka 'The Thatch'. Raby at this time offered little opportunity for either employment or further accommodation.

It is likely that Ned left school at the age of ten years and would have sought employment opportunities elsewhere on the Wirral peninsular. The big drawback however was transport. At the turn of the twentieth century, Ned, being an enterprising sort of lad, found the solution by becoming the owner of a 'Penny Farthing' cycle. This bizarre contraption had one enormous wheel at the front and a tiny one at the rear. The rider sat very high up and moved pedals attached directly to the front wheels. If one had set out to deliberately design and build the most potentially unstable device known to man, the Penny Farthing would have been the result.

Eventually the Penny Farthing, the forerunner to the modern 'safety' bicycle, became widely available to folk on a limited income. Ned roamed far and wide on this dangerous contraption. Little more is known of his life until 1914, when he joined the army. After an initial period of training in this country, Ned was sent to France. Not only did he suffer at the hands of a far better equipped and more efficient German Army - but also from the many well publicised deprivations of existence in the trenches.

Of the five brothers, three fought in France, the other two brothers being too young to fight .One brother was killed in 1916 at The Somme and the third was Tom, my father.

Neither Ned nor Tom would talk about their nightmare experiences, but by 1917 Ned had been wounded several times and was invalided out of the army. His disabilities entitled him to a miniscule pension, which forced him to seek employment, even to maintain a mediocre lifestyle.

Subsequently Ned married a girl called Mary and by 1921, the year of my birth, they had two children. Now living in Birkenhead, Ned managed to secure employment as a tram driver.

The first street trams in Britain were built in Birkenhead, from 1860 onwards by an extrovert American from Boston, one George Francis Train. Although the early trams were horse drawn, iron rails were soon laid and the changeover from horse drawn to electric powered, went smoothly. For a few years, Ned managed to support his family, just, with his wages and the small war pension. As the economic downturn evolved from the aftermath of the Great War, a desperate government, anxious to cut public spending, sought to save outgoings wherever possible. Servicemen's pensions therefore became a 'legitimate' target and in due course Ned was summoned to appear before a medical tribunal.

Just a few days before the hearing, Ned was driving his tram from the suburbs of Birkenhead to Woodside, the terminus for the ferry crossing to Liverpool. The last few hundred yards from Hamilton Square to the pier head, consists of a gradual slope down to the River Mersey. At this point Ned collapsed at the wheel. Fortunately he was just able to slam the handbrake on before he blacked out. Due to the terrified passengers and a highly concerned tram company, Ned chose to depart gracefully.

The medical council decided to continue paying Ned's pension . . .

At about the same time, Cammell Laird the Merseyside ship builder, laid off thousands of workers due to the slump in shipping orders. Lever Brothers, the soap manufacturer based at Port Sunlight, just five miles away, were however, rapidly expanding to become the premier employer on the Wirral. Ned successfully applied for the newly created position of commissionaire at Lever's head office and could be seen proudly standing at the main entrance, resplendent in his uniform, not to mention his war medals.

Status Quo reigned until 1931 and the Great Depression. Once again Ned was summoned to appear before a medical council, whose object was to terminate his pension.

On the Monday prior to the meeting, Ned was at his usual position. At about 9am and just as a group of senior managers walked by, Ned collapsed to the ground. He was subsequently taken to the adjacent Port Sunlight Hospital, built by the Lever consortium, as there was no NHS in those days.

At the subsequent meeting of the medical board, the decision was made to commute Ned's pension into a small lump sum, to be paid in lieu of the weekly pension.

Ned and his family were living in the north end of Birkenhead, not far from the docks which handled much of the Irish traffic and also smaller tramp steamers. Ned now needed an alternative income. He chose to invest in a two up- two down house, together with a shop and some outbuildings. He decided to start – wait for it – an ice cream factory! Elbowing to one side the fact that Ned had had no ice cream manufacturing experience whatsoever, the main problem lay in obtaining the products required to produce high quality ice cream - primarily the milk. A solution was found at a farm at Sealand, twenty-five miles away on the boundary of Cheshire and North Wales. Transport costs would however have been prohibitive.

Ever the entrepreneur, Ned solved the problem by purchasing a 1927 Ivy Karryall. It was in effect, a three wheeled motorcycle which had two wheels at the rear. This machine had a covered van top and sides and a flimsy windscreen and the whole contraption was powered by a Raleigh 350 cc side valve engine. It did not have a reverse gear, so the road fund tax, as it was then called was just four pounds a year. The machine returned upwards of fifty miles to the gallon, petrol then costing one shilling (5p) per gallon.

I can well remember Uncle Ned's first visit to Lancelyn Farm with the Karryall. At that time I would have been about twelve years of age and was fanatical about motorcycles. Although the rear van section had a sound floor, the driver's cab did not. As I clambered into the front I straddled the flat petrol tank and placed my feet onto large boards – similar to the 'running boards' fitted to the outside of cars of that period.

The sit-up and beg handlebars housed all the controls except those for the gears and rear brake. There were levers which controlled - brakes, petrol flow, air intake and clutch. There was a lever which operated the magneto (forerunner to the battery) and before attempting to start the devilish machine, a brass pump was used to inject oil into the engine! After all the controls had been correctly set, the rider selected neutral and then, hopefully, kick started the engine into life.

I have tried to explain the operating requirements, to highlight just how much work there was for a disabled person to cope with. The milk collection entailed a long journey for this type of vehicle, which was very heavily loaded on the return trip, unstable in high winds and rain and had a long steep hill to cope with, on each leg of the journey. All of this with a rickety underpowered machine, prone to punctures and breakdowns, and probably seven or so years old when purchased by Ned.

And thus it was that Ned's ice cream business got off the ground. One can only marvel at the determination and nerves of steel required by a middle aged man with severe mobility problems, working long hours for seven days a week, merely to survive financially, physically and mentally.

The Great Depression of 1931 followed the General Strike of 1926 and the aftermath of a government pursuing a means-tested social policy. Anyone in receipt of pension or 'dole' was forced to disclose all personal details to what would be called, today 'the social'.

My grandfather and grandmother, in the early 1930s, were two such victims. Consequently, all surviving male relatives were interviewed by a local government officer and forced to declare their earnings - there was no PAYE tax then. My father, a struggling tenant farmer was assumed to be the wealthiest and had to contribute five shillings (25p) to his parents, to subsidise their meagre old age pension. Uncle Ned was second on the list and his 'donation' was three shillings (15p) per week. The three younger brothers, on lower incomes, probably contributed between one and two shillings (5 – 10p). In such hard times, these sums of money were not easy to find but somehow each brother managed to pay his dues – just in case they should ever falter, the man from 'the social', would never be far away.

This now brings the history of Uncle Ned up to September 1939 when WW II was declared. By God's good grace, Ned had managed to survive a hard childhood, endured insecure employment, fought for three years in a most disastrous war and despite his disabilities, struggled to survive for twenty tough post war years. Now, due to food and fuel rationing, Ned's tiny business was forced to close.

Ned however still remained cheerful and set about converting his shop into a fruit and vegetable retail establishment. The motorcycle/van, now in a state of disrepair, was exchanged for a pony and trap.

By this time I had joined the RAF. I had been sent to Cardigan for attestation and once registered, was sent home to await re call in a few month's time. As I was still living at home, I was expected to work on the farm seven days a week and for long hours.

One of my tasks involved taking a team of horses, on a Tuesday and a Friday, to Birkenhead to supply greengrocers and chip shops with potatoes and vegetables. Uncle Ned's premises were at the limit of my deliveries. To save time and expense he would travel some distance to meet me. Never once did I hear him complain or be ill tempered, although life must have been far from easy for a man, now in his late fifties, continually ill but working as hard as ever. His shop probably only broke even, supplying barely a living wage, so once again Ned needed supplementary income.

Birkenhead boasted not only the Argyle Theatre but also several good cinemas. One of these, The Savoy, was situated at the river end of Argyle Street. Ned applied, successfully, for the position of commissionaire. During the day he managed the shop and carried out deliveries with the pony and trap.

In the evenings he would stand in front of the box office resplendent in his colourful uniform, once again proudly displaying his medals. Now on an even keel financially, Ned beamed delightedly to all and sundry, both day and evening.

During the course of 1940, Ned continued to juggle his time between his two occupations - until August of that year. Convoys using the English Channel and eastern and southern UK ports were attacked and suffered severe losses. Consequently the Port of Liverpool quickly replaced Portsmouth and Southampton.

Many convoys were re-routed via the south west coast of Ireland, to the Mersey and Liverpool. Consequently Liverpool began to handle ninety per cent of all war material imported into the UK. Intelligence rapidly alerted the Germans to this fact - and from about 20 August onwards, heavy raids were carried out on Liverpool and Birkenhead.

At this time the Luftwaffe was probably three times larger than Bomber Command and perhaps more significantly, had more modern and faster aircraft. Germany's bomber force expanded rapidly from 1933 onwards. It had been tried and tested to destroy innocent and neutral towns (and their inhabitants). Firstly during the Spanish Civil War and later against Warsaw and on 14 May 1940, against Rotterdam. This latter was in an attempt to create a base for 'Operation Sea lion', the proposed German invasion of Great Britain.

Shockingly the Dutch were already negotiating a surrender when they were blitzed! Bomber Command, had previously refrained from attacking any areas where the killing of 'civilian' population might occur. This despite the fact that the majority of civilians were directly engaged in assisting the German war effort.

The day after the attacks on Rotterdam, Bomber Command started to attack industrial targets in the Ruhr valley.

The bombing raids on Merseyside increased in intensity from September 1940 and lasted until late May 1941. The anti-aircraft defences were totally inadequate and night fighter defences almost non-existent. As they controlled the whole area from France to Norway, the Germans only had to cross the Channel, or the North Sea, to find their targets. They had radio beams for navigation and bombing, and only had to fly down the Mersey in order to locate Liverpool and Birkenhead. Never the less, indiscriminate bombing of civilian areas did happen. Liverpool became the most heavily bombed UK city outside of London.

In October 1940 Uncle Ned's house received a direct hit and sadly both my uncle and aunt were killed.

Concurrently London was into its second month of heavy German bombing. During one particularly intensive night raid, Air Vice Marshal 'Bomber' Harris dragged the Chief of Air Staff, Sir Charles Portal onto the Air Ministry roof to watch the conflagration. Quoting a biblical text, Harris said: 'They've sown the wind, now they will reap the whirlwind'. By 'sowing the wind' Harris was referring to German bombing attacks on Warsaw, Rotterdam and London.

The ideas of AVM Harris regarding the allied bombing offensive, had not been formed in the comfortable enclaves of Whitehall but many years earlier in France. In 1917, a twenty five year old Harris had flown his Sopwith 1 ½ Strutter of 45 Squadron, above the battle raging to wrest control of the Passchendaele ridge from the German army.

During a period of some four months, Harris had witnessed first-hand, the appalling conditions and the carnage being enacted below him. A mud bath which could drown men and horses and which produced at the very least 250,000 casualties and approximately 100,000 dead. From that time Harris became convinced that bombing could save the lives of land forces.

During my time with an active Bomber Command Squadron, I met many people who had lost 'Uncle Neds' - or had lost their family homes to the Luftwaffe bombings of 1940 – 41. All had one aim – not to kill German civilians - but to subjugate aggressive German territorial ambitions – FOREVER.

APPENDIX II   The Short Life of Keith Gosling Part 1

Keith Gosling – aged 19 years – special operator (SO) with 101 Squadron – 15 June 1944 – until his untimely death on 21 July 1944.

By early June 1944, Keith, from Bradford England, had qualified as an RAF wireless operator who spoke German as his second language. Due to this he had volunteered to serve as a 'special', operating Airborne Cigar (ABC) 'jamming' equipment, with 101 (special duties) Squadron, at Ludford Magna, Lincolnshire. Unlike the seven 'normal' members of a Lancaster aircrew and apart from take-offs and landings, the SO would NOT be live on the crew intercom system for the duration of the flight.

Keith's first flight with the James' crew was on the 'disastrous' Reims raid of 22 June 1944, which ended in our crash landing at Thorney Island, on the return journey.

Keith's sixth and last flight with our crew, was on a daylight raid on 18 July to Manneville, where we were subjected to intense ack ack fire. During all these operations Keith displayed levels of stoicism and maturity one would have expected of an older man.

The James' crew was not detailed to fly on the 21 July. There were more aircraft than special operators. Keith Gosling therefore *was* required to fly - with a Canadian pilot, P/O DLW Meier RCAF, and his crew (six Canadians and one British), in Lancaster K-King. This was to be the first operation over enemy territory that the entire Meier crew had flown. Meier himself had taken part in one trip as 'second dicky', to gain experience with a seasoned crew and captain.

The raid was planned to target a synthetic oil refinery, at Homberg in the Ruhr Valley. On the morning of 22 July, we were horrified to hear that of two 101 Sqn Lancasters missing on the Homberg raid, one was that of P/O Meir and crew. On board that Lancaster of course - was 'our' special operator, Keith Gosling.

During August and September 1944, news filtered through that the bomb-aimer, Flt/Sgt Gwlliam (Canadian) had managed to bail-out over Namur, Belgium, before the aircraft eventually crashed at Cambrai in France. The news was that he had been hidden by the local resistance, but that the remaining seven members of the crew had all died in the crash. Gwlliam was returned to England in autumn 1944.

After interrogation, Flt/Sgt Gwilliam was deemed medically unfit for operational flying and returned to Canada. There were also outstanding questions regarding why K-King had been flying over Belgium at all, when the return flight plan was to head for the North Sea over Holland?

There followed a trying and poignant period during which Keith's mother, Mrs Gosling wrote to both Fred James and several crew members. Mrs Gosling wanted to know the reason that Keith had been lost flying with another crew - and also the whereabouts of his personal possessions? Keith's father had left the family home some years before the outbreak of war. Keith, an only child, had been brought up single-handedly by his mother. She had worked hard to provide Keith with the best possible education - and was anxious to ensure that her ex-husband did not benefit from Keith's demise. This was easy enough to understand but it was impossible for any of us to help - all correspondence had to be passed over to the squadron adjutant. Nevertheless it was a testing time for all concerned.

Now - fast forward to 1998, just after I had made my first contact with the 101 Squadron Association. We attended the annual reunion which was held, on that occasion, at RAF Waddington. On the Saturday evening, we were travelling in a courtesy coach from our hotel to Waddington, for the annual dinner. During the course of the trip I became engaged in conversation with one of the other guests, one Sam Brookes. We soon discovered that we had served on the squadron at the same time in 1944. Sam advised that he had been a special operator – his first question was, of course: 'What was the name of your SO'? My reply that it was Keith Gosling, elicited a gasp of astonishment from my questioner.

Sam Brookes and Keith Gosling had trained together, arrived at Ludford together, received their commissions together and had become personal friends. Furthermore, Sam and his wife had only recently returned from visiting the burial site of the Meier crew. They were surprised to find that instead of seven graves (the crew of eight minus the bomb-aimer) there were only six! In addition Keith Gosling had been listed as the PILOT of the aircraft?

By now our coach reached the RAF base and the conversation was put on hold until the return journey, after the dinner. What we weren't to know however, was that two former luminaries, both ex 101 Sqn COs in fact, were to give an impromptu piano and guitar singalong after dinner. This reunion was to see the association chairmanship handed over, from ex Vulcan era Air Vice Marshal Eric Macy, to ex VC 10 Captain,

Air Commodore Jim Uprichard - the very two musicians whose charismatic performance took our eyes off the time – and caused us to miss the coach for the return journey to the hotel back in Lincoln!

We assumed that Sam Brookes had not been so engrossed, as he was nowhere to be seen. Our paths failed to cross at the Sunday reunion at Ludford and so I missed the resumption of the Keith Gosling saga.

It was to be another four to five years before the next revelations were forthcoming. During a meeting between Sam Brookes and our former pilot Fred James, further information came to light. The pilot P/O Meier, despite his name appearing in the Squadron 'Roll of Honour', it would seem, had not been killed at all! Meier had in fact bailed out of the aircraft some considerable time after the exit of the bomb-aimer. This was one explanation as to why the authorities assumed that Keith Gosling must have been the pilot. We should remember that 101 Sqn was unique in having a crew of eight in their Lancasters, rather than the usual seven. It is perhaps understandable then that the authorities became confused!

Meier had been captured and taken a prisoner by the Germans. However, after the end of the war when the allies released the POWs, Meier had simply disappeared.

I have to say at this point, that I was uncomfortable with the established facts. It is well known that the Lancaster was not an easy aircraft from which to escape. From the landing point of the bomb-aimer and the crash site of the Lancaster, it appeared that he (the BA) had bailed out *well before* the doomed aircraft hit the ground, so let us take him out of the equation. Standard procedure in an emergency, would be for the pilot to hold the aircraft as level as possible to enable the crew to escape, then the captain would attempt to leave the aircraft himself. By this time the plane was often out of control and frequently on fire and the pilot, like the captain of a ship, would perish. Time and again we would hear of only two or three Lancaster crew escaping - but not the pilot. It was most unusual to hear that the pilot had successfully bailed out but not one other member of his crew.

This was especially so as the bomb-aimer had exited through a miniscule hatch in his compartment but none of the six aircrew had managed to escape via the much larger and more accessible rear main door!

The next piece in the puzzle was that in the early 1950s, there was proclamation of a divorce by Meier's English wife, of Meier himself.

By this time Mrs Meier was ready to re marry. There was certainly no evidence to believe that he was either in England or indeed Canada, while the divorce took place – so, where was he? There is no need to divorce a dead man, so we can only presume that evidence existed to prove that Meier was alive at this time?

Release of British, Commonwealth and American POWs was in many cases not as speedy as it could have been – but it was inconceivable that, five or even more years after cessation of hostilities, Meier was being held against his wishes.

Once again the trail went cold – until the 101 Squadron Association reunion of, I think, September 2008. We were at Ludford for Sunday's usual church service and wreath laying. Following the latter and in time honoured fashion, we retired to the WI for tea and sandwiches. I sat at a table when Fred James approached me. He said: 'Ron, there's a couple of fellows who would like to talk to you'. I got up and followed him to the rear of the room where five men were sitting. Fred introduced me and went back to his wife. I would say that four of the men were in their late fifties or early sixties. The fifth was probably no older than forty-five. One of the older men introduced himself and the other three as - Canadian relatives of WW II 101 Sqn airmen. He introduced the younger man as - a historian of RCAF activities during WW II.

It didn't occur to me at the time but no surnames were offered. During the early part of the twenty-first century, many of the aircrew who had survived the war were now dead. More than a few Commonwealth relatives, especially Canadians, attended the Squadron reunion to research their father's / uncle's / grandparent's wartime activities. Frequently a book would be subsequently published. Also I had presumed that Fred James must have known these men. The younger man assumed 'the chair'. He asked me whether I had flown with Keith Gosling and for what duration. He then asked how well I knew Keith. As I told them all I knew he paused and added softly:

'Ron, do you think Keith would have wanted, for any reason to defect to the enemy, during his flight with P/O Meier'?

As I started to reply, I noticed that the other four leant forward slightly and exchanged nervous glances. I was I admit, astounded at this question but out of loyalty to not just Keith but also his doting mother, I felt that I must scotch whatever traitorous opinions these people had. I repeated all I knew of Keith's background and character.

I particularly stressed that his mother had scrimped and saved to ensure her son obtained a good education. I added how much Keith was looking forward to going to Oxford at the end of the War. Due to the circumstances, Keith would have only known Meier and his crew for a few hours before take-off. He had settled well with the James' crew and was no doubt looking forward to returning to tried and trusted crew mates, after the trip with Meier. I also added that 101 Squadron's special operators were out of intercom contact with the rest of the crew apart from during take offs and landings. I offered my personal opinion that it was out of the question for Keith to even consider desertion. I now wish that I had thought at that time to ask what prompted them to think that Keith or indeed any other crew member would want to defect to the enemy.

For another, say ten minutes, the younger man told me that the bomb aimer, Flt/Sgt Gwilliam had bailed out of Lancaster K-King, approximately thirty minutes into the return flight - but some *twenty minutes before the aircraft crashed at Cambrai*. P/O Meir had on the contrary, exited the Lancaster almost immediately before it crashed, incarcerating six crew members.

The men then bombarded me with a series of questions. These were centred around issues such as how capable a pilot would the flight engineer have made, after P/O Meier had bailed out – could he have flown all the way back to the UK and landed safely? They seemed particularly interested in the operating mode of 'George' the automatic pilot – how reliable was it. Would I have expected the other crew members to have bailed out at the same time as Meier? Could I think of reasons why they would not have?

I responded that I would have expected that at least two or three of the six remaining crew should have been able to escape, provided that the aircraft could have remained on automatic pilot for say five or ten minutes. All of this however would be dependent on what sort of trouble the aircraft was in at that time. I explained that, without specific pilot training, a flight engineer would have difficulty controlling a stricken Lancaster for more than a minute or two if the auto pilot was not engaged or was not functioning. During the flight the pilot's parachute forms a part of his seat. When he bails out he removes this part of the parachute.

Anybody else would experience additional difficulty sitting at the pilot's cushionless seat and attempting to control a sick aeroplane.

An announcement came on the tannoy that the BBMF Lancaster was due overhead in twenty-five minutes. At this, the men stood up and thanked me for my help.

My mind was spinning so I took this as my cue and went back to the table. Fred was engaged in conversation for some time. When he had finished I was about to ask who the men were when he said: 'Who were those men'? I told him I had assumed that he knew them! He responded that one of them had approached him by name and asked to speak to his bomb aimer. I told Fred what they had advised me. When we had both turned around to where they had been sitting, there was no sign of anybody. I have heard nothing more, regarding the Meier affair since that time.

On reflection I am convinced that 'those Canadians' knew far more than they told me. Was P/O Meier merely a coward putting his own 'wellbeing' before that of his crew, (a captain deserting a sinking ship) - a heinous enough 'crime' itself. Was there however something much more devious and sinister going on? Was the question as to whether Keith Gosling could have considered desertion, a red herring - or did the Canadians believe that Meier himself had deserted and wanted to establish whether the whole crew could have been implicated - in something which went disastrously wrong? Did Meier manipulate the circumstances relating to the chances of survival of the other crew members, if so why?

My instincts tell me that my Canadian 'friends' knew exactly what had become of Walter Meir, after the end of the war in Europe. If indeed the production of a book was their aim, it, would make sense to reveal as little of the plot as necessary. What sort of an ending would a Frederick Forsythe a Ken Follet or John Nichol devise for this bizarre episode, I wonder?

Keith Gosling Part II.

Almost ten years after my bizarre meeting with the five Canadians at Ludford W.I.I was planning a further update to this book. I re read each chapter myself noting additional or updated material as I went through the book. When I got to Appendix II, The Short Life of Keith Gosling, I reflected that I had heard nothing more regarding the actions of the pilot Walter L Meier with respect to the deaths of six aircrew, (including Keith Gosling).
I made a note that what is now Part I needed no alterations or additions. It was my intension to visit the International Bomber Command Memorial (in Lincoln) and place poppies in the slots adjacent to the names of the twenty aircrew who I had known personally.

To make identification simpler my good friend, researcher and agent Adam James decided to see what information I.B.C.M. had on the names I had given him.

Against Keith Gosling's name was a web site posted by Lawrence Richier and translated from German into French by JL Maillet.[Crash de L' Avro Lancaster LL862 le 21/07/ 1944]

As soon as he saw the French text, Adam realised that there was some valuable material here. Adam worked late into the night translating the French document into English and had become very excited, as a much less opaque picture emerged than the facts I related in Part I.

If we reflect on part 1 of this appendix it was fact that Meier and Gwilliam were the only crew members to escape the Lancaster when it crashed, however there are many gaps and inconsistencies:

Where was Meier after the war ended?
Why did Gwilliam bale out twenty to thirty minutes before the Lancaster crashed at Cambrai?
What instructions did Meier give to the Flight Engineer immediately prior to him (Meier) baling out of the Lancaster.
Why did the aircraft crash almost immediately after Meier baled – out?
And many more!

My main focus however was to attempt to establish **beyond reasonable doubt** the exact cause (or causes) of the death of my crewmate Keith Gosling and the five other crew of Lancaster LL862 SR – K.

After reading the documents collated by Richier I knew that even if the current (2018) discrepancies and missing information continue to be unresolved (as is likely after over seventy years), what actions Meier had taken and perhaps more importantly did not take, answered my outstanding questions regarding the cause of death of my nineteen year old crewmate, Keith Gosling and the other five aircrew members including another Englishman, Sgt Ian Reid.

The bald facts are set out below:

- On a bombing raid to Homburg (Ruhr) on 20/21 July 1944, Lancaster SR – K LL862, piloted by P/O D.LW Meir (R.C.A.F.) dropped its bomb load on, or on the approaches to the target ; the aircraft crashed so there were no photos to confirm exactly where the bombs were dropped.
- After thirty or so minutes into the return trip Flt/Sgt Lowell Gwilliam (the bomb aimer) stated in his 1946 de –brief, that when

- they were at about 18,000 feet the Lancaster went into a dive to port and he was ordered to bale out. Despite the difficulties of escaping at an oxygen rare altitude Gwilliam survived the jump, and after a long hike with an ankle injury and not a little luck, fell into the hands of the local (Belgian) Resistance who kept him safe (despite great risk to themselves and their families) until the end of hostilities.

- The Lancaster flew on after the escape of Gwilliam. Meier announced his intension to defect to Switzerland and wanted the whole crew to join him. They all refused. Meier took a south westerly course instead of the planned northwesterly one which would have taken them over Holland. The aircraft was losing height all the time – it was not hit by flack nor attacked by night fighters (confirmed by local sources).

- Approximately twenty minutes after Gwilliam had jumped out of the aircraft, Meier himself baled out of what we have no reason to believe was not a perfectly serviceable Lancaster. He landed adjacent to Cambrai aerodrome. Almost immediately the Lancaster crashed with the remaining six crew members still on board. The burning aircraft was close enough for Meier to see exploding ammunition - indeed Meier thought it was gunfire from Germans searching for him. Meier headed in the direction of the aircraft and surrendered to the Germans.

- The aircrew killed in the crash were:

P/O K. Gosling - A.B.C. Operator
Sgt Reid - Flight Engineer
Sgt Ianuzello - Navigator
W/O2 Nixon - Radio Operator
Sgt Boyle - Mid Upper Gunner
Sgt Douglas – Rear Gunner
Gosling and Reid were English, the others Canadian.

Meier stated at interviews with local Luftwaffe staff at the time of the crash and again eight years later during questioning in Berlin, (by Canadian authorities) that he could not accept going back to England and decided to desert to the enemy. In taking this course of action, Meyer was in derogation of his duty once the bombs had been dropped, to get his crew home without unnecessary loss of life.

What remains is to attempt to discover the circumstances surrounding Meyer's actions from the time he announced his intention to defect until the time Lancaster LL862 SR – K crashed in Cambrai. While Meier had been open about his desertion he was much less so when it came to explaining what provisions he made for the survival of his crew before the aircraft crashed. At the Berlin interview in 1952, Meier merely states that before he jumped he handed over control of the Lancaster to the Flight Engineer. One of the panel at the March 1952, Berlin interview of Meier goes as far as to state.

He expressed much sorrow but only for himself. I do not remember he showed any regret for the six members of his crew who died or their loved ones. Although in general he answered my questions, on some points he was if not evasive at least cautious. For example I could not understand, and moreover still cannot, why his plane crashed almost immediately after he parachuted. He could not or did not want to enlighten me. We left with the impression that something, somewhere was forgotten in the story. I have the idea that he could if he had wanted have given me more information about the crash.

We cannot judge too harshly a man who makes no attempt to mitigate his own treacherous actions in this tragic scenario. I use the word treachery as it means - 'Behaviour that deceives or is not loyal to someone who trusts you'. In every 101 Squadron Lancaster seven highly trained men placed all their trust in their captain to bring them home safely. Never has that trust been more misplaced than in Lancaster LL 862 SR – K. Exactly what happened is pure conjecture but as a front of aircraft crewmember on thirty one completed sorties (and circa eight aborts) this is what I believe happened or indeed failed to happen.

Firstly, it seems incredible that after the departure of Gwilliam over Belgium and with the aircraft on a heading away from the U.K., that no other crew members attempted to leave the aircraft. Assuming the navigators' flight log had been lost, he (the navigator) would immediately realise that the compass heading bore no relation to the original flight plan Keith Gosling would have been off intercom but the remaining crew members would have been aware of Gwilliam's departure and even allowing for the fact that this was the crew's first operation, it seems highly unlikely that any crew member could be so naïve to think that on the departure of the pilot from the plane, the controls could be taken over by the flight engineer. I believe Meier concocted some sort of explanation to gain their confidence to remain on board.

As I explained to the five Canadians in Ludford W.I. (Part 1 of this appendix), circa 2008, the pilot of an Avro Lancaster had his parachute attached to his rear which also served as a seat cushion without which control of the aircraft became much more difficult. I believe that it was highly likely that Meier could have vacated his position at the controls while 'George', the auto pilot was in operation. Once clear of the controls he could have switched 'George' off, descended the step into the bomb aimer's compartment in the nose, and as the escape hatch would be open after Gwilliam's exit, jump out of the aircraft before the plane went out of control. This explanation would account for why the aircraft crashed so soon after Meier's departure. I came to this conclusion before I knew that Gwilliam's 1946 de briefing by the Royal Canadian Airforce Police Service, states that they were investigating – *Allegations that P/O Meier sabotaged the aircraft causing the deaths of his crew in the subsequent crash.* The investigators were pointed in this direction by how quickly the Lancaster crashed after Meier baled out.

So what of Gwilliam, the seventh victim of Maier's treacherous actions? He was not killed like the others but his life was in tatters. When Meier gave himself up to the Germans, he told them that Gwilliam had baled out before him. He had no need to do that. The enemy had a crashed Lancaster with six dead bodies in it and one live pilot. They wouldn't have expected more aircrew. Indeed there was so much confusion that as I related in Part 1 of this appendix, when Sam Brookes visited the graves in circa 1998, he found that his dear friend and fellow special operator Keith Gosling had been listed as PILOT! By giving the Germans a chance to capture Gwilliam, it is a clear demonstration that he was ruthless in wanting nobody around who could tell the truth, either dead or alive. It was no thanks to Meier that Gwilliam fell into the hands of the allies rather than the enemy! Following an 'exciting' two month during which he was moved from hiding place to hiding place when Germans checked his Belgian friend's premises, Gwilliam was repatriated to the UK on 16 September 1944, and de –briefed accordingly Gwilliam was repatriated to Canada on 21 October 1944 and shortly afterwards diagnosed with Psychoneurosis Anxiety State. He recovered sufficiently to fly non - operationally. Gwilliam had no wish to fly again and requested a discharge. When Gwilliam returned to Canada he got in touch with his crewmember's families. He received answers from all except those of Meier and the letters were not returned by the postal authorities. Why do you think that was?

As this level of reaction to his experiences in Belgium, once back home, was unusual in airmen, it was recorded that the cause was flying not escaping. Gwilliam's anxiety state was so deeply embedded that, on short internal flight with a family member, *fourteen years later* , the relative describes him as 'white knuckled' and 'scared to death'. It may be meaningful that Gwilliam described Meyer as being '…sometimes nervous'. To me that could well be a euphemism for Gwilliam lacking confidence in his pilot.

At the age of forty – two years and with a wife and young family Gwilliam drowned in a boating accident in British Columbia in October 1965. I am quite sure that F/Sgt Gwilliam should have been interrogated much more thoroughly when he first returned to England in 1944. He must have been well aware of Meier's mental state after leaving the target area (indeed if not before).Is it not beyond the bounds of possibility that Gwilliam's mental state affected him all his life and just possibly led to a fatal accident that wouldn't have happened otherwise? One can only imagine the final twenty minutes of horror when the remaining crew members realised that their pilot was intent on taking them to their early graves.

As soon as Meier's boots made contact with occupied French soil he actively sought out Germans to whom he could surrender. This was despite locals who offered to hide his parachute and help him evade the enemy! He made first contact with The Luftwaffe who after interrogating him passed him on to the Gestapo. Meier was passed through a succession of P.O.W. camps the final camp being Luckenwalde. Meier was listed as one of the British and Commonwealth P.O.W.'s in the camp on 21 April 1945. The very next day the Russians took over the camp but were in no hurry to repatriate allied prisoners until they had done some bartering for the release of Russian prisoners held in the West

At the end of the war there was no sign of Meier's whereabouts and he effectively disappeared. All attempts by the Canadian authorities to locate him failed. Meier went east to avoid repatriation by the allied forces occupying West Germany. Meier did not intend to return to Canada . . . *'After what I had done.'* Meier was on the run in East Germany - on the run and in fear. Between 1945 -1948 Meier worked on farms then in a uranium mine for the Russians. He had no birth certificate and so passes became difficult to acquire. At one point he was arrested as a British spy and imprisoned for about ten weeks.

In May 1947 Meier was presumed to have died on or since 21 April 1945

In early March 1952, Ivy, Meier's wife (an ex – WAAF) received a letter from her husband, after no contact for almost seven years. The letter was sent from the Russian sector of Germany. The reason for this communication was only that Meier, selfish as usual wanted to know whether the Canadian authorities had granted an amnesty for WW II deserters. Meier had no idea that he was presumed dead or that Ivy was getting a widows pension. Ivy was by this time ready to remarry so the letter confirming that Meier was actually alive must have come as something of a shock.

Ivy was taken to West Berlin before March 24th 1952 by Canadian civil or military, police officers who may have been based in London, as the report was written up there on 24 March. They met Meier in West Berlin and questioned him quite thoroughly. Unconvincingly Meier states that he wrote to his wife during his period of detention but that the letters never arrived. Meier also explained that it was not his intention to 'disappear for good'. He had read that sometime after WW I Canada granted amnesty to deserters. It beggars belief when Meier states that he thought he was only guilty of desertion!

Meier told the interviewing authorities in West Berlin in March 1952 that the last seven years had been hell and that he would willingly return to Canada and 'Face the music' if he knew he would only serve two or three years. He was told that nobody there had the authority to make a deal. He was told that anybody who had deserted between 3 September 1939 and 1 December 1946 and who had not turned themselves in by 30 January 1950 would not even be considered for possible amnesty. As we know, Meier did not re surface until 1952, two years after the deadline!

Meier died in January 1977 in East Berlin (remember 'the Wall' was still in place at that time), at the age of fifty six, a bit young I thought but so what? Well, in 1977 the average age of men dying in G.D.R was sixty seven or sixty eight, eleven or twelve years older.

Having been brought up in the West, Meier should have died at above the average for a man born in East Germany – let us say two or three years longer. This could mean Meier died some fifteen years earlier than could have been expected. Again so what? Meier could easily have succumbed to any of the life ending illnesses just as prevalent in the East as the West. But supposing he did not die of 'natural' causes.

I couldn't find meaningful suicide statistics for G.D.R for 1977, but discovered that a film had been released in circa 2006 called *The Lives of Others*. Surprise, surprise, the film was based on a story line set in **1977**!

The Lives of Others was meant to highlight the dictatorial system of that time, (1977). Controversially the lead character in the film accuses the G.D.R of coldheartedly ignoring people who commit suicide and claims that the state stopped compiling suicide statistics in 1977. While this was not entirely correct it certainly makes a point that 1977 must have been a particularly high point for suicides.

But what reason did Meier have to end his life? The following circumstances contribute to reasons for suicide:

Depression
Psychosis (inner voices)
Impulsive personality
Mistakes made in the past
Personality disorders
Social Isolation (remember East Germans were trapped by the Berlin wall from 1961 until well after Meier's death).

I think what we know about Meier's personality (through his actions) would lead us to believe that all the above contributory reasons could apply to Walter Meier. Considering the additional pressures of living in a dictatorial regime as a foreigner (he must have been under observation), there is every chance that Meier may have taken his own life.

I apologise to readers for this explicit outburst on the moral character of Meier. I visited the I.B.C.C. on 18 April 2018 when I placed a poppy adjacent to the name of GOSLING K Despite the gap of seventy-four years, this action reignited many of the personal traumas created by the loss of Keith. These include the memory of those poignant letters from his loving mother regarding Keith's demise. I felt that the actions of this treacherous person should be publically denounced.

APPENDIX III

Wirral Grammar School for Boys – Bebington

Motto: Wisdom is the Gateway to Life.

I have made reference to the above education centre on a few occasions in the story and feel it is only appropriate to mention three Old Wirralians whom I encountered during my RAF service.

F/Ltn Roy Marsh

In the spring of 1944, I was walking across the parade ground at RAF Lindholme with our rear gunner, George Williams RCAF when we noticed a couple of 'sprog' pilot officers in their gleaming new uniforms. We promptly signalled a first class salute which was duly acknowledged by the two officers. Several seconds later we heard a voice say: 'It's Ron Davies – isn't it'? Turning around I recognised Roy Marsh who had been a year below me at Wirral Grammar. As an undergraduate at Oxford University he had gained a rowing 'Blue' and took part in the Boat Race. He had also joined the University Air Squadron. This meant that when he joined the RAF, he would by-pass a large part of the training.

Roy had now graduated as a pilot with 15 Aqn (3 Group). It was somewhat embarrassing to hear him say: 'It is I who should be saluting you'. Discipline dictated that our meeting was brief. Roy eventually graduated through training to become a Lancaster captain and flew on operations late 1944. On 12-12-1944 Roy, now a captain, of Lancaster HK 627 (LS-F) took off to bomb the steelworks at Witten in Germany. It was a daylight raid and German fighters claimed eight Lancasters out of 140. HK 627 was shot down by flak, burst into flames and crashed near Witten. Roy and his crew all lost their lives. I was unable to make contact with Roy's family.

IBCC (International Bomber Command Centre) panel number 205

F/Sgt Alan Probert

In November 1944 during my brief leave following the completion of our Tour of Operations, I met Alan Probert (who was also on leave). Alan was eighteen months my junior. He explained that he was a navigator with 189 Sqn (5 Group) flying Lancasters. Alan had completed four operations up to that time and was far from optimistic about his future, so we chatted long and hard. As we left I thought that he appeared much more cheerful.

It was some months before I heard the news, immediately after his return from leave, Alan's Lancaster PB 745 (CA – Q), while bound for an operation in Munchen, crashed on take-off, hitting the ground after only just clearing thirty foot high telegraph wires. The sergeant (RAF) rear gunner (Richard Dyson), although burned himself, saved the pilot and was awarded the George Cross for his gallantry. It was too late to save Allen who died of his injuries later that day. Alan was buried in Plymyard Cemetery, Bromborough.

In 1946 on my return from the Far East I visited the family home. Unfortunately I was unable to make contact with anyone.
I was informed that Mrs Probert had become a recluse.

IBCC panel number 87

F/O James 'Jimmy' Masheder

During my embarkation leave in April/May 1945, I met a Mrs Masheder in Church Road Bebington, she was standing by the gateway of her home dressed immaculately. She hailed me as I passed by on my bicycle.

IBCC Memorial : Poppies placed by Ron Davies 2018

Their youngest son Jimmy was some two years my junior and had joined the RAF. Jimmy had also had graduated as a bomb – aimer, on No 77 Sqn (4 Group) flying Halifaxes. On 13 January 1945, he took off in Halifax MZ 812 (KN –X) on a mine laying sortie off Flensberg and Kiel. Four out of thirty two aircraft were 'lost without trace'.

Since that day his mother would wait at the gate every day in case Jimmy should return. I became engaged in a very difficult conversation regarding the possibility of escape. Sadly this hope would never be realised.

This small contribution of information must surely have triggered off the suffering that many mothers would endure, to ensure the future well-being of this country – and still today that anguish continues . . .

School Contacts

Following my contact with the present head teacher Mr David Hazeldine in 2017, I received an invitation to visit the school on 8 December 2016. I duly accepted and almost seventy-six years after leaving the school, I enjoyed afternoon tea in the Head's study. I was also able to read for myself the names of former friends inscribed on the memorial.

Publisher's note: Ron was also invited to attend the annual Wirral Grammar School Christmas Carol service in St. Andrews church, Bebington where he was treated as an honoured guest, seated on the front row along with his son Peter and myself. Ron's father, Tom, is buried in St. Andrews cemetery. In spring 2018 Ron visited the new IBCC and personally placed poppies on the names of Wirral old boys, Marsh, Probert and Masheder.

APPENDIX IV

Lambs to the Slaughter – And a Victoria Cross

'Lambs to the slaughter we were', said Bob Pierce, shaking his head, when I met him and Les Owen in a hostelry in Alford (near Chester). He was referring to the raid on the Cologne / Gremberg marshalling yards, which was carried out during the daylight hours of 23rd December 1944. Even normally taciturn official RAF records admitted that the raid went 'very badly'.

Bob Pierce was the Flt Sgt rear gunner in Walt Reif's crew on that raid. You may remember that the Reif crew was one of *The Original Four crews* (including our own) who had carried out advanced flying training together and joined 101 Squadron at the same time in May 1944.

In mid-July and having completed, like ourselves, nine operations with 101 Sqn, the Reif crew were accepted for a transfer to No. 8 Group, Pathfinder Force. They duly left Ludford Magna to carry out specific training at Warboys.

In chapter twenty while the James' crew was at CCDU Angle, I relate the loss of Walt and four of his crew on the Gremberg raid. Bob Pierce and the MUG, Flt Sgt Jack McLennan bailed out of the stricken aircraft, were captured and spent the remainder of the war as POWs.

Unusually that raid consisted of PFF aircraft only. Twenty seven Lancasters and three Mosquitoes split into three formations, each led by an 'Oboe' equipped Lancaster and with an Oboe Mosquito as reserve leader.

Oboe was one of the most accurate 'blind bombing' navigational aids Bomber Command had at this time. Two 'radio circles' intercepted over the dropping point of the target. The Oboe lead aircraft was piloted on this raid by Sq Ldr R.A.M. (Robert) Palmer DFC (and bar).

Palmer was flying a No. 582 Lancaster (PB 371) with at least two '582' crew members although he and most of the remainder of the crew were on loan from No.109 (Oboe) Mosquito squadron.

On his 110th operational sortie, Palmer had to fly very accurately around the circumference of one 'circle' by following Morse code like 'dot' radio pulses while being told (by British ground controllers) how far he was from the target. The other 'radio circle', when the two intersected, would send Morse code 'dashes' and the bombs / flares/ target indicators could then be dropped. The accuracy of the system meant that the beams were only thirty five yards wide! Close co-operation between the Oboe equipped aircraft's navigator and ground control in England were essential. The aircraft could therefore not stray one iota from its designated path before the dropping zone had been reached.

On approach to the target, the forecast cloud cover failed to materialize and the Cologne ground forces put up an intense flak bombardment which accurately targeted the bomber stream. In consequence an instruction was issued from Bomber Command HQ to forego the fifteen minute, timed Oboe run to the target, to break formation and bomb visually.

As formation leader, Sq Ldr Palmer should have received this instruction. He did not and continued to lead his group into the jaws of the enemy. As if the situation wasn't bad enough, Luftwaffe fighters returning from attacking American bombers entered the fray. Bob Pierce related that their Lancaster was attacked by Messerschmitt Bf 109's (aka Me 109), from below, and cannon shells tore into the underbelly of the aircraft. They did not see the fighters until they had passed by. Walt Reif, the pilot, struggled to right the stricken Lancaster and Bob vividly recalled their skipper screaming at the gunners to bail out.

In front of them they could see that Sq Ldr Palmer's aircraft was also in serious trouble with two engines on fire. Palmer had rejected the option of taking evasive action and continued on the straight and level 'Oboe designated' flight path where, unsurprisingly, his aircraft was hit by both heavy ground ack-ack fire and the Luftwaffe fighters.

Palmer led his formation doggedly and despite his loss of engines and other significant damage, he dropped his bomb load right on target. This provided an aiming point for the remainder of his formation. The Reif crew, by now flying directly behind Palmer, would have seen his aircraft spiraling to earth in flames; only Flt Sgt R K Yeulatt, the rear gunner, escaped, to be held as a POW.

Meanwhile Bob Pierce was having his own problems.

For the first time he was wearing a seat pack parachute (similar to the type worn by pilots) instead of the conventional chest pack. As he attempted to rotate the turret into escape mode it became jammed due to his unfamiliarity with the seat pack.

This gave Bob some additional fraught minutes as he would have known that he didn't have much time before Walt Reif could no longer keep the aircraft level. Once the plane went into a dive, 'G' forces would prevent any crew member from escaping.

The Lancaster crashed into the suburbs of Cologne and Bob Pierce landed in 'someone's back yard', where the townsfolk gathered in a mob...Fortunately the Wehrmacht surrounded him and took him to a police station. Later he was handed over to the Luftwaffe and spent the remained of the war in POW camps.

A Lancaster also from Little Staughton, took off one minute behind Sq Ldr Palmer and one minute in front of Walt Reif and his crew. This aircraft is reported to have been 'Shot down by a fighter over the target area and crashed into a marshalling yard ...from 20,000 ft in a flat spin' [Little Staughton RAF Book of Remembrance - 109 and 582 Squadrons-2000].

Amazingly six of the crew survived and only the Flight Engineer, P.O. K W Hewitt D.F.M, was killed. As I mentioned earlier the Lancaster was not and easy aircraft from which to escape and for six crew members (including the pilot) to survive was indeed exceptional. It is probable that this aircraft went down before those of Palmer and Reif.

The Germans had the view that, without British fighter cover, by maintaining a fixed course to the aiming point in cloudless conditions and minus a main bombing force, the operation was a suicide mission. Who could disagree?

Now to the casualties:

On the way to the target two No. 35 Sqn (PFF) Lancasters collided over the French coast with the loss of all fourteen crew members. At or on approach to the target the three No. 582 Sqn Lancasters, as mentioned above, crashed.

All aircrew who did not survive these crashes were buried at Rheinsberg War cemetery. A fourth No. 582 Sqn Lancaster was abandoned over Oppiter (Belgium) with the loss of three aircrew, the others being captured.

Additionally one Mosquito was shot down by flak and fighters. The loss for this raid of seven aircraft from a total of thirty, means a 23% loss rate – enough said!

Sqn Ldr Palmer (then aged twenty four) received a posthumous Victoria Cross for, amongst other attributes, 'Conspicuous bravery…and prolonged and heroic endeavour'. Palmer received the only 'Oboe' VC of the war. Palmer's VC was also the only medal awarded for this disastrous raid.

Finally, and with a heavy heart, I detail the deceased members of the Reif crew.

Flt Ltn Walt Reif; Pilot RCAF (and ex crop spraying pilot).

Flt Sgt George Owen; W.Op. / air gunner RAFVR.

P.O. Ken Austin; Nav. RCAF.

P.O. Pete Uzelman; B.A. RCAF.

Sgt. John Patterson; Flt Eng. RAFVR.

Both Walt Reif and Pete Uzelman were of German descent. In the early 'thirties' Walt had become a naturalized American while Pete became a naturalized Canadian. To reiterate, the five crew members who lost their lives are buried at Rheinsberg War Cemetary, Kamp Lintford, Nordheim – Westfal, Germany. Ref. Coll. Grave 7.c. 22-25. To compound an undoubted tragedy Walt Reif and his crew were flying the last operation to complete their full tour.

During our visit to the International Bomber Command Centre at Lincoln in 2018 I was able to place poppies on the names of all five Reif crew members.

To conclude: there is an RAF saying that if a VC has to be awarded for an operation, then the operation probably should never have proceeded. I think that says it all.

Acknowledgments

Probert H, 'Bomber Harris – His Life and Times'; Greenhill Books, 2001.

Morpurgo M, 'War Horse':

Whitworth R, 'Merseyside at War';

Harris Sir A, 'Bomber Offensive'; Pen and Sword Military Classics, 2005.

Middlebrook M, & Everitt C, 'The Bomber Command War Diaries'; Penguin Books, 1990.

Crucq Paul M, 'We Never Blamed the Crews'; ADZ, Vlissingen, The Netherlands, 2000.

Crucq Paul M, 'Aiming Point Walcheren'; ADZ Vlissingen, The Netherlands, 2003.

Bowyer C, 'Men of Coastal Command';

Alexander A, 'Special Operations – No 101 Squadron', - 1979.

Richier L 'Crash De L'Avro Lancaster ILL 862 le 21 / 07 / 1944' (translated by J L Maillet)

Aircrew Remembered – Archive Report : 20 / 21. 07 .1944 No 101 Suadron Lancaster I LL 862 SR-K P/O DLW Meier.

Made in the USA
Columbia, SC
20 February 2019